SPIRAL GUIDES

Trave...

G000125745

CALIFORNIA

Contents

the magazine 5

✦ Cliché? No Way ✦ Motion Picture Perfect ✦ What's the Rush ✦ Whole Lotta Shakin' Goin' On ✦ Trials & Errors ✦ Phantom Relics ✦ Artistic License ✦ California Timeline

Finding Your Feet 31

✦ First Two Hours ✦ Getting Around
✦ Accommodations ✦ Food and Drink ✦ Shopping
✦ Entertainment

San Francisco and the Bay Area 41
In Three Days
Don't Miss ✦ Alcatraz Island and Fisherman's Wharf
✦ Chinatown and North Beach ✦ South of Market
✦ Golden Gate Park
At Your Leisure ✦ 23 more places to explore
Where to... ✦ Eat and Drink ✦ Stay ✦ Shop
✦ Be Entertained

Northern California 71
In Five Days
Don't Miss ✦ Sonoma–Mendocino Coast ✦ The Wine Country
✦ Sacramento and the Gold Country ✦ Yosemite National Park
At Your Leisure ✦ 4 more places to explore
Where to... ✦ Eat and Drink ✦ Stay ✦ Shop
✦ Be Entertained

The Central Coast 99
In Three Days
Don't Miss ✦ The Monterey Peninsula ✦ Big Sur
✦ Hearst Castle ✦ Santa Barbara
At Your Leisure ✦ 6 more places to explore
Where to... ✦ Eat and Drink ✦ Stay ✦ Shop
✦ Be Entertained

Los Angeles Area 121
In Three Days
Don't Miss ✦ Hollywood ✦ Beverly Hills
✦ The Getty Center ✦ Disneyland®
At Your Leisure ✦ 13 more places to explore
Where to... ✦ Eat and Drink ✦ Stay ✦ Shop
✦ Be Entertained

Southern California 151
In Four Days
Don't Miss ✦ San Diego ✦ Palm Springs
✦ Death Valley National Park
At Your Leisure ✦ 3 more places to explore
Where to... ✦ Eat and Drink ✦ Stay ✦ Shop
✦ Be Entertained

Tours 179
✦ 1 Coast Highway 1 and the Point Reyes National
Seashore ✦ 2 Santa Barbara and the San Marcos Pass
✦ 3 Mulholland Drive

Practicalities 189
✦ Before You Go ✦ When to Go
✦ When You Are There

Index 195
Atlas 199

Written by Daniel Mangin
Where to sections by Clark Norton

Updated by Daniel Mangin
Update managed by Lodestone Publishing Limited

Copy edited by Janet Tabinski
Page layout by Jo Tapper
Verified by Carole Harley
Indexed by Marie Lorimer

Edited, designed and produced by AA Publishing.

© Automobile Association Developments Limited 2000, 2005
Maps © Automobile Association Developments Limited 2000, 2005
Third edition

The contents of this publication are believed correct at the time of
printing. Nevertheless, the publishers cannot be held responsible
for any errors or omissions or for changes in the details given in this
guide or for the consequences of any reliance on the information
provided by the same.

Published in the United States by AAA Publishing,
1000 AAA Drive, Heathrow, Florida 32746
Published in the United Kingdom by AA Publishing

ISBN 1-59508-035X

Cover design and binding style by permission of AA Publishing

Color separation by Leo Reprographics
Printed and bound in China by Leo Paper Products

10 9 8 7 6 5 4 3 2 1

A01838

the magazine

*B*londe and tanned, surfboards under their arms, they in-line skate down a palm-lined waterfront sidewalk. He calls everyone "dude." She chats away on a cell phone, the other ear plugged to an iPod. The ultimate California cliché, they're as real as can be – everyone in LA has seen them. But do they tell the whole story of the Golden State? No way, dude!

CLICHÉ?
No Way

During the 20th century, California became known for funnin' and sunnin', fancy cars, movie stars, face-lifts, trend-setting fashions, and wacky cults and cultural movements. In the process, "California" and "airhead" became synonymous. "You lose 10 points off your IQ every year you stay there," went a line in one of Woody Allen's early movies.

But beneath its frivolous exterior, California has for the last 150 years been about serious business – mining, agriculture, railroad building, moviemaking, oil refining,

Hunks, babes, ripples and tans

Previous page: Los Angeles cityscape

defense contracting and technological innovation. With all its residents have accomplished – the state's economy, the world's fifth largest, generates 13 percent of America's gross national product – it's a wonder there's time to hit those myriad beaches at all.

"The Californians are an idle, thriftless people, and can make nothing for themselves," griped Richard Henry Dana in *Two Years before the Mast*, published in 1840. Had Dana arrived a century earlier, before the Spanish began colonizing in earnest, he might have marveled at the self-sufficiency of the Native American population. And had he dropped by a decade or so after he did, when the Gold Rush was in full swing, he might have seen how an international influx of talent had inspired no end of entrepreneurial spirit. Three different Californias, all in the space of a century.

The real clichés about the state have to do with its diversity – California will shortly become the first state in the continental U.S. to have a non-Caucasian population of more than 50 percent – and its encouragement of risk-taking. People have come here to "start over" since the first Asiatic explorers arrived around 20,000 BC, and they've done it side by side with pioneers of many cultures. There's often been friction, but the general impetus has been toward coexistence.

Old images die hard, though, which brings us back to our surfer dude and dudette. They remain a potent icon, but to paraphrase California-born writer Richard Rodriguez, these days the guy's just as likely to be Filipino as Caucasian and his girlfriend's likely to be Chinese. The one constant: He's calling everyone "dude."

Now You Know

California contains the highest point (Mt. Whitney, 14,495 feet/ 4,418 meters) and the lowest point (Badwater, 282 feet/86 meters below sea level) in the 48 contiguous states – both visible from Dante's View. About 90 percent of the wine made in the United States and nearly all the commercially grown artichokes come from California.

LA style: Red Caddy heads down Sunset Boulevard

Motion Picture Perfect

(California's got everything filmmakers want)

"You know what's remarkable is how much England in no way looks like Southern California," gushes Mike Myers during a chase scene in "Austin Powers: The Spy Who Shagged Me." It's an inside joke, for the scene was shot near Los Angeles, and England was merely one of the many places California has, when not playing itself, impersonated over the years.

Plentiful sunshine and striking scenery made Los Angeles a natural for film production. In his memoir, Mack Sennett, who produced the Keystone Kops comedies, described how silent-era filmmakers would zip around the city with their equipment, set a comedic routine into motion, and let the cameras roll. Another asset of Los Angeles, though, was its distance from the East Coast and its proximity to Mexico. Many early filmmakers, using equipment that violated the movie-camera patent held by East Coast inventor Thomas A. Edison, often needed to slip south of the border to avoid prosecution by his trust.

But not all the action was in the Southland. Northern California was a major player, too. East of San Francisco in Niles, the Essanay Film Manufacturing Co. produced several hundred one-reel films, most of them Westerns, between 1912 and 1916. Many films were also shot in San Francisco, Santa Cruz and Marin County.

George Lucas operates the biggest Northern California studio these days, Marin County's Skywalker Ranch, where he makes films such as "Star Wars: Episode 1 – The Phantom Menace." In addition, his Industrial Light and Magic division provides special effects for countless big-screen efforts. Lucas's presence is a key reason the San Francisco Bay Area has developed into the nation's third largest center – after LA and New York – for film and TV production.

Movies are shot all over the state, even in the sparsely populated north, though sometimes the natural setting doesn't satisfy fussy set directors (make-up was applied to Humboldt County's redwoods to make them look more "realistic" in the 1952 Technicolor picture "The Big Trees"). Still, the majority of production takes place within a 30-mile (48-kilometer) radius of Hollywood, where on any given day as many as 150 movies, TV shows, commercials and music videos are shot. Los Angeles has been losing ground in recent years to other regions, among them Vancouver and Toronto, but it remains the nexus of filmmaking in North America. The movies produced here are responsible for more than half of all tickets sold worldwide.

Moses (Charlton Heston) took orders from the master – Cecil B. DeMille

Hollywood Superstars

D. W. Griffith
As a New York-based director, Griffith helped define film-shooting and -editing techniques. But it was in California that he produced his first two epics, "The Birth of a Nation" and "Intolerance."

Cecil B. DeMille
The great showman had a reputation for salacious films during the silent era but got away with it because many of his pictures were Biblical tales. He starred as himself in "Sunset Boulevard," showing kindness in the film to Gloria Swanson, who in real life he'd molded into a star.

Mary Pickford
Audiences adored "America's Sweetheart," the personification of innocence, but Mary Pickford was also a savvy investor who loved snapping up corner lots in Beverly Hills and elsewhere. She and four other big talents – Douglas Fairbanks Sr. (her second husband), Charlie Chaplin, D. W. Griffith (some say she made the director's reputation) and Westerns star William S. Hart (only briefly involved) – formed United Artists.

Sid Grauman
Remembered these days for building the Chinese Theatre (► 126) in Hollywood, Grauman erected many other Los Angeles movie palaces. His biggest theaters presented lavish "prologues" – stage shows – that often outshone the pictures that followed.

Irving Thalberg
The "boy wonder" executive at MGM in the 1920s and 1930s was in large part responsible for its quality productions. He was only 37 when he died of pneumonia.

Hollywood diva-dealers: Mary Pickford, right, and Barbra Streisand, above

The Warner Brothers

The four Warner Brothers – Jack, Harry, Albert and Sam – backed the winning system for adding sound to pictures and produced the great gangster films of the 1930s.

Barbra Streisand

She's won all kinds of awards – two Oscars, a Tony and numerous Emmys and Grammys – and she's as accomplished behind the scenes as out front. With "The Prince of Tides," Streisand became the first woman ever nominated for a Best Director Oscar for a film she'd also starred in.

George Lucas

The Modesto-born producer-director scored early with "American Graffiti," a homage to the California of his youth. Much of the film was shot in downtown Petaluma, near the Wine Country. The state's terrain pops up as various outer-

Steven Spielberg is this era's great showman

space locales in the "Star Wars" movies.

Steven Spielberg

Spielberg got his start directing television episodes and the modest "The Sugarland Express" but quickly graduated to blockbusters such as "Jaws" and "Close Encounters of the Third Kind." He's shown his serious side with pictures such as "The Color Purple" and "Schindler's List."

Hitchcock and California

London-born Alfred Hitchcock said his mission in life was "to simply scare the hell out of people," and he often subverted California's sunny image to accomplish this. He made two of his creepiest films in Sonoma County. In "Shadow of a Doubt," Teresa Wright played a young girl in staid Santa Rosa shocked to realize that her uncle, played by Joseph Cotten, is a murderer. And in "The

Birds," peaceful, small-town Bodega Bay (Hitch also mixed in shots from nearby Bodega, Bloomfield and Valley Ford) turns into a living hell when birds begin attacking the citizenry. The suspenseful "Vertigo" is a veritable postcard of late-1950s San Francisco. Many of Hitch's productions were shot on back lots in Southern California. The tram tour at Universal Studios (► 137) passes by the Bates Motel in "Psycho."

What's the Rush?

how gold changed the face of California

"This is a curious rock, I am afraid that it will give us trouble," said James Marshall, who, on January 24, 1848, discovered a piece of quartz he thought contained gold. He was right about the gold – and the trouble, at least for himself. Within months, the stampede to the Sierra foothills east of Sacramento had begun in earnest. By the time the gold dust settled, the face of California had changed forever.

Gold fever struck first among the state's residents, who realized they had but a few months' lead on the rest of the world. Sailors jumped ship; farmhands and even farm owners abandoned their crops. "Every seaport as far south as San Diego, and every interior town, and nearly every rancho – has become suddenly drained of human beings," reported the *California Star* newspaper in 1848.

When President James Polk confirmed in a December 1848 speech that the rumors of gold discoveries in California were true, Easterners began heading west via two grueling routes. One involved crossing up to 3,000 miles (4,825 kilometers) of plains, mountains and desert. The other option was by sea to Panama, by land across the Isthmus of Panama (there was no canal back then) and by sea again to San Francisco.

Fewer than 1,000 people lived in San Francisco in 1847. More than 30,000 lived there by the end of 1849 – the term "Forty-Niners" refers to that year's influx of "argonauts" – and towns sprang up all over Northern California. Most miners were lucky to break even after months of hard labor, and success often begat as much grief as happiness. Law enforcement was nearly nonexistent and thieves were everywhere. When justice was meted out, though, it tended to be swift and complete – hangings by vigilantes were commonplace.

Most Easterners and foreign-born prospectors planned to return home after they made their fortunes, so they didn't bring their wives and children. Women were so scarce that one miner was said to have charged for the privilege of seeing his bride. Even at $5 per look, he had many takers. Prostitutes headed West as well; many made more money than the miners did, though disease and poor living conditions took their toll.

Gold Rush-era buildings in Nevada City

The Gold Rush changed California forever, and not all for the better. Downsides included mining techniques that devastated the environment and the theft of land from Native American peoples. The freer atmosphere of the camps and cities such as San Francisco gave rise to an independent spirit, however. Historians have noted that California became a place where it was permissible to fail, as indeed many miners did. The lack of a stigma encouraged the entrepreneurial spirit that transformed the Golden State from an economic backwater into a powerhouse.

The legendary bandit Joaquin Murieta (► 14) was "preserved" for posterity

24-Karat Characters

John Sutter (1803–80)

Colonel John A. Sutter, in 1848 one of California's richest residents, had set about establishing farms in the Sacramento area and mills in the Sierra foothills. He dispatched James Marshall to build a sawmill at Coloma. When Marshall discovered gold, Sutter wrote, "Instead of feeling happy and contented, I was very unhappy, and could not see that it would benefit me much." He was correct. His claims weren't honored, and the prospectors who flooded into the region ravaged his farms for food and his mills for lumber to build shacks.

James Marshall (1810–85)

The man whose discovery ignited the Gold Rush profited little from it. He died broke and bitter in 1885, having been unable to enforce his claims.

John Sutter came to California (then part of Mexico) in 1839

Irish-born Lola Montez was a flamboyant and glamorous character

Sam Brannan (1819–89)

Merchant Sam Brannan realized from the start that he could make a fortune supplying miners with the necessities of life – food, clothing and mining tools. After hearing about Marshall's find, he stocked up his general store in Sacramento and headed to San Francisco to announce the discovery of gold. Brannan charged high prices, loaned money at exorbitant interest rates and took whatever advantage he could. He became Gold Rush California's first millionaire but lost his shirt in later investments, including some spas in the Napa Valley town of Calistoga. He died a pauper.

Lola Montez (1818–61)

Born Eliza Gilbert in Ireland, Montez became notorious in Europe as the beautiful consort of artists, among them composer Franz Liszt and author Alexandre Dumas. King Ludwig of Bavaria was dethroned in part because of his association with Montez. She'd been run off the Continent by the time she landed in California, where she whipped up a sensuous "spider dance" to enchant the women-starved men. The act fared well for a time in San Francisco, but when enthusiasm waned she struck out for the mining towns, ending up in Grass Valley. After embarking on a disastrous tour of the United States and Australia, she settled in New York, where she died penniless in 1861 at the age of 42.

Joaquin Murieta (1830?–53?)

Of all the Gold Rush legends, that of Joaquin Murieta is the most difficult to trace. Some historians dispute even the existence of this Mexican-born bandit, who allegedly began his life of crime to avenge his torture, the rape of his wife and the murder of his brother by Yankee miners. A fun-loving guy, he'd plunder by day and party by night in the southern mine country near Sonora. A posse supposedly captured and killed him in 1853 and preserved his head in a large jar of whiskey and arsenic (some say it was brandy). Then again, he may simply have gone back to Mexico. Writers of Westerns refashioned Murieta's tale along the lines of Robin Hood. Hucksters made many dollars touring the Gold Country with Murieta's head, which was said to have been lost in San Francisco following the 1906 earthquake. The head was purportedly rediscovered in the late 20th century in Sonoma County.

Bret Harte (1836–1902)

The actual sight of writer Bret Harte (born Francis Brett Harte) often dismayed fans of the man who shaped the fiction of the American West: He was more of a dandy than a rough-and-tumble guy. Truth was, he didn't so much experience life in Gold Rush-era mines as hear about it. But he was a good listener. "The Luck of Roaring Camp" and other stories contain vivid, even moving portraits of the hardships miners endured – though in real life the men and women of the Gold Rush were cruder and more hard-bitten than Harte let on. Harte published his early poems and stories in the *Overland Monthly*, which he edited. He abandoned the West not long after achieving fame and never repeated his early success. He died a mostly forgotten man in England in 1902.

Bret Harte gained notoriety as a journalist before taking teaching jobs around Angels Camp

Black Bart (1829–1917)

The Wells Fargo Company's stagecoaches, which carried large sums of money, were inevitable targets for bandits. The most famous of these outlaws was the debonair Black Bart, who never stole from the passengers ("I only want Wells Fargo's money," he'd say), never actually loaded his shotgun and was unfailingly polite. At least twice he left behind a poem, signed "Black Bart, Po8." (Po8 – poeight – stood for poet.) Bart robbed coaches from 1875 to 1883 and was only caught because he left his handkerchief behind during a difficult heist. When detectives traced the laundry mark, they discovered he was a San Francisco-based mining engineer named Charles E. Bolton (given name: Charles E. Boles). Now, a few lines from the famous po8, addressed to bankers whose money he stole:

> " I've labored long and hard for bread
>   For honor and for riches
>   But on my corns too long you've tread
>   You fine-haired son [sic] of bitches. "

Whole Lotta
SHAKIN'
Goin' On

**Shattering facts about
California's geology**

Earthquakes have a way of getting under the skin – literally – of even the most blasé Californians. Years will go by with only desultory trembling, quakes that register 3.5 or 4.2 on the Richter scale. To some newcomers it even seems like fun. "Did you feel the shaking yesterday?" At around 5.0 people take notice, but damage is usually minimal – ceramic objects fall and break, loose plaster becomes dislodged.

Then along comes a whopper like Southern California's Northridge earthquake of 1994 (6.7) or Northern California's Loma Prieta quake of 1989 (7.1). Streets buckle and undulate like waves, glass pops out of windows and huge billboards flap like flags in a breeze. Buildings and freeways collapse, and everyone finally "gets" it: terra firma is a relative term. For six or eight months afterward, stomachs tighten at the slightest aftershock as humans' flight-or-fight reflexes kick in. Even a heavy truck rumbling by makes some folks feel queasy.

Young ladies smile for the camera while San Francisco burns

Earthquake Facts and Figures

What Causes a Quake?
Here's the simple version: The continents sit on top of plates on the Earth's crust. When one continent's plate shifts against another's – this happens along what are called faults – an eruption occurs. The shock of this eruption is felt on the Earth's surface, causing land, buildings, trees and other objects to shift.

Focusing on the Epicenter
Scientists call the underground point where an earthquake occurs – where those plates shift – the focus. The place where the quake erupts at the earth's surface is called the epicenter. The deeper the focus, the more treacherous the earthquake.

The Richter Scale
A Southern Californian named Charles Richter invented the scale that bears his name in 1935 as a way of calculating magnitude, or size, of earthquakes. The scale, which uses data supplied by seismographs, is logarithmic, which means that a magnitude 7.0 earthquake is about 31 times more powerful – in terms of earth-shaking energy

– than a 6.0 one, and over 900 times more powerful than a 5.0 quake.

How Big Was S.F.'s Big One?

The San Francisco earthquake of 1906 would have measured 8.3 on the Richter scale. The quake caused a 250-mile (400-kilometer) section of the San Andreas Fault to shift 21 feet (6.5 meters) in mere seconds. Seven hundred people died and damage came to more than $400 million in 1906 dollars, about $7.6 billion these days. Ironically, much of the damage was caused by people who set their own buildings ablaze because they were insured for fire but not earthquakes.

It Ain't Over Till It's Over

Fifty-seven people died and more than 1,500 were seriously injured in the Northridge earthquake that rocked the Los Angeles area in 1994. It caused more damage than any quake in the United States since the 1906 San Francisco one. During the three weeks following the initial tremor, nearly 3,000 aftershocks were recorded.

What, Me Worry?

None of the 50 most destructive earthquakes in recorded history has taken place in the Golden State. Some seismologists believe that the 1989 and 1994 quakes have for the short term eased pressure underground and that no huge quakes are likely in the first decade of the 21st century.

Experiencing That Trembling Feeling?

In case of an earthquake:
Get beneath a doorway or something sturdy.
Use your arms to protect your head.
Don't run outside – falling objects could hit you.

Fissure perfect: The San Andreas Fault

"People, I just want to say, you know, can we, can we all get along?" asked a plaintive Rodney King during the full-scale riot that followed the acquittal of four Los Angeles police officers who'd been accused of using excessive force after stopping him for a routine traffic violation. On that tumultuous day in 1992, getting along appeared quite out of the question – television news cameras captured the mayhem even more vividly than an amateur video had documented King's 1991 travail. This time the camera exposed a truth that many Californians try to gloss over, namely that as mellow as things *can* be here, folks haven't always gotten along. In the interest of full disclosure, and because everyone loves a good scandal, below are a few other notorious trials and errors – strikes, union-busting, cultural clashes, sensational murders – in Golden State history.

TRIALS & ERRORS

Infamous moments in California history

"Gifts" for the Natives

Before the Spanish came to California in 1542 about 300,000 native people moved freely throughout the region. By the end of the Mission era, in the 1830s, that number was 150,000. The chief culprit was infection – the native peoples had no immunity to diseases Europeans brought such as smallpox, measles and syphilis. By 1870, 20 years after California became part of the United States, the Native American population was about 30,000. Genocide was the primary cause for this later decline.

Thanks for the Help

Chinese men were among the waves of immigrants to California during the Gold Rush, later working on levees in the Central Valley and on the western portion of the transcontinental railroad. To keep the future population of Chinese as low as possible, severe restrictions were placed on the immigration of women from China. In 1870, out of more than 63,000 Chinese in California, fewer than 5,000 were women. During periods of low employment, anti-Chinese riots were common, as were attempts to force Chinese to repatriate.

Fatty's Fateful Party

Silent-film comedian Fatty Arbuckle liked to zip up the coast from Los Angeles to San Francisco to unwind. In 1921, he threw a bootleg-liquor party in his suite at the still-extant St. Francis Hotel. A young actress named Virginia Rappe got sick

at the party and died a week later. The police charged Arbuckle, then one of America's highest-paid performers, with rape and murder. Goaded by William Randolph Hearst's *San Francisco Examiner*, the city's District Attorney, who had designs on higher office, put the actor through three trials. No end of prosecutorial foul play took place before the third jury acquitted Arbuckle and apologized for his ordeal. By then, his career was in tatters. "It was only business," Hearst allegedly told Arbuckle about his newspaper chain's coverage when they met later in the 1920s. Amazingly, five years after the trial, Hearst hired Arbuckle to direct a picture, but the effort ended in failure.

Strikebreaking Effort Prompts Bloody Thursday Riots

In May 1934, San Francisco's longshoremen (dockers) called a strike to force shipowners to allow true unions (as opposed to the existing ones controlled by the companies). In early July, with nearly 100 ships sitting idle in the port, the owners, with the help of city police, moved to break the strike. A riot later known as Bloody Thursday ensued, and the National Guard was called in to assist the police. The four-day general strike that followed led to a longshoremen's victory that solidified union power in San Francisco for two generations.

Funny gal
Thelma Todd
came to an
unfunny end

Greatest Forced Migration in American History

"Japanese on West Coast Face Wholesale Uprooting," read the headline in the *San Francisco News* on March 4, 1942. What the paper described as "the greatest forced migration in American history" saw nearly 100,000 Issei (Japanese aliens, many eligible for United States citizenship) and Nisei (American citizens of Japanese descent) interned in camps throughout California. The government feared that Issei and Nisei might aid Japan in an attack on the West Coast, though American residents of German or

All hell broke loose in LA after the King verdict

Italian descent were not interned. Many Japanese lost their property or sold it at a fraction of its value.

Unsolved Hollywood Mysteries

A great Hollywood scandal of the 1930s involved the murder of comic actress Thelma Todd, a party girl par excellence. So many people had reasons to cover for the killer that it took 50 years for a solution to surface – at which point two did. In one version, gangster Lucky Luciano, whom Todd had dated, killed her because she knew too much about his gambling rackets and infiltration of Hollywood unions. In the other, her business partner, director Roland West, accidentally caused her death.

The victim in another famous mystery went by the name the Black Dahlia because of her dyed black hair and dark attire. Born Elizabeth Short, she was an aspiring actress whose body was found, severed, in 1947. The lurid details of the story captured the public imagination. More than four dozen people confessed to the murder, most for the publicity. In 2003, a retired Los Angeles police detective published a book fingering his own father as the killer, though, like Todd's case, this one officially remains unsolved.

Kennedy Wins Primary, But Loses Life

On June 5, 1968, U.S. Senator Robert F. Kennedy had just finished his victory speech at the Ambassador Hotel in Los Angeles. He'd won the California presidential primary, making him the probable nominee of the Democratic Party to face the likely Republican, Richard M. Nixon, in the general election. He exited the dais and was escorted into the hotel's pantry, where he was shot. Police

Conspiracy theorists still debate what happened the night RFK was shot

Manson now serves his time in the Central Valley at the state prison in Corcoran

arrested a Palestinian immigrant named Sirhan Bishara Sirhan, who was convicted of the crime. Conspiracy theorists think it unlikely Sirhan acted alone, though, and enough discrepancies between the forensic reports and eyewitness accounts emerged to keep people suspicious. The Ambassador, once one of LA's premier hotels, went out of business in the 1990s.

The Manson Murders

Roman Polanski was out of the country the day in 1969 that members of Charles Manson's cult murdered the director's eight-months-pregnant wife, actress Sharon Tate, at their Los Angeles home. Four others also died. Trial documents later revealed that Richard Burton, Elizabeth Taylor, Frank Sinatra, Steve McQueen and Tom Jones were among the other targets of the Manson gang. Their visit to the Tate house may have been a mistake, however. They were supposedly looking to settle a score with actress Doris Day's son, Terry Melcher.

The O.J. Simpson Case

Few murder trials received coverage as intense as that following the 1994 murder of Nicole Brown Simpson, ex-wife of football star and actor O.J. Simpson, and her friend Ron Goldman. According to the Los Angeles District Attorney's office, hundreds of pieces of evidence implicated Simpson, but his so-called Dream Team of attorneys skillfully countered this

evidence. Unlike at the criminal trial, in a later civil case Simpson was required to testify. He was found to have caused the two deaths, but this verdict resulted in punitive damages, not jail. Simpson's much-photographed mansion in Brentwood was demolished by its new owner in the late 1990s.

Did he or didn't he? One jury acquitted O.J., the other disagreed

PHANTOM RELICS

California reinvents itself so often that its past sometimes gets lost in the shuffle. Following are descriptions of bona fide ghost towns once in the thick of the state's action, along with re-created villages with tales to tell.

Indian Village of Ahwahnee

The Southern Miwok people, who had lived in the Yosemite Valley area for 4,000 years, fiercely resisted the encroachment of miners during the early 1850s before finally succumbing. Within a century, the Miwok way of life had all but vanished, but a re-created village at Yosemite National Park reveals some of their heritage. Among the site's structures, many made of local cedar, are a ceremonial roundhouse and a sweathouse. Other intriguing buildings include a cone-shaped bark-covered house and an acorn granary (black acorns were a Miwok staple).

Missions such as La Purísima were beautiful but isolated

✉ Behind Yosemite Valley Visitor Center (➤ 87)

Mission La Purísima Concepcíon

The handsome missions in cities such as San Diego, Santa Barbara and San Francisco hardly convey the isolation and vulnerability early Spanish settlers experienced. Not so with Mission La Purísima, which Franciscan friars founded in 1787 on a still solitary site about 60 miles (97 kilometers) north of Santa Barbara. Exhibits at the restored mission show how daily life unfolded for the settlers and native peoples.

✉ Mission Gate Road, off Highway 246 (head west from US 101 or east from Highway 1) ☎ (805) 733-3713 🕐 Daily 9–5; closed Jan 1, Thanksgiving and Dec 25 💲 Inexpensive

Fort Ross

Russia's brief foray into California culminated in the establishment of Fort Ross in 1812. Perched high on a bluff with clear Pacific views – the better to spot invading ships – the fort was composed of redwood buildings. The Ross Colony served mainly as a base for fur trappers. By 1821, when the fort was completed, the Russians had nearly rendered their main quarry, the sea otter, extinct. The colonists – Russians and many Aleuts – grew crops for Russia's Alaskan territories for two more decades, then departed. John Sutter, at whose Sierra Nevada mill gold was discovered in 1848, bought the fort in the early 1840s and moved most of its contents to Sacramento.

✉ Fort Ross State Historic Park, 19005 Coast Highway 1, Jenner ☎ (707) 847-3286 🕐 Daily 10–4:30; closed Jan 1, Thanksgiving and Dec 25 💲 Inexpensive

Malakoff Diggins

Ecology wasn't the strong suit of gold-mining companies. Their most destructive technique, hydraulic mining, consisted of blasting hillsides with water to dislodge gold and other ore. Malakoff Diggins was, from 1855 until 1884 – when a court order stopped the practice – the site of one such operation. The scars of the past remain visible, as do rusting pipes and equipment, yet there's a haunting quality to nature's reclamation of the landscape. Restored buildings in the nearby town of North Bloomfield include the drugstore, general store and town hall.

✉ Malakoff Diggins State Historic Park (from Nevada City take Tyler-Foote Crossing Road north to Lake City Road east) ☎ (530) 265-2740

◉ Park: daily dawn–dusk. Museum: daily 10–4:30, late May to early Sep; Sat–Sun 10–4, rest of year
💲 Inexpensive

Bodie Ghost Town State Historic Park

The last resident of the gold-mining boomtown of Bodie departed in the late 1940s, leaving behind a house that's part of a fascinating state park whose 170 buildings are preserved in what's dubbed a state of "arrested decay." Bodie, 8,375 feet (2,552 meters) up in the Sierra Nevada, may look like Nowheresville, but in the late 1800s it was one of the wildest mining camps in the West, famous for its wicked citizens, worse weather, wide streets and bad whiskey. Boozing, brawling, gambling and gunslinging were typical activities in this wild and crazy place. (The miners had a lot of pent-up energy to release.) A small museum documents the town's history, and you can peek into or enter miners' cabins, the schoolhouse, stores, mine shafts and a Methodist church. Guided tours through part of the stamp mill – where ore was pulverized into powder to extract gold and silver – take place daily in the afternoon during the summer.

"Rustic Russian" best describes Fort Ross's architecture

✉ Highway 270 (last 3 miles/5 km to town unpaved), east of US 395 ☎ (760) 647-6445 ◉ Park: daily 8–7, late May to mid-Sep; at least 8–4, rest of year. Museum: daily 10–6, May–Oct; often closed rest of year 💲 Inexpensive

Allensworth

Many Americans trekked west to seek fortune or freedom, among them people of African descent. In 1908, along with four others, Colonel Allen Allensworth formed the town that bears his name. Allensworth, a Civil War Navy veteran who later was U.S. Army chaplain to a unit of the all-black Buffalo Soldiers, hoped to promote economic self-determination for African Americans.

During its early years, the town grew in size (from 20 to 100 acres/8 to 40 hectares) and population (200 people by 1914), but changing water-use patterns, the Great Depression and other events prompted its decline. The town is now being restored to honor its founder's vision.

✉ Colonel Allen Allensworth State Historic Park, Highway 43 (45 miles/72 km north of Bakersfield) ☎ (661) 849-3433 ◉ Daily 9–4 (sometimes till 5; buildings sometimes closed); closed Jan 1, Thanksgiving and Dec 25

artistic license

The Golden State captivates, liberates the creative

California's expansive landscape and its residents' willingness to embrace the unconventional have nourished, even exhilarated, untold artists. Following are just a few painters, poets, musicians, photographers and writers for whom the state has played muse, refuge or both.

Ansel Adams (1902–84)

Ansel Adams – famous for his evocative black and white landscape photography

The famous photographer broke his nose as a lad of four during San Francisco's 1906 earthquake, an occurrence that may or may not have inspired him to examine nature up close. Adams, Edward Weston and Imogen Cunningham were among the Group f/64 photographers of Northern California known for their starkly realistic prints.

Raymond Chandler (1888–1959)

Dames, thugs, losers and the corrupt wealthy mix it up in the deliciously jaundiced detective novels of Raymond Chandler, which evoke Southern California's seamy underside of the mid-20th century. *The Big Sleep* and *Farewell, My Lovely* are two good introductions to the writer's work. "Bay City" in the latter book is Santa Monica.

Jackie Collins (1941–)

Don't laugh. Her prose may be purpler than a

California grape at harvest time, but when Jackie Collins plumbs the psyches of Hollywood wives, she knows whereof she speaks.

R. Crumb (1943–)

The preeminent lunatic of underground comics influenced the psychedelic way San Francisco's 1960s hippie culture perceived itself. Crumb's voluptuously anarchic cover for "Cheap Thrills," the debut album of Janis Joplin's band Big Brother and the Holding Company, turned the world on to his singular talent.

Richard Henry Dana (1787–1879)

In the mid-1830s, Richard Henry Dana interrupted his law studies at Harvard University to sail to California as a merchant seaman. He recounted his adventures, including stops at major ports from San Diego to San Francisco, in *Two Years Before the Mast*.

Joan Didion (1934–)

The contradictory nature of the California dream often surfaces in Didion's essays and fiction, perhaps most poignantly in *Play It as It Lays*, a novel about disaffected Los Angelenos.

Isadora Duncan (1878–1927)

The mother of modern dance, a San Francisco native, made her fame outside California but included the Pacific Ocean and the "waving pine forests of the Sierra Nevada" among the inspirations for her free-form choreography.

Richard Diebenkorn (1922–93)

Jazz, classical music, Henri Matisse, William Butler Yeats, abstract expressionism and the clarity of California sunlight were among the many influences on painter Richard Diebenkorn, who lived and worked in both the San Francisco Bay Area and Los Angeles. Light and color are key themes of Diebenkorn's famous *Ocean Park* series, abstract takes on coastal Southern California.

Jackie Collins – author of several best-selling novels on Hollywood

Painting from Richard Diebenkorn's famous *Ocean Park* series

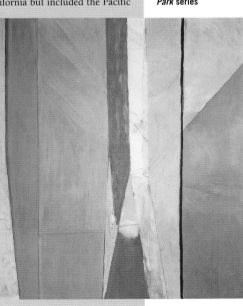

The Grateful Dead (1965–95)

Some bands made the scene earlier and others sold more records, but no group typified the California hippie ethic more than the Grateful Dead. Take a metaphorical toke, put on "Workingman's Dead" and close your eyes. Before you know it you'll be hearing colors you've never heard before.

Helen Hunt Jackson (1830–85)

A half-Native American, half-Scottish woman and her Native American husband suffer untold prejudice in Jackson's 1884 novel *Ramona*. Though sentimental about the mission system, *Ramona* nevertheless resulted in legislation meant to improve conditions for Indians. Unfortunately, in many respects the cure was no better than the disease. The book nonetheless stimulated tourism to California for half a century.

Jack Kerouac (1922–69)

San Francisco figures prominently in Kerouac's groundbreaking novel, *On the Road*. The author hung out in the 1950s in North Beach and elsewhere with Beat-era cronies such as Allen Ginsberg, Neal Cassady, Gregory Corso, Bob Kaufman and Gary Snyder.

Henry Miller (1891–1980)

The author of *Tropic of Cancer* extolled the rugged isolation of Big Sur and the area's convention-flouting residents. One biographer notes that he also appreciated California's "good (and cheap)" wine and "easygoing" women. *Big Sur and the Oranges of Hieronymus Bosch* reflects a particularly jolly period in Miller's life.

Walter Mosley (1952–)

Short on cash, Easy Rawlins accepts a job searching for a missing blonde in Walter Mosley's novel *Devil in a Blue Dress*, later a film starring Denzel Washington. In *Devil, Black Betty* and other books, Mosley, who was born in South Central Los Angeles, delivers a trenchant slice of late-1940s African-American life in Los Angeles. His works explore aspects of the city Raymond Chandler only hints at in his works.

Richard Rodriguez (1944–)

One of contemporary California's most provocative commentators was born in San Francisco and raised in Sacramento. The child of Mexican immigrants, Rodriguez describes himself as the "comic victim of two cultures," namely Latin and Anglo America. In *Days of Obligation: An Argument with My Mexican Father*, he outlines what he's learned from each.

Background picture: Jack Kerouac

Upton Sinclair (1878–1968)

Novelist, socialist and muckraking journalist, Sinclair provided a populist critique of capitalism that caught on with California's electorate in the mid-1930s. Only an orchestrated campaign by the state's economic elite – including the major movie studios, which distorted Sinclair's views in propaganda pieces that played in theaters – kept him from being elected governor. He described his defeat in *I, Candidate for Governor, and How I Got Licked.*

John Steinbeck (1902–68)

The Golden State was the setting for much of Steinbeck's fiction. According to his sister, California was consistently in her brother's "mind – and imagination." Steinbeck's *The Grapes of Wrath* describes life for Central Valley migrant workers. Steinbeck (right) set *Cannery Row* in Monterey's sardine-processing plants.

Amy Tan (1952–)

The recollections of her mother and her mother's friends informed the Oakland-born author's novel *The Joy Luck Club*, about Chinese immigrants and Chinese Americans in the San Francisco Bay Area. The cultural and interpersonal aspects of mother-daughter relationships are the book's principal focus.

Alice Walker (1944–)

California became a haven for Alice Walker, who moved here in the 1970s spiritually exhausted from her participation in the civil rights movement in the Southern states. The author of *The Color Purple* has a home in Mendocino and often stays in San Francisco. She has written in one book that living in Northern California, among other things, provided her the space and perspective to "accept all the parts, good and bad, of my own heritage."

California Timeline

1500
Approximately 300 native tribes live in what is now California.

1542
Portuguese sailor Juan Rodriguez Cabrillo, exploring the New World for the Spanish crown, lands at San Diego.

1769
Mission San Diego de Alcalá, the first of 21 Franciscan missions in Alta California (present-day California), is founded.

1781
Los Angeles, settled by 14 families from Mexico, is officially named "El Pueblo del la Reina de Los Angeles" (Town of the Queen of the Angels).

1821
Mexico achieves independence from Spain; California comes under Mexican rule.

1848
Gold is discovered; California officially becomes a U.S. territory.

1850
California attains statehood.

1869
The Transcontinental railroad links California with the eastern United States.

1873
First navel orange tree is planted in Riverside, spawning the California citrus industry. First cable-car line begins operation in San Francisco.

1886
Fares from the Midwest to Los Angeles drop as low as $1 during railroad price war; thousands emigrate to California.

1906
The Great Earthquake and Fire ravages San Francisco.

1930s
Dust Bowl in the Midwest spurs more immigration.

1937
Golden Gate Bridge opens.

1955
Disneyland opens in Anaheim.

1978
San Francisco mayor George Moscone and gay supervisor Harvey Milk are murdered by Dan White.

1992
Mass rioting ensues when a jury acquits police officers accused of beating Rodney King, an African American, during his arrest in 1991 for a traffic violation.

1994–1995
O.J. Simpson is accused of murdering his ex-wife; the case dominates state and national news for more than a year.

2003
In a special election, voters replace the sitting governor with actor Arnold Schwarzenegger.

Finding
Your Feet

First Two Hours

San Francisco International Airport (SFO), Los Angeles International
Airport (LAX) and San Diego International Airport (SAN) are California's
main gateways. Most major U.S. and international airlines fly into LAX and
SFO, and many serve SAN.

Best Bets for Airport Transfers

- **Taxis** are the foolproof method for getting from all three airports to the city center. In each city, the rate is for the ride, not per passenger.
- **Shared-ride van services** load up with passengers heading to addresses more or less in the same part of town.
- **Public transportation** is not a great option in Los Angeles – it might take you more than two hours to get to your destination – BART trains take a half hour to reach San Francisco. In San Diego public buses can be convenient if you're staying downtown, though a cab ride isn't expensive.
- **Ground transportation fees:** $ = under $12; $$ = $12–20; $$$ = $21–30; $$$$ = over $30, excluding tip. Public transportation from the airports costs less than $5.

San Francisco and the Bay Area

- **San Francisco International Airport** (tel: 650/821-8211) is about 15 miles (24 kilometers) from downtown.
- Queues for **taxis** ($$$$) form on the lower (arrivals) level.
- **SuperShuttle** (tel: 415/558-8500) provides a shared-ride van service ($$). Look for signs (yellow letters on a dark-blue background) on the upper-level traffic islands outside each terminal.
- **Bayporter Express** (tel: 415/467-1800) serves Oakland and other East Bay destinations ($$), also from the upper level.
- **SFO Airporter** (tel: 415/246-2678) makes stops ($$) at major downtown hotels. Board the bus on the lower level.
- **SamTrans** (tel: 800/660-4287) buses ($) serve San Mateo County, where the airport is located, and parts of San Francisco and Palo Alto.
- **BART** (Bay Area Rapid Transit; tel: 650/992-2278) trains are the best public transport option to downtown San Francisco. The trains also travel to the East Bay and parts of northern San Mateo County. From any terminal, walk or take the AirTrain shuttle to the BART station in the International Terminal. Purchase a ticket ($) from machines in the station.
- **If you're driving,** follow US 101 north to the 4th Street exit.
- **Other Bay Area airports:** Oakland International (OAK; tel: 510/563-3300); San Jose International (SJC; tel: 408/277-4759).

Los Angeles Area

- **Los Angeles International Airport** (tel: 310/646-5252) is 18 miles (29 kilometers) from downtown and about 12 miles (19 kilometers) from Beverly Hills and West Hollywood.
- All **ground transportation** can be found on the lower (arrivals) level of all terminals.
- **Taxi fares** vary, depending on where you're going ($$$ for downtown).
- **SuperShuttle** (tel: 310/782-6600 or 800/258-3826) and **Xpress Shuttle** (tel: 310/323-7222 or 800/427-7483) are among the shared-ride vans ($$) offering door-to-door service.
- **Metropolitan Transportation Authority (MTA)** (tel: 213/626-4455 or 800/266-6883) buses ($) leave the airport for many destinations. Some routes (such

as West Hollywood) are direct; others involve complicated transfers. For information, visit the transportation desk near baggage claim.

- **Metro Line** (tel: 213/626-4455 or 800/266-6883) light-rail trains are only convenient if you're going downtown ($). Board the free shuttle bus to the Metro Green Line's Aviation Station. Stay on the train until the Imperial/Wilmington Station and transfer to the Blue Line heading north.
- **If you're driving,** take Century Boulevard east out of the airport to I-405 (the San Diego Freeway, known locally as the 405) heading north. Then take I-10 (Santa Monica Freeway), heading west for Santa Monica or east for downtown.
- For **West Hollywood or Beverly Hills,** get on the 405 but look immediately for the La Cienega Boulevard sign. Head north on La Cienega. (Just before the 405, you'll cross La Cienega, but you'll save time if you access it via the freeway.) Turn west (left) at Wilshire Boulevard for Beverly Hills. Continue north on La Cienega for West Hollywood.
- **Other Los Angeles-Area airports:** Bob Hope Airport (BUR; tel: 818/840-8847) formerly called Burbank; Ontario (ONT; tel: 909/937-2700); John Wayne Airport Orange County (SNA; tel: 949/252-5252).

San Diego

- **San Diego International Airport** (tel: 619/231-2100) is about 3 miles (5 kilo-meters) from downtown. Pick up taxis, shuttles or buses at the Transportation Plaza at Terminal 1 or 2, or curbside at the commuter termi-nal (mostly for in-state flights).
- **Taxis** pick up passengers at all terminals for trips to downtown ($) and beyond.
- **Cloud 9 Shuttle** (tel: 858/505-4998 or 800/974-8885) operates a shared-ride van service ($–$$) to San Diego and beyond.
- **San Diego Transit** (tel: 619/233-3004) bus 992 heads from the airport to downtown.
- **If you're driving,** take North Harbor Drive east for downtown and west for Shelter Island and Point Loma. Harbor Island is across from the airport. To get to La Jolla take I-5 north. For Mission Valley, take I-8 east.

Train Stations

- **Amtrak** (tel: 800/872-7245) trains serve California. San Francisco-bound passengers must disembark at the Emeryville station (5885 Landregan Street) in the East Bay and take a shuttle bus to the city. Amtrak stops in Los Angeles at Union Station (800 North Alameda Street) and in San Diego at the Santa Fe Depot (1050 Kettner Boulevard).

Bus Stations

- **Greyhound** (tel: 800/231-2222) is the state's main long-distance bus company, serving San Francisco (Transbay Terminal, 1st and Mission streets), Los Angeles (1716 E. 7th Street), San Diego (120 W. Broadway), Sacramento (715 L Street) and many other cities.

Orienting Yourself
San Francisco

- Union Square is the hub of downtown San Francisco. Many hotels are here, on Market Street or in nearby SoMa (South of Market Street area), where Moscone Center is located.

San Francisco Visitor Information Center:
✉ Hallidie Plaza, Lower Level, Powell and Market streets ☎ (415) 391-2000
🕐 Mon–Fri 9–5, Sat–Sun 9–3, May–Oct; Sat only, rest of year. Closed Jan 1, Easter, Thanksgiving and Dec 25 🚇 Muni Metro J,

K, L, M, N and BART (Powell Street)

🚌 Muni Bus 5, 6, 7, 21, 26, 27, 31, 38, F-line Trolley; Powell-Mason and Powell-Hyde cable cars

Los Angeles

- Downtown Los Angeles is favored more by business travelers than leisure travelers, who tend to gravitate toward Hollywood, West Hollywood, Beverly Hills or beach towns such as Santa Monica.

Los Angeles Visitor Information Center:
✉ 685 S. Figueroa Street ☎ (213) 624-7300 🕐 Mon–Fri 8:30–5
🚇 Metro Red Line (7th & Figueroa)
🚌 MTA Bus 20, 460; DASH A, E, F

Hollywood and Highland Visitor Information Center:
✉ 6801 Hollywood Boulevard ☎ (323) 467-6412 🕐 Mon–Sat 10–10, Sun 10–7
🚇 Metro Red Line (Hollywood & Highland)
🚌 MTA Bus 163, 210, 212, 217; DASH Hollywood

San Diego

- San Diego sprawls outward from its downtown waterfront. Most tourist attractions are north of downtown.

International Visitor Information Center:
✉ 1043½ W. Broadway, at Harbor Drive
☎ (619) 236-1212

🕐 Mon–Sat 9–5 (also Sun, spring–fall, but call ahead) 🚈 Trolley (American Plaza)
🚌 Bus 30, 992

Getting Around

Driving

You can get by without a car in San Francisco and parts of San Diego, but driving is the easiest way to see most of California. I-5 and US 101 are the major north–south highways. Scenic, winding (i.e., the going's often slow) Highway 1 runs north–south along the coast, merging several times with US 101. I-80 runs east–west through the middle of Northern California. I-10 and I-15 travel east–west through Southern California.

On the Road

- You need a **valid driver's license** from your home state or country to drive in California. The minimum age for drivers is 16; car-rental companies usually require that drivers be 21 or older (some charge more if you're under 25).
- Drivers and passengers must **wear seat belts at all times.**
- Children under 6 years of age or 60 pounds (27 kilograms) in weight must **ride in safety seats;** most car-rental agencies supply them for an additional charge.
- Except where indicated otherwise, **right turns are permitted on red lights** after you've come to a full stop. Turns onto intersecting one-way streets are permitted in the same circumstances.
- Driving with a blood-alcohol level **higher than .08% is illegal.**
- **The speed limit on freeways** is 65 or 70 mph (105 or 112 kph) on rural roads and from 55 to 65 mph (88 to 105 kph) on city freeways. In cities, the speed limit is generally 25 or 30 mph (40 or 48 kph) unless posted otherwise.
- In the San Francisco Bay Area, Los Angeles and San Diego, **avoid commuting hours on the freeways** 7–10 am and 4–7 pm (longer in LA).

In-State Air Travel

- Price wars in recent years have kept fares competitive for flights between Northern and Southern California. If you have the time, though, you may still want to drive to take in the scenery.

City Transit
San Francisco Bay Area

- **Hotels charge a fortune for parking,** and spaces on the street are sometimes difficult to find – two good reasons to take advantage of public transportation. Rent a car for trips farther afield.

- The **Transit Information Line** (tel: 511 or 817-1717 from any area code in the Bay Area) has advice about all public systems.
- **Muni** (tel: 415/673-6864) operates buses, light-rail vehicles, antique trolleys and cable cars in San Francisco. All cost the same amount except cable cars, for which you pay slightly more.
- For above-ground trips on Market Street up to Castro or along the Embarcadero, the **antique trolleys are convenient** (and fun). Exact change is required in dollar bills or coins.
- **Transfers,** valid for about two hours and good for two changes of buses or rail cars, in any direction, are issued free when requested upon boarding.
- **All-day passes** can be purchased at the Visitor Information Center (➤ 33) and elsewhere.
- **BART** trains (tel: 415/989-2278 or 510/465-2278) serve downtown and the southern part of San Francisco and travel to the East Bay and northern San Mateo County. You buy tickets in BART stations.

Los Angeles Area
- It is generally difficult to tour LA by public transit, but it can be done, and in some cases (going to the *Queen Mary*, for instance), it's preferable.
- If you're going to use public transportation, consider staying downtown – subways and bus routes fan out from here. **MTA** buses (tel: 213/626-4455) and **Metro Line** light-rail vehicles serve the metropolitan area. The MTA also operates **DASH** minibuses for short hops around downtown and elsewhere. Santa Monica and other nearby towns operate their own bus systems. Exact change is required except at light-rail stations.

San Diego
- Downtown, Balboa Park and Old Town are well served, and Coronado and SeaWorld receive adequate service, but to get to La Jolla and other places takes a long time, and some locales are under served or nearly ignored.
- **San Diego Transit** (tel: 619/233-3004) operates buses (all over) and trolleys (around downtown, to Old Town and Mission Valley and to California's border with Tijuana, Mexico). Exact change is required on buses; you can purchase trolley tickets at vending machines in the stations.

Taxis
Taxis are difficult to hail in all three cities. You're generally better off calling for one or joining the line at a hotel taxi stand.
- **San Francisco:** Yellow Cab (tel: 415/626-2345) and Veteran's Cab (tel: 415/552-1300).
- **Los Angeles:** Independent Cab Co. (tel: 323/255-2525) and United Independent Taxi (tel: 323/653-5050).
- **San Diego:** Silver Cabs (tel: 619/280-5555) and Yellow Cab (tel: 619/234-6161).

Admission Charges
The cost of admission for museums and places of interest mentioned in the text is indicated by price categories
Inexpensive under $7   **Moderate** $7–13   **Expensive** over $13

Safety
Though often highly publicized, incidents of violence against travelers in California are rare. However, it's wise to be prudent. Ask at visitor centers about neighborhoods you should avoid.

Accommodations

Standards are high throughout the state, but in general the best accommodations are available in San Francisco and Los Angeles – each of which has a number of world-class hotels – and in resort areas such as the Wine Country, the Monterey Peninsula, Santa Barbara and Palm Springs.

Hotels and Motels

- Hotels and motels are the **most common types of lodgings.** Hotels tend to be the best options in big cities and motels are kings of the highways.
- **Full-service hotels** in California often include such amenities as fitness rooms, indoor pools, laundry service, in-room modems and safes, valet parking and concierges. Motels often offer outdoor swimming pools and hot tubs, along with amenities such as cable TV and hair dryers.
- Many hotels and motels allow children (of varying ages) **to stay free** with their parents in a room. Some allow pets. Most do not include meals in the rates – except for the occasional Continental breakfast.
- **One drawback with motels** is security because the door to your room opens directly to the outside world.

Bed-and-Breakfast Inns

- B&Bs in California often charge high rates comparable to big-city hotels or full-service resorts. They generally require two-night minimum stays on weekends and three-night minimum stays on holidays. Many are also geared toward romantic couples and are not friendly to young children.

Resorts

- California has a number of high-end, full-service resorts, with such amenities as golf courses, tennis courts and multiple swimming pools.

Best Inexpensive Option

- California has a number of hostels that charge $10–25 per night per person. Most have dormitory-type rooms where sexes are segregated, some have rooms for couples or families. Most limit stays to a few days at a time. **American Youth Hostels** (tel: 301/495-1240).

Booking Accommodations

- Book well in advance, if possible, for big-city hotels, national-park lodgings (especially crowded Yosemite) and resorts in high season.

Diamond Ratings

- AAA tourism editors evaluate and rate lodging establishments based on the overall quality and services. AAA's diamond rating criteria reflect the design and service standards set by the lodging industry, combined with the expectations of our members.
- Our one (♦) or two (♦♦) diamond rating represents a clean and well-maintained property offering comfortable rooms, with the two diamond property showing enhancements in decor and furnishings. A three (♦♦♦) diamond property shows marked upgrades in physical attributes, services and comfort and may offer additional amenities. A four (♦♦♦♦) diamond rating signifies a property offering a high level of service and hospitality and a wide variety of amenities and upscale facilities. A five (♦♦♦♦♦) diamond rating represents a world-class facility, offering the highest level of luxurious accommodations and personalized guest services.

Food and Drink

Culinarily, the state is one of the most cosmopolitan places in the world, reflecting its melting-pot population.

Regional Specialties

- California's fertile fields provide local chefs with a **multitude of fresh produce and other ingredients** such as Sonoma lamb, Castroville artichokes, Gilroy garlic, Modesto almonds and Coachella Valley dates.
- **Seafood is another specialty.** One of the most savored local delicacies is the Dungeness crab, known for its sweetness. San Francisco is the home of **cioppino,** a richly seasoned shellfish stew.
- San Francisco is also **renowned for Asian food.** Dim sum – a selection of Chinese dumplings and other tasty morsels – is a must for lunch, as is phó, a delicious Vietnamese noodle soup usually containing beef and vegetables. In general, Asian restaurants offer some of the best bargains.
- Developed in California over the past quarter-century or so, and always evolving, **California cuisine** relies on fresh local ingredients to create innovative, often light fusion dishes that blend American, Asian, Mediterranean and Latin influences.
- **New American cuisine** can perhaps best be thought of as high-class meat and potatoes. A pork chop, for instance, may be cooked fairly rare and served with a gravy containing fresh herbs; the mashed potatoes on the side may be infused with garlic. Regional and ethnic influences are sometimes evident, and natural and organic ingredients are often highlighted.
- **Latin American food** is prevalent throughout the state, especially the areas closer to Mexico.

Drink Specialties

- **California wines** rank among the finest in the world. While vintages from the Napa and Sonoma valleys are best known, don't overlook those from other regions, such as near Monterey or Santa Barbara.
- **The martini,** said to have been invented in California, has regained its former cachet. Fine martini bars now dot the big cities. Irish coffee – coffee spiked with Irish whiskey and whipped cream – is claimed to have been born at the **Buena Vista Café** (➤ 69) in San Francisco. **Margaritas,** though a Mexican import, have virtually been adopted as the California state drink.
- Recent years have seen a renaissance of **local microbreweries** producing a variety of flavorful specialty beers, now available throughout the state.

Best Brew Pubs

- **Beach Chalet,** San Francisco (➤ 64).
- **Gordon Biersch Brewery and Restaurant,** San Francisco (➤ 69).
- **Father's Office** (1018 Montana Avenue, Santa Monica; tel: 310/393-2337).

Dining Options

- California's trendiest restaurants are the new bistros and cafés springing up around the state that are often casual in look and feel but serious about good food. Celebrity chefs often helm the kitchens. Hot restaurants include **Boulevard** (➤ 64) and **Rose Pistola** (➤ 66) in San Francisco, and **Patina** and **Spago Beverly Hills** (➤ 146) in LA.
- Many of the hottest restaurants have **full bars** where you can walk in without a reservation, sit down and order a meal – sometimes from a special bar menu, sometimes from the full menu.

- **Lounges and brew pubs** that specialize in drinks, but also serve excellent food, are another trend.
- **You can't always tell the quality** of a restaurant by its exterior. In Los Angeles, a fine restaurant may be hidden away in a small shopping mall. In San Francisco, what appears to be a modest neighborhood ethnic spot may serve some of the best food in the city.

Some Bests
The following restaurants are recommended for their special attributes:
Best for al fresco meals:
- **Campanile,** Los Angeles (➤ 144)
- **George's at the Cove,** San Diego (➤ 173)
- **Tra Vigne,** St. Helena (➤ 94)

Best for California cuisine:
- **Café Beaujolais,** Mendocino (➤ 93)
- **Chez Panisse,** Berkeley (➤ 64)
- **Mustards Grill,** Napa Valley (➤ 94)

Best neighborhood ethnic cuisine:
- **La Super-Rica,** Santa Barbara (➤ 117)
- **Slanted Door,** San Francisco (➤ 66)
- **Ton Kiang,** San Francisco (➤ 66)

A Practical Guide to Eating Out
- **You can dine very well for $10 a person or even less,** especially at a neighborhood ethnic restaurant. Keep in mind that tax, tip and drinks can add 50 percent or more to the total cost of a meal.
- Eating hours typically are: **breakfast** from about 7 to 9:30/10 am (though some diners serve breakfast all day and night); **lunch** from 11:30/noon to 2/2:30 pm; **dinner** from 5 to 9:30/10 pm or until late.
- **Call ahead.** Restaurants often change their opening hours and days or occasionally close for private parties.
- Except for informal diners and cafés, **most restaurants accept reservations,** and it's a good idea to book well ahead at trendy restaurants in big cities.
- **Tipping is an expected practice in California,** though usually the amount is left to the discretion of the customer. Tips can range between 10 and 20 percent, with 15 percent most common. Some upscale restaurants routinely add a service charge (around 15 to 18 percent) for groups of six or more people.
- Even in the big cities, **casual dress is widely accepted** in California restaurants. However, some establishments do impose a dress code – a jacket or jacket and tie for men – or occasionally have a policy barring jeans, shorts or sneakers.
- By law, **smoking is banned indoors** in all California restaurants. Some allow cigarette smoking on outdoor patios. Indoor bars are now also legally non-smoking, though some are lax in their enforcement.
- Credit cards are accepted at most restaurants, but not all. If you aren't sure, **it's wise to carry plenty of cash or traveler's checks,** which are widely accepted.

Diamond Ratings
As with the hotel ratings (➤ 36), AAA tourism editors evaluate restaurants on the overall quality of food, service, decor and ambiance – with extra emphasis given to food and service. Ratings range from one diamond (💎) indicating a simple, family-oriented establishment to five diamonds (💎💎💎💎💎) indicating an establishment offering superb culinary skills and ultimate adult dining experience.

Shopping

In California you can get everything from exquisite Asian silks to colorful Mexican pottery. If you're looking for more home-grown products, consider hand-made jewelry from local artists, Native American baskets, or California wines, almonds or dates. Certain types of purchases may fall somewhere in the middle; chances are that the surfer wear that says "L.A." all over it is actually made in Southeast Asia, but it still makes a suitable souvenir.

Local Specialties

On the North Coast, especially in the Mendocino area, look for paintings and jewelry by local artists. Carmel, along the Central Coast, is another town lined with art galleries. The San Joaquin Valley is good for buying almonds and, in the town of Reedley, near Fresno, Mennonite quilts (World Handcrafts, 1012 G Street, Reedley, tel: 559/638-3560). San Francisco offers a bonanza of Asian imports in its Chinatown and Japantown districts. Los Angeles is the place to buy movie memorabilia, while LA's Olvera Street and San Diego's Old Town are good for Mexican and Central American imports. The Palm Springs area is strong on Native American crafts.

Pricing

Full retail-price clothing is not particularly good value in California; price tags are generally higher than on the East Coast, for instance. Factory outlet shops, however, generally provide bargains on designer fashions. Imports from Asia and Latin America are often very good buys. And you won't find better prices on California wines, canned nuts, dried fruits and other local food products.

Practicalities

- **Hours:** Shops and stores may open anywhere from 9 am to noon; the latter is most common among small specialty shops, and on Sundays for many stores. Most stores stay open until 5 or 6 pm. though stores in malls or shopping plazas often don't close until 9 pm or even later. Some stores stay open late one night a week, usually a Thursday or Friday, and a fair number of smaller stores close on Sunday or Monday.
- **Payment methods:** Most stores accept credit cards and traveler's checks.
- **Etiquette:** Browsing is permissible almost everywhere, and most sales persons do not rely on high-pressure tactics. In fact, service in stores is often too relaxed – it's not always easy to find someone to wait on you.

Top Shopping Districts

- **For chic shopping,** the ultimate is Rodeo Drive in Beverly Hills (➤ 149).
- **For good-value standard shopping,** you'll usually do best at a big-city or sub-urban mall. But one district that can provide surprising value, considering its popularity with tourists, is San Francisco's Fisherman's Wharf. There you'll find a huge **Cost Plus World Market** store (2552 Taylor Street, tel: 415/928-6200), loaded with inexpensive imports of all kinds, as well as several big shopping complexes – Ghirardelli Square, the Cannery, the Anchorage and Pier 39 among them (➤ 69 for all) – that, combined, offer hundreds of specialty shops, food courts, bay views, and free street performers and other entertainment. Though you'll have to hunt down the good values among the overpriced schlock, they're there.
- **For the best department stores,** San Francisco's Union Square (➤ 68) is *the* place to go. Macy's, Neiman-Marcus and Saks Fifth Avenue line the square, and a Nordstrom is nearby at the **San Francisco Shopping Centre** (➤ 68).

Entertainment

The state's varied terrain lends itself to a wide variety of outdoor activities, while the cities and resort areas are centers for nightlife and the arts.

Information

- The best sources for current entertainment listings are **local newspapers.**
- Several cities and resort areas have 24-hour, toll-free, hot-line numbers that give upcoming events. **Most regional visitor bureaus and information centers** (➤ 33, 34) produce annual guides or seasonal brochures that list groups offering music, theater and dance productions. Check phone directory.

Nightlife

Los Angeles, San Francisco and, to a lesser extent, San Diego and Palm Springs, are the nightlife capitals of California.

- **Bars:** The best selection is in San Francisco, ranging from classy hotel lounges and sleek bars in trendy restaurants to atmospheric dives in color-ful neighborhoods (➤ 69–70).
- **Nightclubs:** For sheer raucous entertainment, Los Angeles, especially the Sunset Strip, has the top nightclubs and dance clubs (➤ 150).
- **Culture:** San Francisco's Civic Center area, with world-class opera and sym-phony, and its nearby Theater District, which presents touring productions of Broadway-style shows along with other stage plays, is a top site for the performing arts (➤ 70 for information). In Los Angeles the cultural divi-sions are more dispersed but center on several downtown performing arts venues (➤ 150).

Spectator Sports

California has five major league baseball teams, three National Football League teams and four National Basketball Association teams. In addition, the state has women's professional basketball teams, three National Hockey League teams, several thoroughbred racing tracks, a number of professional and amateur soccer teams and numerous college teams in many sports.

Outdoor Activities

California is one of the world's premier regions for outdoor sports and activities.

- Thousands of miles of **scenic and often challenging hiking trails** crisscross the state's mountains and forests.
- Dozens of **top-flight downhill ski and snowboarding resorts,** as well as thou-sands of miles of scenic cross-country ski and snowshoe trails, are located in the Sierra Nevada and other mountain ranges.
- Mountain biking, horseback riding and rock climbing are other sports **popular in rugged California landscapes.**
- **Water sports** – canoeing, fishing, kayaking, river rafting, sailing, swimming, surfing, waterskiing and windsurfing among them – thrive along the long ocean coastline, as well as in the state's huge network of rivers and lakes.
- **Whale-watching expeditions** set out in winter from Monterey and other coastal communities during gray whale migrations.
- Road biking, running and jogging are **favorite pastimes along many paved trails,** such as the 32-mile (51-kilometer) Jedediah Smith Memorial Bicycle Trail along the American River Parkway near Sacramento.
- **Hot-air ballooning,** most common in the Wine Country but also found in Southern California and the Sierra, offers a bird's-eye perspective on it all.

San Francisco and the Bay Area

In Three Days 44 – 45
Don't Miss 46 – 54
At Your Leisure 55 – 63
Where To 64 – 70

Getting Your Bearings

Good food, carefree living and an active cultural scene have been San Francisco trademarks since the frisky Gold Rush days. Writing in 1880, Robert Louis Stevenson credited the city's convivial ambiance to its international citizenry. "The town is essentially not Anglo-Saxon; still more essentially not American," he wrote. "The shops along the streets are like the consulates of different nations. The passers-by vary in features like the slides of a magic lantern."

Elsewhere in his writings Stevenson acknowledged the clashes of culture that characterized 19th-century San Francisco. More than almost anywhere in America, though, this city of shapely hills and water views has been a place that tolerates and even celebrates eccentricity and diversity. It's no accident that Beat writers, psychedelic rockers and budding performance artists all flourished here, not to mention the pioneers in the feminist, human-potential and gay-liberation movements.

The agreeable climate attracted the earliest settlers, Ohlone people who lived near what is now Mission Dolores. Spanish seafarers discovered what one called a "very noble and very large harbor" beyond the strait later named the Golden Gate. But it took the discovery of gold to prompt mass migration. San Francisco boomed for 50 years, until the earthquake and fire of 1906 destroyed it.

By the time the city recovered, Los Angeles was on the rise and business had begun moving south. San Francisco continued to attract entrepreneurs and artists, though, and it has remained the hub of Northern California life. The sense of history is palpable, but with multimedia and Internet companies thriving, a 21st-century dynamism is amply evident as well.

5 Golden Gate Bridge

(101)

0   1 mile
0   2 km

Palace of Fine Arts 9

Baker Beach

BLVD

PRESIDIO
Golden Gate National Recreation Area

LINCOLN

6 California Palace of the Legion of Honor

CALIFORNIA STREET

Cliff House 7

GEARY   BOULEVARD

Seal Rocks

RICHMOND   **SAN FRANCISCO**

FULTON   STREET

Ocean Beach

GREAT HIGHWAY

8

Golden Gate Park

HAIGHT ASHBURY

LINCOLN   WAY

19TH AVENUE

7TH AVENUE

Twin Peaks

Previous page: San Francisco's Transamerica Pyramid at dusk

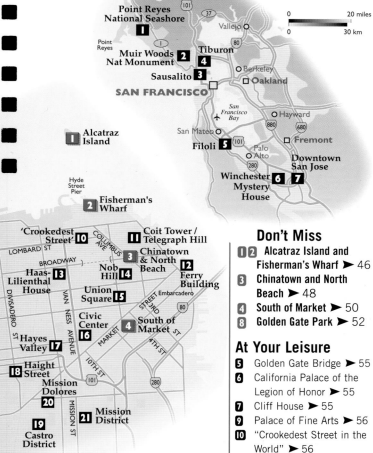

Don't Miss

1 2 Alcatraz Island and
Fisherman's Wharf ➤ 46

3 Chinatown and North
Beach ➤ 48

4 South of Market ➤ 50

8 Golden Gate Park ➤ 52

At Your Leisure

5 Golden Gate Bridge ➤ 55

6 California Palace of the
Legion of Honor ➤ 55

7 Cliff House ➤ 55

9 Palace of Fine Arts ➤ 56

10 "Crookedest Street in the
World" ➤ 56

11 Coit Tower/Telegraph Hill
➤ 56

12 Ferry Building ➤ 57

13 Haas-Lilienthal House
➤ 57

14 Nob Hill ➤ 58

15 Union Square ➤ 58

16 Civic Center ➤ 58

17 Hayes Valley ➤ 59

18 Haight Street ➤ 59

19 Castro District ➤ 59

20 Mission Dolores ➤ 60

21 Mission District ➤ 60

Farther Afield

1 Point Reyes National Seashore ➤ 61

2 Muir Woods National Monument ➤ 61

3 Sausalito ➤ 62

4 Tiburon ➤ 62

5 Filoli ➤ 62

6 Winchester Mystery House ➤ 63

7 Downtown San Jose ➤ 63

A proper taste of San Francisco includes its famous sights but also its simpler pleasures – a tree-lined staircase and a bayside stroll.

San Francisco and the Bay Area in Three Days

Day 1

Morning
A hearty breakfast will fortify you for an early-morning ferry ride to **1 Alcatraz Island** (➤ 46–47), home to the famous prison (left).

Afternoon
Head into **3 North Beach** (➤ 48–49), where you can lunch Italian at Rose Pistola (➤ 66) or L'Osteria al Forno (519 Columbus Avenue, tel: 415/982-1124) and browse through the shops on Columbus and Grant avenues. From North Beach, continue into **3 Chinatown** (➤ 48–49).

Evening
Catch the sunset or twilight views from the Top of the Mark (➤ 69) cocktail lounge. Dinner is a real event at Masa's (➤ 65). For a delightful time that's less of a splurge, head to the always bustling Zuni Café (➤ 66).

Day 2

Morning
Take the Powell-Mason line to the **Cable Car Museum** (➤ 58). Walk north or hop on another cable car and get off at Greenwich Street. Walk east four blocks to visit **11 Coit Tower** (➤ 56), afterward descending the Greenwich and Filbert steps.

Afternoon
Have lunch at Fog City Diner (➤ 65). Walk south along the waterfront side of the

Embarcadero, savoring the East Bay views and breezes. Then catch an F-line antique trolley and head up Market Street. Disembark at 3rd Street and walk south into the **4 SoMa** district (➤ 50–51), where you can sit in Yerba Buena Gardens or enjoy cultural and entertainment options that include museums, galleries, a high-tech video arcade, the kids-oriented Zeum (above) and an old-fashioned carousel.

Evening
Tea at the café or a cocktail at the bar of the swank W San Francisco hotel (181 Third Street, tel: 415/775-5300) should revive you in time for dinner at the postmodern-chic Hawthorne Lane (22 Hawthorne Lane, tel: 415/777-9779).

Day 3

Morning
The hubbub of the city recedes in gorgeous **8 Golden Gate Park** (➤ 52–54). Begin your explorations with the flora in the park's eastern section at the Conservatory of Flowers and the nearby Rhododendron Dell, then walk west to Strybing Arboretum and stroll through the botanical exhibits there. Reflect on the morning's sights over tea at the restful Japanese Tea Garden (right).

Afternoon
Have lunch at the Beach Chalet (➤ 64), then walk north along the Ocean Beach sidewalk to the **7 Cliff House** (➤ 55–56).

Evening
Have an early Chinese seafood dinner at fancy Harbor Village (➤ 65) or less-expensive Yuet Lee (1300 Stockton Street, tel: 415/982-6020). After dinner, watch San Francisco have a good laugh at itself at the long-running *Beach Blanket Babylon* show (➤ 70). Order your tickets way in advance, especially during summer.

Alcatraz Island and Fisherman's Wharf

The tiny fleet that sails in with the morning catch is among the few remnants of the San Francisco waterfront's once prosperous fishing industry. But even when fishing was king, tourist amusements were part of the mix: In the 1800s you could watch an "educated" pig play cards at Cockney White's museum. You can't escape the ultracommercial tourist attractions of today's wharf, but several fine nautical attractions dock here, and ferries depart for Alcatraz Island.

Many inmates tried to escape "The Rock," but none succeeded

Many people declare the ferry ride and visit to Alcatraz Island and its former maximum-security penitentiary to be the highlight of their trip to San Francisco. The 15-minute ferry ride, breezy setting and great city vistas supply some of the thrills, but what fascinates even more is the tour of "The Rock," where notorious gangsters such as Al Capone and "Machine Gun" Kelly did time. As if the walk through the cell blocks and into the exercise yard didn't provide a vivid (yet never grim) portrait of prison life, the self-guided audio tour, well worth the nominal extra fee, includes enlightening – at times even heart-warming – commentary by former guards and inmates. The federal prison operated from 1934 to 1963, and

Alcatraz Island's illustrious history also includes a stint as a military post and an occupation from 1969 to 1971 by Native Americans who claimed the island on behalf of all U.S. Indian tribes. Allot four hours minimum for the ferry ride and tour, and in summer make reservations a few days ahead.

➕ Off map 200 C5 ✉ Pier 41 ☎ (415) 773-1188 (boat schedules and information); (415) 705-5555 or (800) 426-8687 (credit-card ticket orders) 🕐 Ferries daily 9:30–4:15 (evening tours 6:30 and 7:30), late May to Aug; 9:30–2:15 (evening tour 4:20), rest of year 💵 Moderate (evening tours expensive) 🚌 30-Stockton, 19-Polk; Powell-Hyde cable car; F-line antique trolleys (east on Market Street and around the Embarcadero)

Waterfront Attractions

In addition to Alcatraz, boats and ferries along the waterfront depart for bay cruises and excursions to **Sausalito** (► 62), **Angel Island** and other points. For a great nature-oriented day trip, pack a picnic lunch and head to Angel Island, a state park that previously served as a processing center for immigrants. Once on the island you can ride a tram or bike (rentals at dock) or hike past historic and scenic sites.

Shops, restaurants, the Aquarium of the Bay, the Hard Rock Cafe and a carousel lure millions of people to **Pier 39** (Powell Street and Embarcadero). The most entertaining attraction, though, is free: Highly photogenic sea lions on the pier's western side that loll, bark and vie for supremacy.

T-shirt and trinket shops, street vendors and artists, and seafood restaurants keep things frenetic at **Fisherman's Wharf** (Pier 45), centered on a few piers west of Pier 39. The more interesting of the two boardable World War II-era vessels docked here is the **USS *Jeremiah O'Brien*** (tel: 415/544-0100). It took part in the D-Day invasion of Normandy (June 6, 1944) and the 50th-anniversary festivities there. The engine room appeared in the movie "Titanic." The gadgetry aboard the **USS *Pampanito*** (tel: 415/775-1943), a submarine that served with distinction in the Pacific, seems amusingly antiquated.

TAKING A BREAK

Outdoor stands near Pier 47 sell fried clams, shrimp cocktails and other delicious seafood offerings. Also try Pier 39.

Snack al fresco to bay breezes and the sound of sea lions at Pier 39

Excursions

✉ Piers 39, 41, 43½ ☎ (415) 705-5555, Blue & Gold Fleet; (415) 447-0591 or (800) 229-2784, Red & White Fleet 💲 Moderate–expensive

THE WHARF AREA: INSIDE INFO

Top tip At the splendid **Hyde Street Pier** you can board historic vessels, among them a schooner and a side-wheel ferry. The pier is part of the **San Francisco Maritime National Historical Park**, which includes a nearby museum (admission free) that's open daily 9–5. (Hyde and Jefferson streets, tel: 415/561-7100, open: daily 9:30–5:30, mid-May to mid-Sep; 9:30–5, rest of year. Closed Jan 1, Thanksgiving and Dec 25. Admission: inexpensive.)

Hidden gem At the child-friendly **Basic Brown Bear Factory**, on the second floor of the Cannery (► 69), you can watch and participate in the creation of a teddy bear.

Chinatown and North Beach

Chinese settled Chinatown and Italians populated adjacent North Beach in the 19th century. More so than any other immigrants, both groups clung with pride to old-country traditions. People from all over Southeast Asia now call Chinatown home and few Italians remain in North Beach, but the influence of these captivating neighborhoods' pioneers remains palpable.

Beat poets and others have sought "inspiration" at Vesuvio for decades

Broadway, just north of the Financial District, has been the traditional border between Chinatown and North Beach. From Columbus Avenue and Broadway you can make two leisurely loops (about 1 hour each), first through Chinatown and then through North Beach.

Chinatown

In recent decades, Chinatown has burst beyond its traditional borders of Broadway and Bush, Kearny and Stockton streets. Some residents complain that little here is authentic, least of all the architecture, which has been called a travesty of Chinese design. Keep this in mind on touristy Grant Avenue, whose shopkeepers proffer mostly tacky souvenirs and overpriced jewelry (the gems and prices are better on Stockton Street). To see the "real" Chinatown, such as it exists, meander down the side streets and alleys.

➕ 201 D3 and 200 C4 🚌 1 California (Chinatown only), 15-Kearny, 30-Stockton, 41-Union

From Broadway near Columbus, walk south on Grant Avenue. Turn right on Jackson and left onto Ross Alley to watch the bakers at **Golden Gate Fortune Cookies Co.** (56 Ross Alley) whip up batch after batch. Continue south on Ross and cross Washington Street for a look at **Superior Trading Co.** (837 Washington), a large herbal pharmacy.

Just east of Superior Trading is Waverly Place. Walk south on Waverly to **Tin How Temple** (125 Waverly Place, 3rd floor), where incense fills the air. A flier explains the history of the small Buddhist temple (open 10–4).

At Clay Street, head west (right) a half-block to Stockton Street. Peking duck, soy-sauce chicken and barbecued pork hang in shop windows. Some stores specialize in dried delicacies such as black and white fungus, shark fin, sea scallops (the best are priced at $85 a pound) and abalone. Walk north (right) on Stockton to Jackson and turn right. Turn right again at Grant. Rest your feet at **Ten Ren Tea Co.** (949 Grant), where you can sample exotic tea blends. Continue north on Grant to Broadway.

Chinatown delicacies include the familiar and the exotic

North Beach

Back at Broadway, head south a few steps on Columbus Avenue. Beat writers such as Jack Kerouac (➤ 28) read or sold their works at still-bohemian **City Lights Books** (➤ 69) and hung out at nearby **Vesuvio** (➤ 69).

Cross Broadway at the traffic light, walk north briefly on Columbus to Grant Avenue and make a right. Designer clothing boutiques and quirky shops line the next few blocks of Grant, along with a few old-timers such as the **Italian French Bakery** (1501 Grant Avenue), which serves terrific focaccia. You can rest your feet in Washington Square park, heart of North Beach during its Italian heyday, and still a neighborhood nexus. From here you can either walk south down Columbus Avenue toward Chinatown or head to **Coit Tower** (➤ 56).

TAKING A BREAK

Caffe Trieste (601 Vallejo Street), a Beat haunt, serves invigorating espresso drinks, as does **Caffe Puccini** (411 Columbus). **Golden Gate Bakery** (1029 Grant Avenue) sells tasty mooncakes and other Chinese pastries. Chinese dim sum – meat-filled dumplings and other morsels – is served from early morning until mid-afternoon at **New Asia** (772 Pacific Avenue).

CHINATOWN AND NORTH BEACH: INSIDE INFO

Hidden gem Julia Morgan, the architect of Hearst Castle (➤ 108–109), designed the stylish **redbrick building** (formerly the Chinese YWCA) at 965 Clay Street, west of Stockton Street.

South of Market

Business, culture and entertainment converge in SoMa.
Trade shows and conventions take place at Moscone Center,
the San Francisco Museum of Modern Art tops an eclectic
roster of cultural institutions and the diversions range from a
century-old carousel to virtual-reality games. With many of
its highlights less than a decade old, SoMa has become a hot
hangout for locals and visitors.

SoMa stretches from just west of the Embarcadero to Division
Street. The western part contains some happening nightclubs
and restaurants, but SoMa's core is the **Yerba Buena Gardens**
complex, home to restaurants, a bowling alley, a skating rink
and the **Zeum** children's museum/activity center. **Moscone
Convention Center** is here as well. The Sony-operated
Metreon complex contains IMAX and conventional theaters,
along with futuristic play areas – the HyperBowl video bowling's a kick – for kids and adults. You could spend a fortune
amusing yourself at Yerba Buena or not a penny: Willows,
pines and other trees border the grassy knoll within the tranquil **East Garden,** perhaps the city's most pleasant small park.
At the garden's southern edge is a waterfall dedicated to Martin
Luther King Jr. that provides a scenic and sonic backdrop.

Swiss architect Mario Botta designed the **San Francisco
Museum of Modern Art (SFMOMA)**, a snazzy 1995 modernist structure. Some even snazzier recent acquisitions over
the past decade have enhanced the prestige of the city's classiest museum. Matisse, O'Keeffe, Warhol and Richard
Diebenkorn (a Bay Area resident for many years, ➤ 27) are
among the painters represented. The photography collection
is one of California's finest.

SFMOMA (opposite) and Yerba Buena Gardens (below) are among SoMa's varied cultural offerings

Yerba Buena Gardens
🕂 201 D2 ✉ Bordered by Mission, 4th, Folsom and 3rd
streets 🚇 Muni Metro J, K, L, M, N and BART (New
Montgomery) 🚌 9-San Bruno, 14-Mission, 15-Kearny,
30-Stockton

San Francisco Museum of Modern Art (SFMOMA)
🕂 201 D2 ✉ 151 3rd Street ☎ (415) 357-4000
🕐 Thu–Tue 10–6 (also Thu 6–9), late May to early Sep;
from 11 am, rest of year 💰 Moderate

Cartoon Art Museum
🕂 201 D2 ✉ 655 Mission Street ☎ (415) 227-8666
💰 Inexpensive

California Academy of Sciences
🕂 201 D1 ✉ 875 Howard Street ☎ (415) 750-7145
💰 Moderate

The **Cartoon Art Museum,** which exhibits comics, cartoons and animation cels, and the respected **California Academy of Sciences**, which has an aquarium and natural history exhibits, are among the cultural organizations occupying the periphery of Yerba Buena Gardens. The Mexican Museum and the Contemporary Jewish Museum will relocate here in 2005.

TAKING A BREAK

Metreon's ground floor contains several restaurants. The **Firewood Café** and **Sanraku** (Japanese) grill are two good choices. On a fine day, you can take your food to the **East Garden** or a terrace overlooking it.

SOMA: INSIDE INFO

Top tips To appreciate Yerba Buena, sit for at least a few moments in the East Garden – one entrance is off Mission Street, mid-block between 3rd and 4th streets.
• Muni Metro and BART stop one block from Yerba Buena; if you're driving, there's a garage at 5th and Mission streets.
• **Several outlet shops** do business in SoMa (➤ 69).

Hidden gems Pop into the **Palace Hotel** (New Montgomery and Market streets) for a look at the fancy Garden Court restaurant (you can see it from the main lobby) and the **Pied Piper Bar** (nearer to Market Street), named for the large Maxfield Parrish painting within.

Golden Gate Park

About 75,000 people drop by Golden Gate Park on a sunny weekend, just one indication of this more than 1,000-acre (405-hectare) urban getaway's vital role in city life.

Magical without being showy about it, the Golden Gate Park is a place where the whole is greater than the sum of its parts – in this case lakes, gardens, groves, playgrounds, a herd of buffalo, windmill and a brew pub with ocean views. The primary reason to come here is to stroll amid nature both rustic and manicured, especially until the new spaces of the primary cultural facilities – the M.H. de Young Memorial Museum and the California Academy of Sciences – open in 2005 and 2008 respectively. The main sights are in the park's eastern and western ends. John F. Kennedy Drive passes by or near several of the park's delights along the 3 miles (5 kilometers) from Stanyan Street to Ocean Beach.

Greenery is such a trademark of Golden Gate Park it's hard to imagine that nearly the entire area was once sand dunes. Much of the credit for the land-scaping goes to John McLaren, the park's intrepid superintendent from 1890 to 1943, but he was partly just lucky: Golden Gate Park sits atop several under-ground streams, which he tapped as water sources for the vegetation he nurtured so creatively.

Above: Visitors enjoy a quiet moment on Stow Lake, one of the highlights of Golden Gate Park
Below: The well-groomed Japanese Tea Garden

If your time is limited, concentrate on the eastern part. Drive or take the 5-Fulton bus to 8th Avenue, walk east on John F. Kennedy Drive to the Conservatory Garden, then loop back west on Kennedy Drive past the Rhododendron Dell to the attractions between 8th Avenue and Cross-Over Drive. These include the Japanese Tea Garden and Strybing Arboretum. If you have more time, drive or catch the 5-Fulton bus west to the ocean. At 36th Avenue walk south on Kennedy Drive to the **Buffalo Paddock** or continue on to 47th Avenue, near the **Dutch Windmill** and **Cliff House**.

Park Highlights

The **Conservatory of Flowers**, a copy of the original, which graces the Royal

🔲 Off map 200 A1   🚃 N-Judah (south side of park)
🚌 5-Fulton (north side of park)

Conservatory of Flowers
✉ John F. Kennedy Drive at Conservatory Drive   ☎ (415)
666-7001   🕐 Tue–Sun 9–4:30 (last entry; open until 5)
💷 Inexpensive

M.H. de Young Memorial Museum
✉ 75 Tea Garden Drive, off John F. Kennedy Drive
☎ (415) 863-3330, de Young   🕐 Reopens in summer
2005; call for hours   💷 Moderate

Japanese Tea Garden
✉ Tea Garden Drive, off John F. Kennedy Drive   ☎ (415)
752-4227   🕐 Daily 8:30–6, Mar–Oct; 8:30–5 (or 5:30),
rest of year   💷 Inexpensive

Strybing Arboretum and Botanical Gardens
✉ 9th Avenue at Lincoln Way   ☎ (415) 661-1316
🕐 Mon–Fri 8–4:30, Sat–Sun 10–5   💷 Free

Botanical Gardens in Kew, England, has been beautifully refurbished since being damaged in a mid-1990s rainstorm. The 19th-century structure merits a peek, however, as do the tropical and subtropical plants inside the seasonal gardens. To the west on the other side of the street is the lush Rhododendron Dell. South of the Conservatory, on Bowling Green Drive, lies the serene **National AIDS Memorial Grove**, and beyond that the **Children's Playground**, whose carousel was built in 1912.

The rust-orange new building of the **M.H. de Young Memorial Museum** was designed by the architectural firm of Herzog & Meuron, among whose other commissions are the Tate Modern in London. The de Young's strengths include the works of the John D. Rockefeller III Collection of American Paintings and the African and Native American holdings.

Ponds, pagodas and bamboo-lined paths create a tranquil atmosphere at the **Japanese Tea Garden**. Magnolias, camellias, azaleas, Japanese maples, dwarf pines and other plants and trees grow in the garden, which was developed for Golden Gate Park's 1894 Midwinter Exposition. You can contemplate the scene over a cup of tea in the teahouse. Crowds of summer tourists can shatter the tea garden's calm, so you may find things more peaceful at the nearby **Strybing Arboretum and Botanical Gardens**. The 55-acre (22-hectare) arboretum contains biblical, fragrance, succulent and primitive plant gardens, along with the trees and other vegetation of several continents. One entrance is about 100 feet (30 meters) west of the Japanese Tea Garden. Natural history is another major focus here.

TAKING A BREAK

The wide windows of the upstairs brew pub at the 1925 Spanish Colonial-style **Beach Chalet** (➤ 64) look out on Ocean Beach, making this a splendid spot for a sunset drink. Lucien Labaudt's stunning wraparound mural on the first floor, painted in the fresco style, depicts 1930s San Francisco.

Left: The Victorian-style Conservatory of Flowers has been beautifully refurbished

GOLDEN GATE PARK: INSIDE INFO

Top tips Weekends are great days to come to the park because many streets are closed to traffic.

• If you're planning to visit the Japanese Tea Garden in summer, be sure to **arrive by 9:30 am** to beat the crowds. If you're feeling energetic you can rent bicycles and skates at several shops on Stanyon Street between Page and Waller streets.

Hidden gems From east to west, **additional park highlights** include the Music Concourse and its bandshell, the Rose Garden, Stow Lake, the Buffalo Paddock and the Dutch Windmill.

At Your Leisure

5 Golden Gate Bridge

One of San Francisco's most exhilarating views is that of the 1.7-mile (2.7-kilometer) icon that connects the city with Marin County. The suspension bridge's towers taper slightly as they rise gracefully to a height of 746 feet (227 meters). The distinctive color, international orange, complements the surroundings: blue sky, the often dark-gray waters of the bay, the brown to green hillsides, and the multihued San Francisco skyline. (Imagine this: The U.S. Navy wanted to paint the bridge black and yellow so ships could see it better.) A stroll across this sturdy yet elegant structure can be superb on a sunny day, but if it's cloudy or the wind is gusting, be ready for one bone-chilling excursion. The vista points at either end have magnificent views, but for a loftier perspective – with the bridge's cables framing the city – take the Alexander Avenue exit from the north (Marin) side and take the first left. You will pass under US 101; turn left again and head up Conzelman Road to the Marin Headlands.

➕ Off map 200 A4 ⏰ 24 hours, cars, bicycles; 5 am–9 pm, pedestrians

6 California Palace of the Legion of Honor

The French neoclassical Legion of Honor, completed in 1924, is a tasteful three-quarter-scale adaptation of the 18th-century Palais de la Légion d'Honneur in Paris. The windswept cliff-top setting itself rates a stop, with views of the city unfolding to the east and south, and glimpses through gnarled cypress and pines of the Golden Gate to the north. But the museum's collection also entices. Key holdings include prints and drawings, pre-20th-century European art, English and European porcelain and sculptures by Auguste Rodin.

➕ Off map 200 A2 ✉ 34th Avenue at Clement Street
☎ (415) 863-3330 ⏰ Tue–Sun 9:30–5 (also first Sat of month 5–8:45) 🚌 2-Clement, 18-46th Avenue, 38-Geary 🎫 Moderate

7 Cliff House

Folks have been coming to the Cliff House complex for more than a century to have a drink or a meal and enjoy the ocean view. Just offshore is **Seal Island,** a favorite hangout of birds and, despite

Map labels: Golden Gate Bridge 5, Baker Beach, LINCOLN BLVD, California Palace of the Legion of Honor 6, Cliff House 7, RICHMOND, GREAT

The Golden Gate Bridge links San Francisco with Marin County

The "Crookedest Street in the World"

the name, sea lions. Fun to roam through if it's not too windy, are the ruins of the **Sutro Baths**, a gigantic swimming and bathhouse facility (just north of the Cliff House) that burned down in the 1960s. Expect no-great-shakes American fare – though brunch isn't bad, and you really can't beat those vistas.

🔲 Off map 200 A2 ✉ 1090 Point Lobos Avenue ☎ (415) 386-3330 🕐 Mon–Fri 9 am–10:30 pm, Sat 8:30 am–11 pm, Sun 8:30 am–10:30 pm (bar nightly until 2 am) 🚌 18-46th Avenue; 38-Geary (but only the ones marked Point Lobos or Fort Miley)

🟦 Palace of Fine Arts

San Francisco's civic leaders produced the lavish Panama-Pacific International Exposition of 1915 to proclaim the city's recovery from the 1906 earthquake and fire. The fair's temporary buildings were torn down, leaving only the classical-style Palace; it was so beloved by locals, that it was replicated in permanent materials in the 1960s. Its graceful colonnade skirts the edge of a lagoon lined with benches. Inside the palace is the **Exploratorium,** a warehouse-like space full of amusing interactive displays that elucidate principles of natural and applied science.

🔲 Off map 200 A4 ✉ Beach and Baker streets ☎ (415) 561-0360 (Exploratorium) 🕐 Exploratorium: Tue–Sun 10–5 (also most Mon holidays). Closed Thanksgiving and Dec 25 🚌 30-Stockton 🎟 Moderate (free first Wed of month)

🔟 "Crookedest Street in the World"

You've got better things to do with your time. But, hey, you're on vacation, so go ahead, take the irresistible plunge down San Francisco's novelty block, where eight switchbacks deliver cars from the top of the hill to the bottom. It's one-way only.

🔲 200 B4 ✉ Lombard Street between Hyde and Leavenworth streets (enter on Hyde) 🚌 19-Polk; Powell-Hyde cable car

🔟🔟 Coit Tower/Telegraph Hill

Lillie Hitchcock Coit, an eccentric fan of city firefighters, bequeathed the money that built the 210-foot (64-meter) Coit Tower that honors them. The bay and downtown views from the 1933 structure are unparalleled, and interior murals depict Depression-era California. If you find yourself suddenly feeling amorous, you'll know why readers of a local newspaper voted Coit Tower the city's premier spot for lovers. Two sets of plant- and flower-lined steps lead

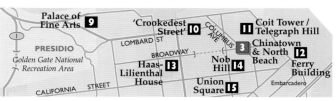

past Craftsman bungalows and other lodgings down the east slope of Telegraph Hill from Coit Tower's base. The **Greenwich Steps** descend to Montgomery Street, where a few feet to the south the wood-plank **Filbert Steps** continue east. At the bottom of Telegraph Hill you can catch a bus on Battery Street to downtown or walk north a few blocks to Fisherman's Wharf. A fine few hours can be had walking from North Beach (➤ 49) to Coit Tower and down the steps.

➕ 201 D4 ✉ Telegraph Hill Boulevard and Greenwich Street ☎ (415) 362-0808 🕐 Daily 10–7:30, late May to early Sep; 10–6, rest of year 🚌 39-Coit (from Washington Square park, Union Street side) 🎫 Inexpensive

🔢 Ferry Building

The 1896 Ferry Building survived San Francisco's two major earthquakes, not to mention the indignity of having its façade blocked by a freeway for three decades, only to emerge – after a complete makeover that shows off the structure's spectacular skylit nave – as a popular upscale marketplace. Local purveyors of gourmet produce, meats, fish and prepared foods have permanent bodegas, and a farmers' market is held year-round on Tuesdays (10–2) and Saturdays (8–2) and,

The view east from the Fairmont Hotel's glass elevators takes in a wide sweep of the city and the bay (➤ 58)

except in winter, on Thursdays and Sundays (10–2). This is a great place to pick up a gourmet snack for a waterfront picnic.

➕ 201 D3 ✉ Embarcadero and Market Street ☎ (415) 693-0996 🕐 Mon–Fri 10–6, Sat 9–6, Sun 11–5 (individual business hours vary; some restaurants open later). Closed Jan 1, Thanksgiving, Dec 25 🚇 Embarcadero Station (BART and all Muni); F-line antique trolleys 🚋 1-California

🔢 Haas-Lilienthal House

Many mansions along broad Van Ness Avenue were dynamited in 1906 to halt the advance of the fires that followed the earthquake. The imposing Queen Anne-style Haas-Lilienthal House, one block west, was one of the beneficiaries of this strategy. With 24 period-decorated rooms, the home, built in 1886 for German-born immigrant William Haas, a prominent merchant, was modest compared to the destroyed mansions. But it's still a grand setting, and on the one-hour, guided tours you'll get a feel for the taste and style of prosperous San Franciscans of the late 19th century. Walking tours of Pacific Heights leave from the house on Sundays at 12:30.

➕ 200 A3 ✉ 2007 Franklin Street, near Washington Street ☎ (415) 441-3004 🕐 Wed noon–4 (last tour at 3), Sun 11–5 (last tour at 4) 🚌 1-California, 27 Bryant, 47–49 Van Ness/Mission 🎫 Moderate

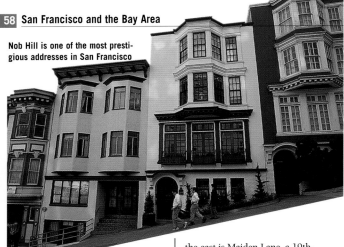

Nob Hill is one of the most prestigious addresses in San Francisco

⒕ Nob Hill

Nob Hill, a mostly residential neighborhood, has some of the city's finest views. It became *the* place to live when the 19th century's "Big Four" railroad barons – Charles Crocker, Leland Stanford, Mark Hopkins and Collis Huntington – spent thousands of dollars erecting mansions near California and Mason streets. **Grace Cathedral** (California and Taylor streets) stands on the site of Crocker's mansion, which, like those of his friends, was destroyed in the 1906 earthquake and fire. The Fairmont Hotel (California and Mason streets), just about to open, was gutted, but its shell survived, as did that of the brownstone James Flood Mansion (now the Pacific Union Club), across Mason Street. To take in the views, head to the **Top of the Mark** (➤ 69) the skyline bar at the Mark Hopkins-Intercontinental hotel (California and Mason streets).

🕂 200 B3 🚋 1-California bus; all cable-car lines

⒖ Union Square

The hub of downtown's shopping and financial districts is home to Niketown, Tiffany & Co., and the Neiman Marcus and Macy's department stores. On the west side of the square is the Westin St. Francis, the scene of the party that ended Fatty Arbuckle's career (➤ 19). On the opposite side of the square to the east is Maiden Lane, a 19th-century red-light district that's now the locale of fancy shops. The circular ramp at the gallery at 140 Maiden Lane is said to have been architect Frank Lloyd Wright's test run for the Guggenheim Museum in New York City. Three blocks south of Union Square on Powell Street are the San Francisco Visitor Information Center (➤ 33) and the turnaround for two cable-car lines.

🕂 200 C2 🚋 3-Jackson, 30-Stockton, 38-Geary, Powell-Hyde and Powell-Mason cable cars

⒗ Civic Center

Shafts of light and the marble stairs of its massive rotunda seem to

What Makes a Cable Car Go?

Cables loop continuously beneath Powell, Hyde, Mason and California streets. To get a cable car going, the operator uses a long pole called a grip, which grabs the cable, causing the car to move along with it. To stop, the operator releases the grip. In the basement of the **Cable Car Museum,** you can view the wheels actually moving the cables. (Mason and Washington streets, tel: 415/474-1887, open: daily 10–6, Apr–Sep; 10–5, rest of year. Closed Jan 1, Thanksgiving and Dec 25. Bus: 1-California; Powell-Hyde and Powell-Mason cable cars. Admission: free.)

cascade from above onto the main floor of San Francisco's debonair **City Hall** (Polk and McAllister streets), completed in 1915 in the French high-baroque revival style. Free tours (tel: 415/554-6023) of City Hall – where baseball player Joe DiMaggio

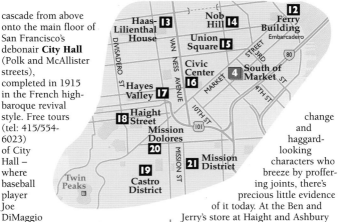

married actress Marilyn Monroe – take place daily. Across Civic Center Plaza sits the superb **Asian Art Museum** (Larkin and McAllister streets; tel: 415/379-8801; moderate), with objects on display from more than three dozen countries.

➕ 200 B1 🏛 Asian Art Museum:
Tue–Sun 10–5 (also Wed 5–9)
🚇 Civic Center (BART and all Muni);
Van Ness Avenue (all Muni)
🚌 5-Fulton, 19-Polk, 21-Hayes,
47-Van Ness Avenue

🟦 Hayes Valley

Shops and galleries – smart, but not too fancy, offbeat but not too funky – lie west of Van Ness Avenue along Hayes Street. To revive yourself after your shopping excursion drop by funky-artsy **Frjtz** (579 Hayes Street, tel: 415/864-7654) for crêpes, Belgian fries and DJ-mixed sounds.

🟦 Haight Street

A San Francisco rock critic wrote a few years back that the "Summer of Love" never happened in 1967 – journalists dreamed it up, he claimed. Which would make it all the more ironic that the corner of Haight and Ashbury streets, ground zero during the Flower Power days, remains a major pilgrimage for San Francisco visitors. Whether there was a "Summer of Love" or not, except for waifs in tie-dye shirts seeking spare

change and haggard-looking characters who breeze by proffering joints, there's precious little evidence of it today. At the Ben and Jerry's store at Haight and Ashbury you can, however, buy Cherry Garcia ice cream, named for the late Grateful Dead musician Jerry Garcia, who lived nearby at 710 Ashbury Street. One oasis of 1960s idealism and activism is the **Red Victorian Bed, Breakfast & Art** (1665 Haight, near Cole Street). At its Peace Center Arts Gallery are posters, T-shirts, Haight Street hagiographies and even a meditation room. The most interesting stretch of Haight Street is between Masonic Avenue and Shrader Street.

➕ Off map 200 B1 🚌 7-Haight,
33-Ashbury, 71-Haight-Noriega

🟦 Castro District

Gay folk settled this middle-class neighborhood in the 1970s, and before long it had garnered an international reputation as a homosexual mecca. The new residents helped elect Harvey Milk, who ran a camera shop on

Off the Beaten Track
You can see north to Marin County and east to Oakland from **Twin Peaks**, the second highest spot in San Francisco. It can get windy up here, but the views are sublime. (Twin Peaks Boulevard off Portola Drive; take Market Street west from Castro. Bus: 37-Corbett from north side of Market Street west of Castro Street.)

Castro Street, the first openly gay member of the San Francisco Board of Supervisors. Another supervisor, Dan White, murdered Milk and Mayor George Moscone in 1978. White had resigned from the board and when he wanted to be reinstated – something only the mayor could do – they had declined to support the notion, igniting his murderous rage. A huge rainbow flag, a symbol of the gay community, flies above Harvey Milk Plaza, at Castro and Market streets, and two landmarks can be found across Castro from it. The **Twin Peaks Tavern** (401 Castro) was one of the first gay bars whose windows looked out on the street. The need to hide behind curtains or shutters became less pressing in the early 1970s as San Francisco became more tolerant. A few doors down stands the Spanish baroque-style **Castro Theatre** (429 Castro), built in 1922 as a silent-movie house. An organist plays the Mighty Wurlitzer between shows almost every night. Gay-owned stores dot the neighborhood.

➕ Off map 200 B1 Ⓜ Muni (K, L, M), F-line antique trolleys 🚌 24-Divisadero, 33-Ashbury, 37-Corbett

🔟 Mission Dolores

San Francisco's oldest standing structure, erected in 1791 of wood and stucco, is officially called Mission San Francisco de Asis. The 4-foot (1.2-meter) thick adobe walls of the chapel have survived numerous major earthquakes. The original bells, which were cast in Mexico, remain, as do some of the original redwood roof

support beams. Vegetable dyes were used to create the ceiling design, based on Ohlone Indian baskets.

➕ Off map 200 B1 ✉ Dolores and 16th streets ☎ (415) 621-8203 🕐 Daily 9–4 Ⓜ J-Church (Muni), F-line antique trolley; BART (16th and Mission streets) 🚌 22-Fillmore 💲 Inexpensive

🔟 Mission District

Mission Dolores anchors the northern edge of the Mission District, for many years a major Latin American neighborhood but now evolving as Asians, Arabic people and upwardly mobile professionals have moved in. One popular section is the Valencia Corridor, the eight blocks of Valencia Street between 16th and 24th streets, where thrift stores, cheap eateries and bookstores thrive. On 24th Street, between Mission and Bryant streets, the Latin American influence remains strongest. At the **Precita Eyes Mural Arts & Visitors Center** (2981 24th Street, near Alabama Street, tel: 415/285-2287, open: daily), you can pick up a map with directions to the area's murals, many by Latino artists. **Galeria de la Raza/Studio 24** (2857 24th Street, at Bryant Street, tel: 415/826-8009, open: Wednesday to Sunday), exhibits and sells the work of American-born and international Latino artists.

➕ Off map 200 B1 Ⓜ BART (16th Street, 24th Street) 🚌 14-Mission, 22-Fillmore, 26-Valencia; 27-Bryant, 48-Quintara/24th Street

The Mission District is known for its colorful and dramatic murals

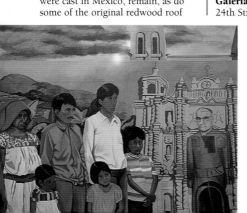

Farther Afield

❶ Point Reyes National Seashore

Quite possibly the most beautiful wilderness in the entire Bay Area, what is now the Point Reyes National Seashore was settled centuries ago by Coast Miwok Indians. A good first stop is Bear Valley Visitor Center, 38 miles (61 kilometers) northwest of San Francisco, off Highway 1 in Olema, where you can pick up maps and view exhibits about the seashore's wildlife and vegetation. The shortest of two easy-to-walk paths that leave from the center's parking lot ends at **Kule Loklo,** a re-created Miwok village. On the slightly longer Earthquake Trail, part of which passes over the San Andreas Fault, stands a fence that shifted 16 feet (26 meters) during San Francisco's 1906 earthquake. Solitary **Point Reyes Lighthouse,** a 21-mile (34-kilometer) drive from the visitor center, sits on a rocky promontory at the bottom of 308 very steep steps. The bluff above it is billed, correctly it would seem, as the windiest spot on the American West Coast. A visit to Point Reyes and Muir Woods National Monument (➤ next) makes for a fine day trip from San Francisco.

➕ 202 B1   ✉ Highway 1 (from San Francisco take US 101 north to Mill Valley/Stinson Beach exit and follow signs)   ☎ (415) 464-1500, visitor

Windswept Point Reyes

center; (415) 669-1534, lighthouse   ⓘ Park: daily 24 hours. Visitor center: Mon–Fri 9–5, Sat–Sun 8–5. Lighthouse: Thu–Mon 10–5 (steps close at 4:30)   🎟 Free

❷ Muir Woods National Monument

The coastal redwood grows to heights of 200 feet (60 meters) or more in this forest 12 miles (19 kilometers) north of the Golden Gate Bridge. If your California travels won't be taking you past the state's other redwood groves, visit Muir Woods. The only drawback is the park's popularity (from May to October it's best to visit before 10 am or after 4 pm), but most visitors don't leave the paved and boardwalked trails. For a good introduction to the park's flora and fauna, walk the main trail to Bridge 4, but loop back to the entrance via the less-traveled Hillside Trail. The 2-mile (3-kilometer) hike (trail maps at the park entrance) takes a little more than an hour.

➕ 202 B1   ✉ Muir Woods Road, off Panoramic Highway (from San Francisco take US 101 north to Mill Valley/Stinson Beach exit and follow signs)   ☎ (415) 388-2595   ⓘ Daily 8–dusk   🎟 Inexpensive

3 Sausalito

This town across the bay from San Francisco has gotten so gosh darn cute that few traces of its risqué past remain. Rumrunners and sailors hung out in the 19th century, and during the mid-20th century artists and other bohemian types settled here. It costs too much for most artists to live in Sausalito now, but the superb San Francisco views and jolly atmosphere remain. A great way to visit the walkable town is via boat – either the **Golden Gate Ferry** (tel: 415/923-2000) from the Ferry Building (Market Street and the Embarcadero in San Francisco) or the **Blue & Gold Fleet** (tel: 415/773-1188) from Pier 41. Bridgeway, the town's main drag, contains shops and restaurants. For a cocktail with a view, walk up the staircase across Bridgeway from Plaza Vina del Mar to the **Alta Mira Hotel.** From the outdoor deck on a clear day you can peer over pines and palms at Alcatraz, the Bay Bridge and points beyond. Weekend brunch here is a popular event.

202 B1 Off US 101 (take Alexander Avenue exit at north end of Golden Gate Bridge, follow signs to downtown) Route 10/Golden Gate Transit

4 Tiburon

On a beautiful day, few activities are more enjoyable than having lunch on the wharfside decks at **Sam's Anchor Café** (27 Main Street, tel: 415/435-4527) or the adjacent **Guaymas** restaurant (5 Main Street, tel: 415/435-6300). Sam's, which serves American comfort food, is a local institution, but the Mexican cuisine at Guaymas is much better. After lunch, you can spin past Main Street's shops. **Ferries** (tel: 415/435-2131) depart from here for windswept Angel Island State Park, whose attractions include a station where Asian immigrants were processed (and often sent back to their homelands) from 1910 to 1940.

202 B1 Tiburon Boulevard off US 101, 14 miles (22 km) north of San Francisco (take Tiburon Boulevard/East Blithedale exit, turn right on Tiburon Boulevard and right on Main) Route 8/Golden Gate Transit; also Blue & Gold Ferry (415/773-1188) from Ferry Building (Mon–Fri) or Fisherman's Wharf (daily)

5 Filoli

Sixteen acres (6.5 hectares) of formal gardens surround the 43-room home, 26 miles (42 kilometers) south of San Francisco, built for William Bowers Bourn II, whose holdings included the **Empire Mine** (▶ 84). The exterior of the Georgian Revival-style structure stood in for the Carrington mansion on the opening credits of the long-running drama series "Dynasty." If you've visited European manors or

Some Sausalito residents live on houseboats docked off Bridgeway

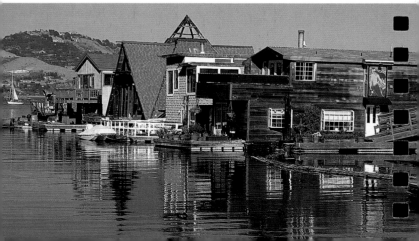

even California's Hearst Castle, you may find the house tour (only the first floor is open to the public) less than spectacular. The gardens, though, designed as a series of "rooms," are among America's most outstanding.

➕ 202 C1 ✉ Canada Road, west of Edgewood Road exit off I-280 ☎ (650) 364-2880 🕐 Tue–Sat 10–2:30 (self-guided tours), Tue–Thu 10–2:30 (guided tours; reservations recommended), mid-Feb to Oct 🏷 Moderate

🖲 Winchester Mystery House

The gun-manufacturing heiress Sarah Winchester believed the mediums who said she'd die if construction stopped on her mansion, so from 1884 until she died 38 years later, her workers kept building. The resulting 160 rooms contain such oddities as staircases that dead-end into ceilings but also include stylish touches such as Tiffany windows and parquet floors with many inlaid woods.

➕ 202 C1 ✉ 525 S. Winchester Boulevard, off I-280, San Jose ☎ (408) 247-2101 🕐 Daily 9–7, early Jun to early Sep; 9–5, rest of year (also Fri–Sat 5–7). Closed Dec 25 🏷 Expensive

🖲 Downtown San Jose

Though it has roots deep in California history – San Jose was founded by the Spanish in the 18th century and was the state's first capital – you need only visit the immensely popular **Tech Museum of Innovation** (201 S. Market Street, tel: 408/279-7150, moderate) to realize how resolutely the town is oriented toward the future. The mostly inter-active exhibits at the Tech, which outdraws all other downtown attractions combined, survey advances in communications, medical, computer, outer-space and other fields. Across Plaza de Cesar Chavez from the Tech is the **San Jose Museum of Art** (110 S. Market Street, tel: 408/294-2787, moderate), a repository of California-produced modern art that merits a stop for its selection of works by Latino artists. If the **Cathedral Basilica of St. Joseph** (90 S. Market Street) is open, pop in for a look at its stained glass and murals. East of Market Street lies **SoFA** – South of First Street Area – which contains clubs, restaurants and entertainment. SoFA is the hub of downtown nightlife. About a mile west of down-town is the quirky **Rosicrucian Egyptian Museum and Planetarium** (1600 Park Avenue, tel: 408/947-3636, moderate), which houses Babylonian and Egyptian antiquities and a replica of a pharaoh's tomb.

➕ 202 C1 ✉ Downtown San Jose, I-280 to Guadalupe Parkway (Highway 87) north 🚆 Caltrain to Rod Diridon Station (near San Jose Arena, 1 mile/1.6 km from downtown)

Amuse Yourself

Six Flags Marine World (2001 Marine World Parkway, off Highway 37, Vallejo, tel: 707/ 643-6722, expensive), 35 miles (56 km) northeast of San Francisco, combines thrill rides with marine-animal shows. **Paramount's Great America** (Great America Parkway off US 101, Santa Clara, tel: 408/988-1776, expensive), south of the city, has thrill rides and entertainment.

Where to...
Eat and Drink

Prices
Expect to pay per person for a meal, excluding drinks and service
$ under $15 $$ $15–25 $$$ over $25

Absinthe $$–$$$
This sophisticated French bistro in the Civic Center area is one of the best places to come for a drink or meal before or after a performance of symphony, opera or ballet, or simply for an early-morning or late-night meal. The appetizers and entrées are generous and well prepared – try the enticing cold seafood platter – while the banquette seating is comfortable. A full bar with separate food menu beckons as well.

🚼 200 A1 🖂 398 Hayes Street, San Francisco 🕿 (415) 551-1590
🕒 Tue–Fri 11:30 am–midnight,
Sat 10:30 am–midnight, Sun 10:30–10:30. Closed Jan 1–2, Thanksgiving, day after Thanksgiving and Dec 25–26

∇∇∇ Beach Chalet $–$$
Occupying the upper floor of a historic building on the western edge of Golden Gate Park, this combination brew pub and restaurant is one of the most scenic, good-natured spots in San Francisco. You might have to fight the crowds, especially around sunset or at Sunday brunch. If you'd like a meal as well, choose from an eclectic, if not overly imaginative, American menu of seafood, pastas, sandwiches and bar snacks.

🚼 Off map 200 A1 🖂 1000 Great Highway, Golden Gate Park, San Francisco 🕿 (415) 386-8439
🕒 Breakfast Mon–Fri 9–11, Sat–Sun 9–2. Closed Dec 25

Bix $$–$$$
This stylish art-deco supper club on the fringes of North Beach seems right out of the 1930s; the alley entrance suggests a speakeasy. Find a spot at the bar, order a martini or cosmopolitan, and listen to live piano jazz; or ask for a table downstairs or on the mezzanine and savor Bix's updated and often inventive versions of traditional American dishes, such as a surprisingly delicious chicken hash. The menu changes seasonally.

🚼 201 D3 🖂 56 Gold Street, San Francisco 🕿 (415) 433-6300
🕒 Lunch Mon–Thu 11:30–2:30; dinner Mon–Thu 5–11, Fri–Sat 5:30–midnight, Sun 6–10

∇∇∇ Boulevard $$–$$$
Both inside and out, Boulevard is one of the city's most beautiful restaurants. It occupies the entire ground floor of the Audiffred Building, an 1889 jewel on the Embarcadero, and the decor could have been lifted right out of Paris. But Chef Nancy Oakes' menus, which change frequently depending on seasonal ingredients, are primarily Californian, with Mediterranean, Latin and Asian influences. Weekday lunches offer inventive pizzas and more informal service.

🚼 201 E3 🖂 1 Mission Street, San Francisco 🕿 (415) 543-6084
🕒 Lunch Mon–Fri 11:30–2; dinner Sun–Wed 5:30–10, Thu–Sat 5:30–10:30. Closed Jan 1, Thanksgiving, Dec 25 and 31

Chez Panisse $$–$$$
Since the 1970s, Alice Waters' temple of gastronomy in Berkeley has defined and redefined California cuisine, and it remains one of the Bay Area's top restaurants for a

special occasion. Each night, in two seatings, one menu is served, based on the freshest seasonal ingredients. While this is always a high-end destination, and will pay for, a considerably less expensive than other nights. Upstairs, a casual, more moderately priced café (tel: 510/548-5049) serves both lunch and dinner, with exceptional salads, tasty pizza and other fare.

✚ 202 C1 ⊠ 1517 Shattuck Avenue, Berkeley ☎ (510) 548-5525
🕓 Chez Panisse: Mon–Thu 5–10.30, Fri–Sat 5–11.30. Café: lunch Mon–Thu 11.30–3, Fri–Sat 11.30–3.30; dinner Mon–Thu 5–10.30, Fri–Sat 5–11.30

🍴🍴 Fog City Diner $–$$

One of the city's highest-profile restaurants, with sparkling chrome decor and an enviable location near Fisherman's Wharf, the Fog City Diner pioneered upscale, multi-ethnic diner food in America. Even the ketchup for the cheeseburgers and onion rings is made in-house. Graze through a variety of shareable small plates, or feast on crab cakes or fresh oysters on the half shell. Or, if you prefer, just have espresso and one of the terrific desserts. If all the booths are taken, grab a seat at the bar.

✚ 201 D4 ⊠ 1300 Battery Street, San Francisco ☎ (415) 982-2000
🕓 Mon–Thu 8 am–10 pm, Fri–Sat 8 am–11 pm, Sun 10.30–9. Closed Thanksgiving and Dec 25

Greens $$

This longtime favorite vegetarian restaurant also enjoys a big following among carnivores, who may not even notice that the delicious pizza is topped with Swiss chard rather than sausage or that the terrific enchilada is stuffed with goat's cheese instead of chicken. Greens also serves up some of the city's most soul-stirring bay views. Saturday nights are reserved for special five-course fixed-price dinners; other nights, and lunches, are à la carte. Sunday brunches are a big hit here.

✚ 200 A5 ⊠ Fort Mason Center, Building A, San Francisco ☎ (415) 771-6222 🕓 Lunch Tue–Sat noon–4, Sun 10–2; dinner Mon–Sat 5.30–9; brunch Sun 10–2

Harbor Village $$

Ensconced in a shopping and office complex near the waterfront, Harbor Village is elegant and serves some of the city's best Cantonese-style seafood, fresh from its own tanks. At lunchtime the restaurant dispenses excellent dim sum. One sure sign of the quality: Harbor Village attracts many Chinese families to the teak-and-antique-laden dining rooms.

✚ 201 E3 ⊠ 4 Embarcadero Center, The Embarcadero, San Francisco ☎ (415) 781-8833 🕓 Lunch Mon–Fri 11–2, Sat–Sun 10.30–2.30; dinner daily 5.30–9.30

🍴🍴🍴 Masa's $$$

San Francisco's top French restaurant has retained its reputation through several chefs, each bringing his own strengths to the kitchen. What has not changed is Masa's dedication to the high art of dining. You can expect, and will pay for, a near-perfect gustatory experience, with generous use of ingredients such as foie gras and truffles. The hushed surroundings are flower-filled and formal (jacket and tie are required for men) while service is generally impeccable and the multi-course prix-fixe dinners exquisite.

✚ 200 C2 ⊠ 648 Bush Street, San Francisco ☎ (415) 989-7154
🕓 Tue–Sat 6 pm–late. Closed first week Jul and first 2 weeks Jan

🍴🍴🍴 Postrio $$–$$$

Though celebrity chef Wolfgang Puck spends most of his time in Los Angeles, his San Francisco outpost keeps producing delicious California fare, creatively enhanced with Mediterranean or Asian touches. His famous pizzas are on the bar menu. Postrio's design is as inventive as its food: three levels connecting the bar and dining areas via a wide staircase. At lunch and dinner, the noise can drown out conversation; breakfast is quieter.

✚ 200 C2 ✉ 545 Post Street, San Francisco ☎ (415) 776-7825 ◷ Breakfast Mon–Fri 7–10; brunch Sun 9–2; lunch Mon–Fri 11–2:30; dinner daily 5:30–10:30. Closed Thanksgiving and Dec 25

♨♨♨ Rose Pistola $$

It's noisy and the service can sometimes be scattered, but this gleaming North Beach restaurant packs in a hip crowd devoted to its rustic seafood, antipasto plates and dishes from wood-fired ovens, all served family style. This is a good place to try cioppino, San Francisco's famous fish stew. Sit at a table indoors or on the sidewalk in front; if all are full, opt for the counter or bar area.

✚ 200 C4 ✉ 532 Columbus Avenue, San Francisco ☎ (415) 399-0499 ◷ Lunch daily 11:30–4:45; dinner Sun–Thu 5:30–midnight, Fri–Sat 5:30–1. Closed Jan 1, Jul 4, Thanksgiving and Dec 25

♨♨♨ Slanted Door $–$$

In a city where good Vietnamese food is taken for granted, the Slanted Door ranks at or near the top. Located at the Ferry Building (▶ 57), it draws diners from across San Francisco eager to sample Chef Charles Phan's imaginative dishes. Expect a fair amount of clamor inside the airy space, and to have to wait for a table even with a reservation. The menu, which changes frequently, makes good use of local, seasonal ingredients. Fresh spring rolls, spicy squid and caramelized shrimp all explode with flavor.

✚ 200 E3 ✉ Embarcadero and Market Street, San Francisco ☎ (415) 861-8032 ◷ Lunch daily 11:30–2:30, dinner 5:30–10

♨♨♨ Ton Kiang $

This is one of San Francisco's most beloved neighborhood Chinese restaurants, located along heavily Asian Geary Boulevard, a few blocks from Golden Gate Park. Come for the outstanding dim sum at lunchtime or

fresh Chinese-style seafood at night. Salt-baked chicken and clay-pot seafood dishes are regional specialties.

✚ Off map 200 A2 ✉ 5821 Geary Boulevard, San Francisco ☎ (415) 387-8273 ◷ Mon–Thu 10:30–10, Fri–Sat 10 am–10:30 pm, Sun 9 am–10 pm

Universal Café $$–$$$

In a mixed commercial-residential neighborhood that straddles Potrero Hill and the Mission District, the industrial-chic Universal Café serves bistro-style dishes prepared with a distinctly modern flair. The oft-changing fare might include cherrystone clam chowder as a first course and a pork chop with cannellini beans and broccoli rabe as an entrée. Always on the menu are pizzas, pastas, and a risotto that melts in your mouth. Brunch here is a popular affair.

✚ Off map 200 B1 ✉ 2814 19th Street, San Francisco ☎ (415) 821-4608 ◷ Dinner Sun–Thu 5:30–9:30, Fri–Sat 5:30–10:30; weekend brunch 9–2:30

♨♨♨ Zuni Café $$–$$$

Some customers come for the people-watching – which goes into high gear at the sleek copper bar – and others for the top-notch Mediterranean food orchestrated by chef Judy Rodgers. But eventually, it seems, almost everyone comes to the Zuni, a café that has been a local San Francisco institution for more than two decades. The wood-burning oven turns out a great whole roasted chicken, and the Caesar salad and the hamburger on focaccia are classics. Sit on the balcony for an overview, or opt for oysters, washed down by a martini or Bloody Mary, at the ground-level bar. The Zuni's location, not far from the Civic Center cultural mecca, makes it a good stop before or after an evening at the symphony or orchestra.

✚ Off map 200 B1 ✉ 1658 Market Street, San Francisco ☎ (415) 552-2522 ◷ Tue–Sat 11:30 am–midnight, Sun 11–11. Closed Jan 1–4, Thanksgiving and Dec 24–27

Where to... Stay

Prices

Expect to pay per room

$ under $100 per night   **$$** $100–175 per night   **$$$** over $175 per night

ᔣᔣᔣ Campton Place $$$

Intimate, quiet, luxurious, with just 117 rooms not far from Union Square, Campton Place helps set the standard for top-flight service among San Francisco hotels. Elegance surrounds you from the time you enter the lobby until you settle into your comfortable room, equipped with antique armoire, writing desk and marble bath. Many rooms have sitting areas. The hotel's restaurant, Campton Place (ᔣᔣᔣᔣ), has a long-standing reputation in its own right as one of the city's top places to dine.

🚇 200 C2 ⊠ 340 Stockton Street, San Francisco, CA 94108 ☎ (415) 781-5555 or (800) 235-4300; fax: (415) 955-5536; email: reserve@campton.com

ᔣᔣᔣ Chancellor Hotel $$

The 15-story Chancellor is a moderately priced bargain, offering comfort without extravagance. Rooms are of medium size, with high ceilings and ceiling fans. Deep tubs add a touch of luxury to the bathrooms. Most of the 137 rooms sleep no more than three people, but a few two-room connecting suites are available. The hotel also has a restaurant and bar.

🚇 200 C2 ⊠ 433 Powell Street, San Francisco, CA 94102 ☎ (415) 362-2004 or (800) 428-4748; fax: (415) 362-1403; email: info@chancellorhotel.com

ᔣᔣ Commodore Hotel $$

One of the best values in San Francisco, this cheerful hotel – whose whimsical lobby resembles an old-fashioned ocean liner, complete with an attached restaurant called the Titanic Café – is located just three blocks west of Union Square. Rooms, each with a name and theme based on a different San Francisco landmark, are uncluttered, attractive and surprisingly spacious for the money.

🚇 Off map 200 A2 ⊠ 825 Sutter Street, San Francisco, CA 94109 ☎ (415) 923-6800 or (800) 338-6848; fax: (415) 923-6804; email: commodorehotel@jtvhospitality.com

ᔣᔣ Greenwich Inn $-$$

Motels for the budget-conscious line Lombard Street west of Van Ness Avenue. Among the quietest and fine value is the Greenwich, a block south of Lombard. This is a no-frills motel: the rooms are on the small side, but they're clean and decorated with cheerful touches, and parking is free. Buses to downtown stop across the street, and inexpensive meals can be had at several nearby restaurants.

🚇 Off map 200 A4 ⊠ 3201 Steiner Street, San Francisco, CA 94123 ☎ (415) 921-5162 or (800) 280-3242; fax: (415) 921-3602; email: info@greenwichinn.com

ᔣᔣ Hotel Monaco $$$

Near Union Square, the Hotel Monaco makes one of the most striking impressions in the city. From its Beaux Arts facade to its eye-catching lobby – where you can sip complimentary evening wine before the huge fireplace and beneath the painted vaulted ceiling – to its vividly decorated rooms, some with whirlpool tubs, the Monaco lives and breathes hip. Stop by for a look around even if you don't stay here. Its stunning Grand Café, with an 88-seat bar, evokes the Europe of 1900.

🚇 Off map 200 A2 ⊠ 501 Geary Street, San Francisco, CA 94102 ☎ (415) 292-0100 or (800) 214-4220; fax: (415) 292-0111

▼▼▼ Hotel Rex $$-$$$

Replicating the sophisticated look of San Francisco's 1920s-era artistic and literary salons, the Rex has a lobby lined with walls of old books and guest rooms filled with restored walnut armoires and original artworks. Marble baths add a touch of luxury. The lobby harbors a clubby lounge.

✚ Off map 200 A2 ⊠ 562 Sutter Street, San Francisco, CA 94102 ☎ (415) 433-4434 or (800) 433-4434; fax: (415) 433-3695; email: resrex@jdvhospitality.com

▼▼▼▼ Ritz-Carlton $$$

The Ritz-Carlton may be San Francisco's finest hotel. Everything here bespeaks luxury. The neoclassical building is itself a stunner; inside, the lobby and hallways are lined with antiques and paintings, the rooms are ample and richly furnished, the baths are laden with Italian marble. But despite the opulence, you'll find the service remarkably gracious. The Dining Room (▼▼▼▼) is one of the city's best restaurants; elegant afternoon tea is served in the Lobby Lounge.

✚ 200 C3 ⊠ 600 Stockton Street, San Francisco, CA 94108 ☎ (415) 296-7465 or (800) 241-3333; fax: (415) 291-0288

▼▼▼ White Swan Inn $$-$$$

Of San Francisco's numerous bed-and-breakfast inns, the White Swan is the most elegant in the downtown area. Inside this 1908 building, just a few blocks from Union Square, the decor is so Edwardian you might think you'd just stepped into an English town house. That feel extends more informally to the good-sized rooms, which have fireplaces, four-poster beds and floral wallpapers, and in the clubby library, where afternoon hors d'oeuvres are served. Buffet-style breakfasts may be taken in your room or in the parlor.

✚ 200 C2 ⊠ 845 Bush Street, San Francisco, CA 94108 ☎ (415) 775-1755 or (800) 999-9570; fax: (415) 775-5717; email:whiteswan@jdvhospitality.com

Where to...
Shop

In San Francisco, one of America's great shopping cities, shopping is closely identified with neighborhoods, each with its distinct personality. Union Square unites the city's major department stores, for instance, while Fisherman's Wharf is geared toward tourists. North Beach maintains its strong Italian influence, and the Haight-Ashbury lives up to its funky reputation by offering a number of retro clothing shops.

Union Square is the heart of the downtown shopping district. Major department stores include Macy's, Neiman Marcus and Saks Fifth Avenue. Upscale boutiques such as Armani, Gucci, Polo, Vuitton, Hermes, Tiffany and Cartier also dot the immediate area. **Wilkes Bashford** (375 Sutter Street, tel: 415/986-4380), a men's clothier, and **Gump's** (135 Post Street, tel: 415/982-1616), which carries high-quality antiques, glassware and porcelains, are longtime local favorites. Giant national book, music and toy chain stores, such as Virgin Megastore, Williams-Sonoma, Niketown and Borders Books and Music, are also on hand. Nearby, the **San Francisco Shopping Centre** (865 Market Street, tel: 415/495-5656) has spiral escalators leading to dozens of specialty shops, as well as Nordstrom, a department store known for its service.

In the **Financial District**, the glass-domed **Crocker Galleria** (50 Post Street, tel: 415/393-1505) has three levels of shops and restaurants, plus rooftop gardens. Near the waterfront, the towering **Embarcadero Center's** four office buildings contain more than 100 shops on their lower levels, including book, travel and clothing stores. **Jackson Square**, on the fringes of the Financial District, is home to several stores selling fine antiques.

Union Street in the Marina District is known for its ritzy boutiques, antiques stores and fine jewelry shops.

Four major shopping complexes stand out in the **Fisherman's Wharf** area: **Ghirardelli Square** (900 North Point Street, tel: 415/775-5500), **The Cannery** (2801 Leavenworth Street, tel: 415/771-3112), **The Anchorage** (2800 Leavenworth Street, tel: 415/775-6000) and **Pier 39** (Embarcadero at Beach Street, tel: 415/981-7437). All have dozens of specialty shops where you'll find everything from kites to music boxes, gourmet chocolate to redwood furniture. Fisherman's Wharf is also the easiest place in town to find a souvenir T-shirt for everyone you know. (See **Top Shopping Districts, ▶** 39.)

North Beach is known for its Italian delis and bakeries, as well as quirky boutiques, art galleries and bookstores. **City Lights Books** (261 Columbus Avenue, tel: 415/ 362-8193) is the city's most famous.

Hayes Valley, along Hayes Street near the Civic Center, has become a center for trendy art galleries and shops selling vintage collectibles.

Budget shoppers can head to discount and factory outlet stores in the **South of Market** area. Among them are **Jeremy's** (2 South Park Avenue, tel: 415/882-4929) and **Nordstrom Rack** (555 Ninth Street, tel: 415/934-1211). **Chinatown** and **Japantown** are other good areas to search for bargains, mostly Asian imports.

The **Haight-Ashbury** is the place to rummage for retro-chic items such as 1960s vintage apparel and art-deco home accessories; **Revival of the Fittest** (1701 Haight Street, tel: 415/751-8857) is one good shop. The cutting-edge shops in the **Castro** district are geared toward gays and lesbians.

Where to...
Be Entertained

Check the city's two free weeklies, the *Bay Guardian* and the *SF Weekly*, and the Sunday edition of the *San Francisco Chronicle*, for detailed listings.

NIGHTLIFE

North Beach, the South of Market area (SoMa), the Mission District and the Castro are among the liveliest districts at night.

HOTEL BARS

The **Top of the Mark** in the Mark Hopkins Inter-Continental Hotel atop Nob Hill (999 California Street, tel: 415/392-3434) is one of the classiest lounges, where dance music, martinis and city views

combine to make for dazzling evenings. The art-deco **Redwood Room** at the Clift Hotel (495 Geary Street, tel: 415/775-4700) and the **lobby lounge** at the Ritz-Carlton Hotel (▶ 68), are other classics.

BARS AND CAFÉS

The **Buena Vista Café** (2765 Hyde Street, tel: 415/474-5044), near the Wharf, is credited with inventing Irish coffee. **Specs'** (12 Saroyan Place, tel: 415/421-4112) and **Vesuvio** (255 Columbus Avenue, tel: 415/362-3370) both exude old-time North Beach ambience. Singles crowd into **Gordon Biersch** (2 Harrison Street, tel: 415/243-8246), a brew pub along the Embarcadero, and the **Balboa Café**

(3199 Fillmore Street, tel: 415/921-3944), in the Marina District. Gay bars are centered in the Castro, Polk Street and South of Market areas, while lesbian bars can be found on Valencia Street in the Mission District.

MUSIC

For jazz, head to **Bruno's** in the Mission District (2389 Mission Street, tel: 415/648-7701), a retro cocktail bar; the **Café du Nord** (2170 Market Street, tel: 415/861-5016) in the Castro; **Enrico's** (504 Broadway, tel: 415/982-6223), a North Beach landmark; or (for blues and occasional jazz) the **Boom Boom Room** (1601 Fillmore, tel: 415/673-8000) in the Fillmore.

The **Great American Music Hall** (859 O'Farrell Street, tel: 415/885-0750), the **Fillmore** (1805 Geary Boulevard, tel: 415/346-6000) and **Slim's** (333 11th Street, tel: 415/255-0333) all present top rock, blues or country-music acts.

The highly regarded **San Francisco Symphony** (201 Van Ness Avenue, tel: 415/864-6000) and the **San Francisco Opera** (301 Van Ness Avenue, tel: 415/864-3330) are in the Civic Center area.

THEATER AND CABARET

Pick up half-price, same-day tickets (Tue–Sat) for various theater performances at **TIX Bay Area** (tel: 415/433-7827) on the western edge of Union Square.

Several theaters host touring productions of Broadway musicals and plays, including the **Orpheum** (1192 Market Street), the **Golden Gate** (Golden Gate Avenue at Taylor Street) and the **Curran** (445 Geary Street). Check shows at all three by calling 415/551-2000. The non-profit **American Conservatory Theater** stages plays at the **Geary Theater** (405 Geary Street, tel: 415/749-2228).

Club Fugazi (678 Green Street, tel: 415/421-4222) in the North Beach district hosts the long-running *Beach Blanket Babylon*, a musical revue that features outlandish costumes – including absurdly high hats – and clever lyrics about San Francisco.

DANCE CLUBS

Mezzanine (444 Jessie Street, tel: 415/820-9669), hip dance, gallery and performance space, while south of Market, the **DNA Lounge** (375 11th Street, tel: 415/626-1409) presents alternative rock and hip-hop bands. The **Metronome Ballroom** (1830 17th Street, tel: 415/252-9000) is popular for ballroom dance, including swing.

SPORT

The **San Francisco Giants** baseball team (tel: 415/472-2000 for tickets) plays at SBC Park in China Basin. The East Bay's **Oakland A's** (tel: 510/638-4627 for tickets) play baseball at Network Associates Coliseum, the same stadium that hosts the **Oakland Raiders** (tel: 510/762-2277) of the National Football League. The NFL's **San Francisco 49ers** (tel: 415/656-4900) play football at Candlestick Park, but tickets are difficult to obtain. Call **BASS** (tel: 510/762-2277), or check the classified ads in the *San Francisco Chronicle*. The **Golden State Warriors** (tel: 510/762-2277 for tickets) play NBA basketball at theArena in Oakland.

San Francisco is a wonderful city for participant sports. You can bike for miles in Golden Gate Park or by the ocean or bay, go sailing on the bay or rent small boats at Golden Gate Park's Stow Lake, and fish at Lake Merced.

Golden Gate Park has 16 public tennis courts (tel: 415/753-7001), and a par-3 golf course, but most golfers head for the more challenging links at **Lincoln Park** (tel: 415/221-9911), **Harding Park** (tel: 415/664-4690) or the **Presidio** (tel: 415/561-4653).

Northern California

In Five Days 74 – 75
Don't Miss 76 – 89
At Your Leisure 90 – 92
Where To 93 – 98

Getting Your Bearings

Northern California beyond the Bay Area encompasses a vast territory. The natural wonders here include craggy coastal bluffs, soaring redwoods, hot springs, the granite cliffs of the Sierra Nevada, spectacular caverns and the allegedly magical Mount Shasta. Oh yes, and as miners declare in Hollywood movies about mid-1800s California, "There's gold in them thar hills."

Many winery tours make a stop in the aging cellar

A travel writer in the 1960s characterized Northern California as "not seductive," by which he meant it's not flashy and doesn't nurture a swinging social scene. The region has its upscale locales – the chic Wine Country for one – and handsome bed-and-breakfast inns dot the coastal and inland areas. But Northern California is composed mainly of farming areas and small towns with regular folks going about their business. Their activities just happen to have one of the world's most scenic backdrops.

US 101, I-5 and I-80 lead to most of the region's attractions. US 101 heads north from San Francisco, skirting the western edge of the Wine Country before continuing into Redwood Country. More or less parallel to the coast, US 101 is inland for the first 260 miles (418 kilometers) north of San Francisco, then hugs the shore for another 100 until right before the California–Oregon border.

Previous page: Half Dome in Yosemite National Park

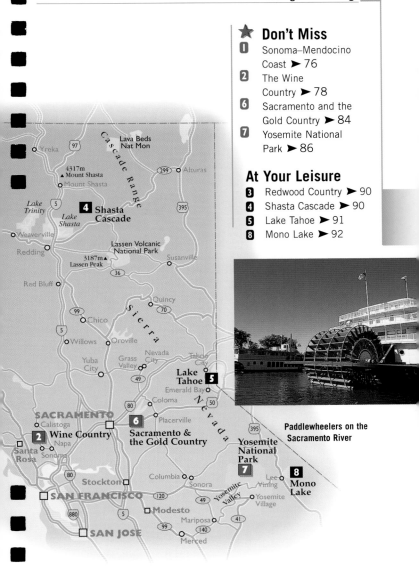

⭐ Don't Miss

1 Sonoma–Mendocino Coast ➤ 76

2 The Wine Country ➤ 78

6 Sacramento and the Gold Country ➤ 84

7 Yosemite National Park ➤ 86

At Your Leisure

3 Redwood Country ➤ 90

4 Shasta Cascade ➤ 90

5 Lake Tahoe ➤ 91

8 Mono Lake ➤ 92

Paddlewheelers on the Sacramento River

I-5 parallels US 101 up the approximate center of Northern California. The road travels through the Shasta Cascade area, which includes Mount Shasta and Lassen Volcanic National Park.

I-80 heads east from San Francisco to the state capital, Sacramento. Farther east off I-80 are the Gold Country and Lake Tahoe. Yosemite National Park and Mono Lake are due east of the Bay Area by various routes.

You can't explore all of Northern California's highlights in five days, but you'll get an inkling of the region's splendor traveling east from the coast into the Wine Country, the Gold Country and Yosemite National Park.

Northern California in Five Days

Day 1

Morning
Drive north from San Francisco on US 101 and west (at Santa Rosa) on Highway 12. Loosen your limbs at ❶ **Bodega Bay** (➤ 76) before continuing north on Highway 1 to ❶ **Goat Rock Beach** (➤ 76), where sea lions do their stretching.

Afternoon
Lagoon and ocean views make lunch at River's End in Jenner (➤ 93) a memorable experience. Take a scenic history lesson at **Fort Ross Historic State Park** (➤ 24) before heading east on Fort Ross Road and south on Cazadero Road to Highway 116. In Guerneville pick up River Road – it's the town's main street – and continue east into the Russian River Valley wine region.

Evening
Have dinner at Healdsburg's Bistro Ralph (➤ 93); if you're lucky there'll be an evening band concert in Healdsburg Plaza.

Day 2

Morning
After a leisurely breakfast, take the 11 am tour at ❷ **Simi Winery** (➤ 80).

Afternoon
Pick up picnic items at the Oakville Grocery (➤ 98) in Healdsburg. Drive south on Healdsburg Avenue and Eastside Road. Veer left (you're still heading south) on Trenton–Healdsburg Road. Just before River Road is the Mark West Estate (7010 Trenton–Healdsburg Road, tel: 707/836-9647), which has picnic tables. Head east on River Road past US 101 to ❷ **Calistoga** (➤ 81).

Evening
Have dinner at a restaurant in downtown Calistoga.

Day 3

Morning
Take a hot-air balloon ride or a hike through Robert Louis Stevenson State Park, 7 miles (11 kilometers) north of downtown Calistoga on Highway 29.

Afternoon
Have lunch at Tra Vigne (➤ 94), then head south to Rutherford. Stop into film director Francis Ford Coppola's **2 Niebaum-Coppola Estate** (➤ 82) or **2 Mumm Napa Valley** (➤ 82), then continue south on Highway 29 and east on Highway 12 and I-80 to **6 Sacramento** (➤ 84), a two-hour drive.

Evening
Have dinner in Sacramento at Biba (➤ 94).

Day 4

Morning
Stroll around Old Sacramento and tour the **California State Railroad Museum** and **Sutter's Fort** (left, ➤ 84).

Afternoon
Shoot east on I-80 and north on Highway 49 and have lunch in **Nevada City** (➤ 84) at Café Mekka (237 Commercial Street, tel: 530/478-1517). Head south on Highway 49, stopping at **6 Gold Country** (➤ 84–85) attractions; don't miss the **Empire Mine** if it's open.

Evening
Spend the night in Sutter Creek (➤ 85).

Day 5

Morning
Drive south on Highway 49 to Highway 120 and head east into **7 Yosemite National Park** (right, ➤ 86–89).

Afternoon
Visit Glacier Point and Yosemite Valley. If it's summer, catch the sunset at Hetch Hetchy Reservoir.

Evening
Have dinner at the Ahwahnee Lodge's dining room (➤ 94) or the Wawona Hotel (Highway 41).

Sonoma–Mendocino Coast

A cross-section of Northern California's wildlife and vegetation – whales, sea lions, ospreys, wildflowers and redwoods – inhabits the coastline near Highway 1 as it slithers north through Sonoma and Mendocino counties. The attractions in this land of rock-strewn beaches and fishing and former logging towns are simple yet simply delightful, among them 19th-century Point Arena Lighthouse and the Mendocino Coast Botanical Gardens.

Only Alfred Hitchcock could have turned the placid village of **Bodega,** just off Highway 1 along Highway 12, and the equally peaceable fishing town of **Bodega Bay,** on Highway 1 itself, into the terror-filled setting for "The Birds" – the church and schoolhouse buildings in Bodega still stand. The remodeled bar and eating areas at the **Tides Wharf Restaurant** (835 Highway 1, tel: 707/875-3652) aren't as atmospheric as they were when Hitchcock filmed on the site, but the fish dishes are tasty. Head north to the **Crab Pot** (1750 Highway 1, tel:

707/875-9970) for salmon jerky, smoked fish or other local delicacies.

Sea lions loll on windswept **Goat Rock Beach,** 10 miles (16 kilometers) north of Bodega Bay in Jenner. Trappers in search of sea otters established **Fort Ross** (► 24), 9 miles (14 kilometers) beyond that. During blooming season (usually May), pink blossoms brighten nearby **Kruse Rhododendron State Reserve.** Here's how Jack London described this part of the coast in *The Human Drift*: "Especially in the Fort Ross section did we find the roads thrilling, while all the way along we followed the sea. At every stream, the road skirted dizzy cliff-edges, dived down into lush growths of forest and ferns and climbed out along the cliff-edges again."

Humpback, killer, blue and pilot whales pass near the coast during their annual migrations

London used to stop at the Gualala Hotel (39301 Highway 1) – the bar hasn't changed since he drank there – in **Gualala.** The Gualala River, which empties into the Pacific Ocean here, separates Sonoma and Mendocino counties. Twenty miles (32 kilometers) north is **Point Arena Lighthouse** (see **Hidden gem,** below), and 20 miles (32 kilometers) beyond that lies tiny down-home **Elk,** a good pit stop with a few shops and cafés.

Artists flocked to **Mendocino,** about 13 miles (21 kilometers) north of Elk, in the 1950s and 1960s. The town's headlands setting and fine restaurants and B&Bs make it a superlative stop. Explore its shops and small museums, walk the headlands and pay a visit to the **Mendocino Coast Botanical Gardens** (18220 N. Highway 1, Fort Bragg, tel: 707/964-4352), whose mild maritime climate supports an astonishing array of plant life (there's also a good café here). A sandy beach and miles of dunes are among the draws at **MacKerricher State Park** (Highway 1, north of Fort Bragg, tel: 707/964-9112).

Sea otter doing the backstroke

The grape-growing region due east of Mendocino, amid the redwoods along Highway 128, has become known for chardonnay, pinot noir and sparkling wines; you'll often have the tasting rooms all to yourself. **Husch** (4400 Highway 128, Philo, tel: 800/554-8724) and the **Roederer Estate** (4501 Highway 128, Philo, tel: 707/895-2288) are good first stops.

TAKING A BREAK

Munch on appetizers or order a meal at **River's End** (➤ 93), which overlooks Goat Rock Beach in Jenner. The best of several fine Mendocino restaurants is **Café Beaujolais** (➤ 93). The clifftops will be crowded, and all sense of awe will be on hold.

SONOMA–MENDOCINO COAST: INSIDE INFO

Top tips On the first day of a two- or three-day excursion from San Francisco you could **drive up the Sonoma Coast,** stopping at a few sights before ending up in Mendocino, where you could spend the next two days.
• You can reach Highway 1 at Bodega Bay by driving west from US 101 in Santa Rosa on Highway 12. The **quickest way to Mendocino** from San Francisco is via US 101 north to Cloverdale, west on Highway 128 and then north on Highway 1. In both cases the longer but more scenic option is to take Highway 1 the entire way.

Hidden gem Clamber up the stairs of **Point Arena Lighthouse** for dizzying views of crashing waves as they spout through a rocky blowhole. The town of Point Arena itself is worth a look. (45500 Lighthouse Road, off Highway 1, tel: 707/882-2777, open: daily 10–4:30, Apr–Sep; 10–3:30, rest of year. Admission: inexpensive.)

The Wine Country

The chardonnays, zinfandels, cabernets and other vintages produced in Sonoma and Napa counties are among the finest in the U.S., and the setting – dense green in much of Sonoma, more arid and a little Mediterranean in quality in Napa – dazzles as much as the wines.

...and the wine is bottled poetry...
Robert Louis Stevenson

Even if you don't drink, the scenery alone is worth an excursion. Diversions that aren't wine-oriented include hiking, cycling, canoeing, primping at classy spas and dining at trend-setting restaurants. But wine is the main attraction, and the two counties contain more than 400 wineries. **Napa** and **Sonoma** are the names of towns, valleys and counties. All are north of San Francisco, with Sonoma County due west of Napa County. The Carneros region straddles the southern edge of the two valleys.

The Wineries and Other Attractions
Buena Vista Carneros Winery Modern California winemaking started at what is now the Buena Vista Carneros Winery, founded in 1857 by Agoston Haraszthy, a Hungarian immigrant. You can peek into 19th-century caves on guided or self-guided tours. Specialties include pinot noirs and chardonnays.

✉ 18000 Old Winery Road, off E. Napa Street, Sonoma ☎ (707) 938-1266 ④ Daily 10–5; tours at 11 and 2. Closed Jan 1, Thanksgiving, Dec 25

When the sunlight filters through the trees along lush, green Arnold Drive, west of and parallel to Highway 12, you'll see what attracted Jack London to the area. From downtown Sonoma take Napa Street west and after Napa becomes Riverside Drive make a left on Solano Avenue and a right on Arnold.

Benziger Family Winery A tram travels into the vineyards as part of the tour at Benziger Family Winery, known for its fine chardonnays and cabernets. The jolly tour is a good one to take if winespeak intimidates you.

    ✉ 1883 London Ranch Road, west off Arnold Drive, Glen Ellen ☎ (707) 935-3000
    🕐 Daily 10–5; tram rides 11:30, 12:30, 2 and 3:30 (extra times in summer). Closed Jan 1, Easter, Thanksgiving, Dec 25

Jack London State Historic Park The park's museum contains London memorabilia. A 1-mile (1.6-kilometer) hike ends at the ruins of the dream house the author built but never occupied (it was destroyed by fire).

    ✉ 2400 London Ranch Road ☎ (707) 938-5216 🎟 Inexpensive

Kunde Homelike Kunde produces an excellent zinfandel from grapes grown on 19th-century vines.

    ✉ 10155 Sonoma Highway (north from north end of Arnold Drive), Kenwood ☎ (707) 833-5501 🕐 Daily 10:30–4:30; tours Fri–Sun 11:30–4. Closed Jan 1, Thanksgiving, Dec 25

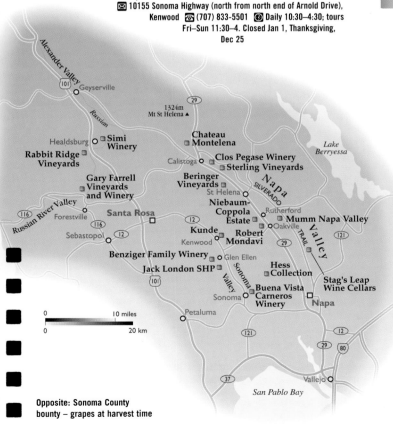

0   10 miles
0   20 km

Opposite: Sonoma County
bounty – grapes at harvest time

Mon Dieu!

At a famous blind tasting in Paris in 1976, French wine experts – much to their later chagrin – awarded top honors to a **Stag's Leap Wine Cellars cabernet sauvignon** and a **Chateau Montelena chardonnay.** "Ah, back to France," wrote one judge about what turned out to be a California wine.

Highway 12 winds north to **Santa Rosa**, where it runs into US 101, which continues north to **Healdsburg.** Shops and restaurants border Healdsburg Plaza, in the center of town.

Simi Winery Founded in the 19th century but employing the latest technology, Simi Winery built its reputation on cabernets, chardonnays and sauvignon blancs. At the large winery, a

Vineyard views near Glen Ellen

good first stop in the Healdsburg area, you can pick up a copy of the free Russian River Wine Road map which will help you to locate smaller operations such as Rabbit Ridge (▶ below).
✉ 16275 Healdsburg Avenue (Dry Creek Road exit off US 101, left at second light), Healdsburg ☎ (707) 433-6981 🕐 Daily 10–4:30; tours 11 and 2. Closed Jan 1, Thanksgiving, Dec 25

Rabbit Ridge Vineyards Chardonnays and zinfandels have made Rabbit Ridge among the most popular of the smaller Russian River Valley wineries.
✉ 3291 Westside Road, Healdsburg ☎ (707) 431-7128 🕐 Daily 11–5 (no tours). Closed Jan 1, Thanksgiving, Dec 25

Gary Farrell Vineyards & Winery Along Westside Road lie several other fine producers, including Rochioli, Porter Creek and, farthest west, Gary Farrell. The winemaker's specialty is reds, particularly pinot noir and zinfandel, but he also makes a full-bodied yet crisp chardonnay.

✉ **10701 Westside Road, Healdsburg** ☎ **(707) 473 2900** ◷ **Daily 11–4; tours. Closed Jan 1, Easter, Thanksgiving, Dec 25**

Continue on Westside Road to River Road which winds east past US 101, where the name changes to Mark West Springs Road. Follow the signs on this road, Porter Creek Road and Petrified Forest Road (all heading more or less east), and you'll wind up in **Calistoga,** at the northern edge of the Napa Valley.

The valley, America's foremost appellation (viticultural region) is compact – less than a mile wide at some points.

Chateau Montelena The oldest sections of the main stone structure here date from 1882. The winery took first prize for its chardonnay at the 1976 blind tasting in France (➤ opposite), but over the years its cabernets have garnered more awards.

✉ **1429 Tubbs Lane, off Highway 29, Calistoga** ☎ **707/942-5105** ◷ **Daily 9:30–4; tours by appointment. Closed Jan 1, Memorial Day, Jul 4, Labor Day, Thanksgiving, Dec 25**

Clos Pegase The postmodern architect Michael Graves designed playful Clos Pegase, where the top varietals include chardonnays, merlots and cabernets.

✉ **1060 Dunaweal Lane, Calistoga** ☎ **(707) 942-4981** ◷ **Daily 10:30–5; tours 11 and 2. Closed Jan 1, Thanksgiving, Dec 25**

Sterling Vineyards An enclosed gondola whisks you to the hill-top headquarters of Sterling Vineyards, whose specialties include merlots, chardonnays and sauvignon blancs. (The fee here is for the ride; tastings are free.)

✉ **1111 Dunaweal Lane, Calistoga** ☎ **(707) 942-3344** ◷ **Daily 10:30–4:30; self-guided tours only. Closed Thanksgiving, Dec 25**

Beringer Vineyards Gables, turrets and ornate carvings set a vaguely Gothic tone at Beringer Vineyards, founded in 1876. The tours of this winery, best known for its chardonnays, cabernets and merlots, include the tunnels Chinese laborers dug into the side of Spring Mountain.

✉ **2000 Main Street, St. Helena** ☎ **(707) 963-4812** ◷ **Daily 10–6, May–Oct; 10–5, rest of year. Tours every half hour. Closed Jan 1, Thanksgiving, Dec 25**

The Treatment You Deserve

You can take a mud bath at one of **Calistoga's spas.** Some folks swear by the usual regimen (the cost runs to about $100): Shower, 10 minutes in the mud, a soak in a hot mineral bath, some time in the steam room, a blanket wrap and a massage. The "mud" is actually volcanic ash, and in most spas is mixed with peat. It's heated to boiling point after each use to keep things sanitary. The purists at **Indian Springs** (1712 Lincoln Avenue, tel: 707/942-4913) use 100 percent volcanic ash.

The **Mount View Spa** (1457 Lincoln Avenue, Calistoga, tel: 707/942-5789) and **Health Spa Napa Valley** (1030 Main Street, St. Helena, tel: 707/967-8800), two upscale establishments, offer mudless, state-of-the-art treatments.

Culinary Institute of America Greystone, the institute's West Coast campus, has a fine gift shop, a restaurant and a corkscrew display with some technologically amazing specimens. Cooking demonstrations (moderate) take place daily at 1:30 and 3:30; also 10:30 on weekends.

⊠ 2555 Main Street, St. Helena ☎ (707) 967-1100 or (800) 333-9242
🎟 Free

Niebaum-Coppola Estate Niebaum-Coppola Estate produces robust red wines and chardonnays. An on-site museum contains memorabilia from the owner Francis Ford Coppola's "Godfather" series.

⊠ 1991 St. Helena Highway, Rutherford ☎ (707) 963-9099 🕐 Daily 10–5 (also Fri–Sat 5–6, in summer); tour times vary. Closed Jan 1, Easter, Thanksgiving, Dec 24–25

Mumm Napa Valley Winemaking photographs by Ansel Adams (▶ 26), a well-conceived tour and the chance to sip effervescent sparkling wines make Mumm Napa Valley a worthy stop. In the multipaned tasting area you can sample "flights" (three glasses) of recent vintage.

⊠ 8445 Silverado Trail, Rutherford ☎ (707) 942-3434 or (800) 686-6272
🕐 Daily 10:30–6, May–Oct; 10–5, rest of year. Tours on the hour. Closed Thanksgiving, Dec 25

Robert Mondavi You'll get the best overview of the winemaking process at Robert Mondavi, the winery of the man who created fumé blanc. Mondavi is often crowded in summer.

⊠ 7801 St. Helena Highway, Oakville ☎ (707) 259-9463 🕐 Daily 9–5. Tour times vary. Closed Jan 1, Easter, Thanksgiving, Dec 25

Excursions Aloft and Earthbound

Adventures Aloft (tel: 800/944-4408) conducts sunrise balloon rides in the Napa Valley. **Sonoma Thunder** (tel: 707/829-9850) does the same in the Sonoma Valley. Rates run just under $200 per person, which includes breakfast (most flights take place in the early morning).
Sonoma Cattle Co./Napa Valley Trail Rides (tel: 707/255-2900) leads guided horseback rides through state parks.
Getaway Adventures (tel: 800/499-2453) rents bicycles and leads interesting hiking, cycling, sea-kayaking and canoe trips in Napa and Sonoma counties. Some bicycle trips include vineyard tours.

Wine production in this region dates to the 1800s

Hess Collection At the Hess Collection, a mountain hideaway, top-notch modern art (Bacon, Stella and others) vies for attention with valley views and full-bodied cabernets and chardonnays.

✉ 4411 Redwood Road, west of Highway 29, Napa ☎ (707) 255-1144 ⓘ Daily 10–4 (self-guided tours; brief video presentation). Closed Jan 1, Thanksgiving, Dec 25

THE WINE COUNTRY: INSIDE INFO

Top tips To get to the **Napa Valley** from San Francisco, take US 101 north to Highway 37, east to Highway 121, east to Highway 29, then continue north.
• Wineries along the **Silverado Trail** tend to be less busy than their counterparts along the more or less parallel Highway 29.
• To get to the **Sonoma Valley,** take US 101 north to Highway 37, east to Highway 121, north to Highway 12, then continue north.
• North of San Francisco off US 101 are the **Alexander Valley** (take the Healdsburg exit) and the **Russian River Valley** (take the River Road exit and head west).
• Most wineries in Napa and some in Sonoma **charge tasting fees** (from $3 to $10 but usually $5 or under for three or more wines), which are almost always deducted from purchases.
• In summer **it's best to make tour reservations** because some wineries limit the number of participants.
• If you're driving, keep in mind that a **blood-alcohol level of over .08%** qualifies you as legally drunk. Though results vary from individual to individual, the average person reaches that level drinking more than one 4-ounce (118-milliliter) glass of wine.

Don't miss Take at least one winery tour. **Robert Mondavi** (➤ opposite), **Beringer** (➤ 81) and **Simi** (➤ 80) provide a good overview of the winemaking process.

Sacramento and the Gold Country

After gold was discovered in the Sierra foothills, California's politicians moved the state capital to Sacramento. As always, they went where the money went – and there was plenty of it. Sacramento's points of interest yield clues about Gold Rush life, but to see real mines and former mining towns, venture east into the Gold Country.

Sacramento

Sacramento's finest attraction, the **California State Railroad Museum** (125 I Street, tel: 916/445-6645, moderate), exhibits a century-and-a-half's worth of railroad cars and locomotives. The museum is the highlight of slightly too manicured Old Town Sacramento, where wooden sidewalks, restored buildings and old-fashioned signage recall the Gold Rush.

Gold, silver and commerce financed the Roman Corinthian-style **State Capitol** (10th and L streets), which has an impressive rotunda and gardens. **Sutter's Fort State Historic Park** (2701 L Street, tel: 916/445-4422, inexpensive) and the on-site **State Indian Museum** survey local and California history, as does the **California State History Museum** (1020 O Street, tel: 916/653-7524, inexpensive).

Sacramento's Old Town links six blocks of restored 19th-century buildings

Best of the Gold Country

From Sacramento you can explore the Gold Country. I-80 east connects with Highway 49, running north–south through the region.

North of the interstate on Highway 49, 60 miles (97 kilometers) from Sacramento, is **Nevada City,** whose walkable historic district has many Gold Rush buildings. North of town is **Malakoff Diggins State Historic Park** (➤ 24).

Many mines dried up quickly, but the **Empire Mine,** now in **Empire Mine State Historic Park** (10791 E. Empire Street, south from Highway 49, Grass Valley, tel: 530/273-8522, inexpensive), whose lode yielded nearly 6 million ounces (170 million grams) of gold over the years, remained open until the 1950s. Highway 49 winds south for 24 miles (38 kilometers) from Grass Valley back to I-80 and the town of **Auburn.** Eighteen miles (29 kilometers) farther south lies

Marshall Gold Discovery State Historic Park (Bridge Street, Highway 49, Coloma, tel: 530/622-3470, inexpensive). James Marshall (➤ 12) set off the Gold Rush when he spotted a nugget here in 1848.

Placerville, south of Coloma on Highway 49 and 44 miles east of Sacramento on US 50, was known during Gold Rush days as Hangtown, a nod to its townsfolk's preferred method for dispensing justice. The self-guided tour of Hangtown's **Gold Bug Mine** (from Highway 49 take US 50 east and Bedford Avenue north, Placerville, tel: 530/642-5207, inexpensive), a rock-walled horizontal mine, shows the conditions workers experienced as they mined for gold.

Saloons, a Wells Fargo express office and other period buildings at **Columbia State Historic Park** (Parrotts Ferry Road, off Highway 49, Columbia, tel: 209/532-0150, free), 70 miles (113 kilometers) south of Placerville, re-create Gold Rush life.

Twelve square blocks in Columbia have been designated a state historic park

TAKING A BREAK

Try **Fat City** (1001 Front Street, Sacramento, tel: 916/446-6768) for drinks, a snack or a meal.

THE GOLD COUNTRY: INSIDE INFO

Top tips Highway 49 **twists and turns in spots;** the going can sometimes be slow. Summer afternoons can be mighty hot.
• **If you've only a day** to spend in the Gold Country, get a feel for the region touring Nevada City, Grass Valley, Coloma and Placerville. Alternatively, spend the night in **Sutter Creek** and explore its downtown before continuing southward.

Hidden gems The redwoods of **Calaveras Big Tree State Park** (off Highway 4 near Arnold) are hardly "hidden," but the trees here are gems.

Yosemite National Park

What is there to say about Yosemite National Park except don't miss one of America's scenic superstars. The park's waterfalls, the granite monoliths Half Dome and El Capitan, Mariposa Grove with its giant sequoias, and the view of Yosemite Valley and beyond from Glacier Point are all stunners, as is that man-made standard-setter for mountain-rustic chic, the Ahwahnee Lodge.

Seeing the Park

Most visitors charge straight into Yosemite Valley, but consider heading first to **Glacier Point** (take Wawona Road south to Glacier Point Road) for an unforgettable glimpse of the valley – you'll be standing 3,000 feet (915 meters) above it – and perspectives on the major sights except El Capitan. When you see them up close they'll stagger you all the more.

From Glacier Point, head toward Yosemite Valley, back down Glacier Point Road and north on Wawona Road. After you pass through a tunnel, park in the lot to the right and walk across the road to the vista point, which has a head-on view of El Capitan. Then continue a short way to the parking lot for gauzy **Bridalveil Fall,** so called because the slightest wind moves the misty cascade a dozen feet or more from its center.

As you continue east, the name of the road you're on becomes Southside Drive. Stop along the way if something catches your eye – as more than likely it will. Follow signs to Sentinel Bridge and make a left off Southside Drive to reach the Valley

Winter in Yosemite enchants as much as summer does

Visitor Center. Viewing the exhibits here, you'll learn how to distinguish which of Yosemite's features were formed by erosion and which by volcanic eruption. Ancient waters rose to about 9,000 feet (2,745 meters), rounding the rock domes below this elevation. Massive upheavals from beneath the earth's crust – assisted much later by Ice-Age glaciers, which

Happy Trails to You

Yosemite's system of trails includes short and easy hikes and moderately difficult ones such as the 1.25-mile (2-kilometer) path to **Sentinel Dome** or the half loop (6.5 miles/10 kilometers) or full loop (13 miles/21 kilometers) around **Yosemite Valley.** The Four Mile Trail between Yosemite Valley and **Glacier Point** is a relatively short but strenuous climb, though it's easier in the reverse direction, most of which is downhill. If you're heading into the backcountry, stop by the Wilderness Center (it's near the valley visitor center; open late spring to early fall only) for permits and information.

➕ 203 E1   ✉ Entrances: South Entrance (Highway 41), Arch Rock (Highway 140), Big Oak Flat (Highway 120, west side of park), Tioga Pass (Highway 120, east side of park; open only in summer) ☎ (209) 372-0200 for park information, (559) 252-4848 for lodging reservations, (800) 436-7275 for campground reservations (301/722-1257 from outside the U.S. or Canada), (209) 372-1208 for bicycle rentals, (209) 372-8348 for horseback riding 💰 Expensive (per carload, fee good for seven consecutive days)

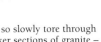

ever so slowly tore through weaker sections of granite – produced the gigantic slabs that jut willy-nilly out of the landscape.

Drop by the **Ahwahnee Lodge,** tucked away to the east of the visitor center. The deluxe lodge contains wide wood-beam ceilings, stone fireplaces and Indian artifacts. Head west from the Ahwahnee on Northside Drive to the parking lot for **Yosemite Falls** – actually three falls that appear almost as one when winter snows are melting. The easy hike to the base of the bottom section, Lower Falls, is a half-mile (.8-kilometer) round trip. **El Capitan,** a bit farther west on Northside Drive, shoots nearly 3,600 feet (1,100 meters) straight up from the valley floor. It's so sturdy that even glaciers, which over millennia ripped ever so slowly through the valley, couldn't reshape its facade.

From El Capitan you can head south on Wawona Road past the cutoff for Glacier

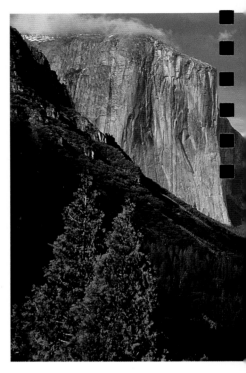

El Capitan, left, and Yosemite Falls are but two of the park's must-sees

Point to the giant sequoias of **Mariposa Grove.** During busy times, instead of driving you'll have to take a shuttle bus that leaves from the Wawona Store, near the Wawona Hotel.

It takes a full day just to breeze past Yosemite's highlights. To truly appreciate the natural setting, though, take your time and venture off the beaten path, if not for a backcountry hike or a bike or horseback ride through the valley, at least to **Hetch Hetchy Reservoir** (➤ opposite) or verdant **Tuolumne Meadows** (Highway 120/Tioga Road east from Big Arch Rock Entrance; Tioga Road closed late fall to late spring).

Getting There

From the San Francisco area take I-580 and Highway 132 east. At Modesto head south on Highway 99. At Merced take Highway 140 east into the park. From the Los Angeles area take I-5 north and Highway 99 north to Fresno; from there, Highway 41 heads north into the park.

TAKING A BREAK

Your splurge in Yosemite Valley is the **restaurant** (➤ 94) at the Ahwahnee Lodge; take a peek at the high-ceilinged room even if you don't stop for a meal, or have a drink in the lobby bar. Fast food is available near the visitor center. There is also fine dining at the Wawona Hotel's main restaurant.

YOSEMITE NATIONAL PARK: INSIDE INFO

Top tips Try to **avoid summer weekends,** when park visitation is highest. Summer weekdays aren't as bad. The weeks just before Memorial Day and after Labor Day are even less trafficked and the weather is mild.
• If you can, **spend at least one night in Yosemite,** either camping (the facilities range from comfortable to primitive) or staying at the plush Ahwahnee Lodge, the historic Wawona Hotel or the casual Yosemite Lodge.
• On the valley floor you can **rent a bicycle** (there are 12 miles (19 kilometers) of mostly flat paths in the valley alone) or arrange **guided horseback rides.**
• You can drive to each sight in Yosemite Valley or **hop aboard the free shuttle bus** that serves each of them and Glacier Point.

Hidden gems Visit the re-created **Indian Village of Ahwahnee** (➤ 24).
• A 1-mile (1.6-kilometer) path (formerly a park road) in the Crane Flat section leads to **Tuolumne Grove,** a stand of 25 giant sequoias. The hike to the grove is easy, but the trip back is moderately strenuous (Highway 120 and Tioga Road).
• A huge valley was dammed to create the **Hetch Hetchy Reservoir,** which supplies San Francisco with much of its water. Steep granite cliffs surround most of the reservoir.

At Your Leisure

🛐 Redwood Country

Northern California's tallest redwoods grow in Mendocino County and points north. The 33-mile (53-kilometer) **Avenue of the Giants** (Highway 254) snakes north from US 101 from north of Garberville to Pepperwood, where it rejoins US 101. (Garberville is just over 200 miles (320 kilometers) north of San Francisco.) Along the avenue, north of Weott, is **Humboldt Redwoods State Park** (tel: 707/946-2409), where you can tour redwood groves.

A few interesting towns north of the park off US 101 are **Ferndale, Eureka** (the best town to stay overnight) and **Arcata**, all of whose downtown historic districts (follow highway signs) contain Victorian-era homes. Still farther north, past Trinidad, is **Patrick's Point State Park** (tel: 707/677-3570), where the ocean views from its bluff are superb.

About 17 miles (27 kilometers) beyond Patrick's Point is the entrance to **Redwood National and State Parks** (tel: 707/464-6101). Stop by the Thomas H. Kuchel Visitor Center (US 101, south of Orick) for directions to Tall Trees Grove and the redwoods within Lady Bird Johnson Grove. **Crescent City,** about 40 miles (64 kilometers) north of Orick, is the last big town before the Oregon border. If you get up this far, check out **Battery Point Lighthouse** (map 202 A5, Battery Point Island, end of A Street, tel: 707/464-3089), which was completed in 1856. It's usually open between 10 and 4 (tides permitting) Wednesday to Sunday from about May to October, but call to be sure during off times to schedule a visit.

🛍 Shasta Cascade

In the far north of California, **Mount Shasta** dominates the terrain between the coastal redwoods and the Cascade Range. With its crisp, clear air and easy to strenuous trails, Mount Shasta is perfect for hikes of a day or longer. The upper slopes of the 14,162-foot (4,317-meter) peak remain snow-covered year-round. Call the **Forest Service Ranger Station** (tel: 530/926-4511) for hiking, camping and other information.

South of Mount Shasta off I-5 are the **Lake Shasta Caverns** (tel: 530/238-2341 or 800/795-2283, expensive), well worth touring (schedule varies). Off I-5 at the lake's southwestern tip is **Shasta Dam** (tel: 530/275-4463, free). You can tour the dam, one of the largest in the U.S. (times vary depending on season and security status).

An interesting stop in **Weaverville,** 47 miles (75 kilometers) west of Redding, is the ornate **Joss House**

The trees at Redwood National Park are so big you can even drive through them

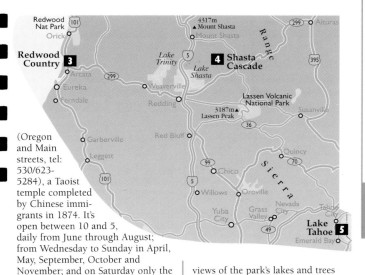

(Oregon and Main streets, tel: 530/623-5284), a Taoist temple completed by Chinese immigrants in 1874. It's open between 10 and 5, daily from June through August; from Wednesday to Sunday in April, May, September, October and November; and on Saturday only the rest of the year.

Lassen Volcanic National Park (tel: 530/595-4444), 49 miles (79 kilometers) east of Red Bluff (take Highway 36 east to Highway 89 north), contains bubbling sulfuric hot springs, cinder cones, lava beds and boiling mud pots. The strenuous Lassen Peak Hike yields spectacular

Emerald Bay. This perfect cove, enclosed by pine forests, has Lake Tahoe's only island, Fannette

views of the park's lakes and trees and beyond to Mount Shasta. The easier Bumpass Hell Trail leads to areas of geothermal activity.

➕ 202 C4 ✉ I-5 ☎ (530) 365-7500 or (800) 326-6944 for tourist information about the Shasta Cascade area

5 Lake Tahoe

The California–Nevada border slices through Lake Tahoe, the largest alpine body of water in North America. Hikers, swimmers and sightseers flock to lakeside beaches and the nearby

mountains in summer, and when the weather turns cold, skiers slalom down slopes at what has long been California's premier ski region. The dichotomy isn't merely seasonal or geographical, however. Year-round, millions eschew the scenic beauty and head straight into the Nevada-side gambling casinos. Lodging costs less around Lake Tahoe than it does nearly anywhere else in the state. Most of the big motel and hotel chains have properties here, and there are some homey B&Bs.

To get the lay of the land, ride the Gondola at **Heavenly** (Ski Run Boulevard, off US 50, South Lake Tahoe, tel: 800/432-8365, moderate

Mono Lake's tufa looks otherworldly, but it's basically just limestone

the 1920s. Or you could drive north, to **Sand Harbor Beach** (Highway 28) or **Tahoe City** (Highway 89).

✚ 203 E2 ✉ US 50 (South Lake Tahoe and Nevada-side casinos); Highway 89 (Tahoe City and lake's western and northern shores) ☎ (800) 288-2463 or (800) 824-6348 (visitor and lodging information)

🔟 Mono Lake

Crusty, coral-like tufa juts out of this beautiful lake east of Yosemite National Park. Take the South Tufa Trail (Highway 120, 5 miles (8 kilometers) east of US 395) to see the most dramatic spires and some of the millions (literally) of migratory birds that flock here. The ghost town of **Bodie** (➤ 25) is 31 miles (50 kilometers) northeast of Lee Vining.

in summer/expensive in winter). The whole Tahoe basin unfolds before you as the gondola climbs the slopes of **Heavenly Ski Resort** to 8,250 feet (2,515 meters) above sea level; at the top you can dine or hike.

You can drive the lake's 72-mile (115-kilometer) circumference in a day, though in summer, when traffic's heavy, a better strategy is to explore a short section, such as the **Pope-Baldwin Recreation Area** and **Emerald Bay**, both along Highway 89 on the south side. If you head to delightful Emerald Bay, visit **Vikingsholm**, a rustic estate built in

✚ 203 F1 ✉ Scenic Area Visitor Center, US 395, Lee Vining ☎ (760) 875-2427 ⊙ Daily 9–5:30, late May to early Sep; times vary, rest of year. Closed Thanksgiving, Dec 25, and Tue–Thu, in winter

Where to...
Eat and Drink

Prices
Expect to pay per person for a meal, excluding drinks and service
$ under $15 $$ $15–25 $$$ over $25

SONOMA-MENDOCINO COAST

⚫⚫⚫ Café Beaujolais $$-$$$
Mendocino's best-known restaurant fits the local look: rustic and relaxed. It is set in a Victorian farmhouse surrounded by gardens. But Café Beaujolais' reputation for pure, fresh ingredients and innovative California country cooking, accented by cuisines from around the world, extends far beyond the Mendocino-Sonoma region. While the menu changes seasonally, you can count on locally grown organic produce, meat from free-range animals, breads baked on the premises. The menu is complemented by an excellent wine list.
➕ 202 A3 ⬛ 961 Ukiah Street, Mendocino ☎ (707) 937-5614
⏰ Daily 5:45–9. Closed Dec–Jan

River's End $$-$$$
The ocean views alone – River's End is at the mouth of the Russian River – would justify a stop here. But the food has enough pizzazz to distract you from those searing orange sunsets and barking sea lions. You can choose from game dishes, such as venison, pheasant or duck, or the freshly caught fish of the day. Dishes may have a French, German or Thai accent. The wine list is extensive.
➕ 202 B2 ⬛ 11048 Highway 1, Jenner ☎ (707) 865-2484
⏰ Thu–Mon noon–3:30, 5–9:30, Apr–Oct; Fri–Sun noon–3:30, 5–9:30, rest of year. Closed Dec 24–25

WINE COUNTRY

Auberge du Soleil $$$
To experience Wine Country living at its most opulent, dine at this longtime favorite whose chef lives up to his Napa Valley counterparts and the exquisite setting. Dining here is a leisurely affair, with multiple courses and ample time to enjoy vineyard views and savor wine from the extensive selection. The cuisine here is French-Mediterranean, with dishes such as Parmesan risotto with Meyer lemon confit, watercress and Maine lobster, veal loin with bacon crust, braised radish and celery, and molasses-glazed sweetbreads. For lighter and less pricey fare, take your meal – or wine and fine cheeses – in the bar.
➕ 202 C2 ⬛ 180 Rutherford Hill Road, Rutherford, CA 94573 ☎ (707) 963-1211 or (800) 348-5406 ⏰ Daily breakfast 7–11; lunch 11:30–2:30; dinner Mon–Thu 6–9:30, Fri–Sun 5:30–9:30

Bistro Ralph $$-$$$
This casual restaurant, situated on the plaza in the heart of Healdsburg, is building a big reputation for home-style California cooking. The owner-chef, Ralph Tingle, makes good use of Sonoma lamb and other local produce. Service is welcoming, and the bar here is a popular gathering place for Wine Country residents; sip some local wines, order some dishes if you'd like and tune in on the local grapevine. The outdoor patio is pleasant on warm evenings.
➕ 202 B2 ⬛ 109 Plaza Street, Healdsburg ☎ (707) 433-1380
⏰ Lunch Mon–Fri 11:30–2:30; dinner daily 5:30–late. Closed Thanksgiving and Dec 25

Copia $-$$$

You'll learn plenty if you choose to participate in the tours and lectures at the dramatic Copia: The American Center for Wine, Food, & the Arts, but this is also a great place to dine. You can choose between the terrace outside the American Market Café ($-$$; eclectic, no reservations) or Julia's Kitchen ($$$; California-French, reservations recommended).

✚ 202 C2 ⊠ 500 First Street, Napa ☎ (707) 265-5701 (café) or 265-5700 (Julia's) ⊙ Café lunch Wed–Mon 11–4; Julia's lunch Wed–Mon 11:30–3, dinner Thu–Sun 5:30–9:30

Mustards Grill $$-$$$

It can get very crowded and noisy at this casual bistro along busy Highway 29 – the crowds are a mix of locals, tourists and Bay Area residents who drive up just for a meal here – but the food is some of the best in the Wine Country and the staff handles the clamor with elan. Preparations and dishes are cutting-edge California, with grilled meats and fish accompanied by fresh local produce; the onion rings are legendary. The wine list is one of the most complete in the region.

✚ 202 C2 ⊠ 7399 St. Helena Highway, Yountville ☎ (707) 944-2424 ⊙ Mon–Thu 11:30–9, Fri 11:30–10, Sat 11–10, Sun 11–9. Closed Thanksgiving and Dec 25

⚅⚅⚅ Tra Vigne $$-$$$

Many Napa Valley habitués consider Tra Vigne the quintessential Wine Country restaurant. This trattoria has it all. Service is friendly and efficient. The surrounding landscape is right out of Tuscany (ask for a seat on the outdoor terrace when you make your reservation), as is the food: fresh pastas, grilled meats and seafood. The inspired wine list, however, concentrates on local vintages. Inside, in the high-ceilinged dining room, there's an attractive bar; try one of the house-made grappas.

✚ 202 C2 ⊠ 1050 Charter Oak Avenue, St. Helena ☎ (707) 963-4444 ⊙ Sun–Thu 11:30–10, Fri–Sun 11:30–10:30. Closed Thanksgiving and Dec 25

SACRAMENTO & GOLD COUNTRY

Biba $$-$$$

This restaurant near the State Capitol owes its popularity to chef-owner Biba Caggiano, author of several Italian cookbooks. Her northern Italian cuisine relies on fresh ingredients and inventive combinations, all attractively presented and efficiently served; some southern Italian dishes are also represented. A grand piano is played nightly in the lounge, where there's a full bar, and the extensive wine list highlights both Italian and California vintages.

✚ 202 C2 ⊠ 2801 Capitol Avenue, Sacramento ☎ (916) 455-2422 ⊙ Lunch Mon–Fri 11:30–2:30; dinner Mon–Thu 5:30–9:30, Fri–Sat 5:30–10:30. Closed Thanksgiving and Dec 25

YOSEMITE NATIONAL PARK

⚅⚅⚅ Ahwahnee Dining Room $$-$$$

While the Ahwahnee Dining Room, the main restaurant of Ahwahnee Lodge, doesn't break any new culinary ground, the well-prepared American dishes, such as grilled steaks and lightly sauced fish, are well suited to the classic lodge surroundings. As you admire the vaulted ceiling that soars 34 feet (10 meters) above, the sparkling chandeliers and the tables set with linen and china, you'll hardly believe that, shortly before, you were out hiking in jeans – which, by the way, violate the dress code here, along with shorts and sneakers. Try to make your dinner reservations well in advance here. Special Christmas and New Year's feasts are so popular that you have to enter a lottery to be chosen.

✚ 203 E1 ⊠ Ahwahnee Road, Yosemite National Park ☎ (209) 372-1489 ⊙ Daily; breakfast 7–10:30, lunch 11:30–3, dinner 5:30–9

Where to... Stay

Prices
Expect to pay per room

$ under $100 per night **$$** $100–175 per night **$$$** over $175 per night

SONOMA-MENDOCINO COAST

👑👑👑 Jenner Inn & Cottages $$-$$$

The Sonoma Coast town of Jenner is one of those settings where the tribulations of travel recede in the face of sweeping vistas and terrain that seems to tumble into the sea. A fitting place to enjoy the scenery and set out for coastal hikes, winery visits and other activities, is this lodging with rooms, suites and cottages, some set amid the trees, others along the waterfront. Some rooms have fireplaces, spas, saunas and kitchens, and to enhance the getting-away-from-it all ambience,

only a few rooms have phones (none has a TV).

🏠 202 B2 ✉ **Route 1, Box 69, Jenner, CA 95450** ☎ **(707) 865-2377 or (800) 732-2377; email: innkeeper@jennerinn.com**

👑👑👑 MacCallum House $$-$$$

As you stroll around Mendocino, you're almost sure to notice MacCallum House. Built in 1882, it's a beautifully restored Victorian with gingerbread trim. A total of 21 rooms in three separate accommodations – the main house, seven cottages and the Barn – are sympathetically furnished with antiques. Some rooms have decks, fireplaces

---

Mountain Room Restaurant $$

The best restaurant in Yosemite Lodge, open for dinner only, serves up Continental cuisine – steak, seafood and pasta – along with some incredible views of Yosemite Falls through the picture windows. You can also opt for the less formal Mountain Room Lounge, where light fare is served, or have a very casual breakfast, lunch or dinner at the food court.

🏠 203 E1 ✉ **Off Northside Drive, Yosemite National Park** ☎ **(209) 372-1274** 🕐 **Daily 5:30–9**

👑👑👑👑 Erna's Elderberry House $$-$$$

One of the state's finest restaurants, Erna's Elderberry House is well worth a drive down from Yosemite; it's in the town of Oakhurst, about 15 miles (24 kilometers) south of the park's southern entrance via Highway 41. Erna's serves one six-course fixed-price dinner per night, with a French-California menu that changes daily to reflect the freshest

ingredients. The indoor dining areas have attractive contemporary touches.

🏠 203 E1 ✉ **48688 Victoria Lane, Oakhurst** ☎ **(559) 683-6800** 🕐 **Dinner; daily 5:30–8:30. Closed first 3 weeks Jan**

LAKE TAHOE

👑👑 Swiss Chalet $$-$$$

If, as for many visitors, Tahoe's alpine air puts you in the mood for Swiss food and decor, head for this family-owned, chalet-style dinner house on Highway 50. Swiss, as well as some German, standards dominate the menu: fondues, wienerschnitzel and other veal dishes, sauerbraten and house-made pastries. Dress is casual, and you can comfortably bring kids along. There's also a lounge with full bar.

🏠 203 E2 ✉ **2544 Lake Tahoe Boulevard (Highway 50), South Lake Tahoe** ☎ **(530) 544-3304** 🕐 **Tue–Sun 5–closing. Closed Easter, 2 weeks in late Nov and Dec 25**

and kitchenettes, and many have water or garden views. The hotel also has a good restaurant and café-bar.

✚ 202 A3 ⊠ 45020 Albion Street, Box 206, Mendocino, CA 95460 ☎ (707) 937-0289 or (800) 609-0492; email: info@maccallumhouse.com

☛☛ Stanford Inn by the Sea $$$

If you're an active – and upscale – traveler, you'll find this woodsy yet stylish lodge a great choice; you can even rent a canoe here for a trip down the nearby Big River. Overlooking the river and ocean, just south of town off Highway 1, the two-story inn has roomy accommodations with fireplaces, CD players and decks that allow you to drink in the views. After a day in the outdoors, return for wine and hors d'oeuvres served by the fire in the lounge, and wake up the next morning to a big vegetarian breakfast, all included in the rates.

✚ 202 A3 ⊠ Coast Highway and Comptche-Ukiah Road, Box 487, Mendocino, CA 95460 ☎ (707) 937-5615 or (800) 331-8884; fax: (707) 937-0305; email: stanford@stanfordinn.com

WINE COUNTRY

☛☛ Comfort Inn Napa Valley North $-$$

This no-frills motel on the edge of Calistoga is not bad for the price. The rooms have the look you might expect, but they're quite suitable and you can unwind from wine touring in the steam room, a small heated pool, or the hot tub. Rates include a modest Continental breakfast.

✚ 202 B2 ⊠ 1865 Lincoln Avenue, Calistoga CA ☎ (707) 942-1112 or (866) 394-2959; fax (707) 942-0318; email: hotelhelp@choicehotels.com

☛☛ Gaige House Inn $$-$$$

Though this bed-and-breakfast is housed in an 1890 Italianate Queen Anne building, some of the sunny rooms inside are decorated with distinct Southeast Asian touches. You can stretch out in the hammock on a backyard deck overlooking Calabazas Creek, or sip premium complimentary wines in the book-lined living room in the evenings. Some rooms here have wood-burning fireplaces, spacious decks and whirlpool baths or clawfoot tubs. Service is solicitous, a concierge is on hand and the full breakfasts are top quality.

✚ 202 B2 ⊠ 13540 Arnold Drive, Glen Ellen, CA 95442 ☎ (707) 935-0237 or (800) 935-0237; fax: (707) 935-6411; email: gaige@sprynet.com ☺ Lodge rooms close some of the winter

☛☛☛ Villagio Inn & Spa $$$

For a Wine Country splurge, check into this stunningly appointed luxury resort in the lower Napa Valley. With prices like these (in the summer, rooms start at around $300), pampering is the order of the day, and the amenities include a bottle of wine upon arrival, a champagne breakfast buffet, and afternoon tea. The spa's worth a visit whether you stay here or not.

✚ 202 C2 ⊠ 6481 Washington Street, Yountville, CA 94599 ☎ (707) 944-8877 or (800) 351-1133; fax (707) 944-8855; email: reservations@villagio.com

SACRAMENTO & GOLD COUNTRY

☛☛☛ Amber House Bed & Breakfast $$

The architectural styles of the four homes that form this inn near the State Capitol range from Craftsman to Dutch Colonial, but the constant here is attention to detail. The rooms are all named for famous artists and writers and decorated accordingly. If you're in a romantic mood, reserve the Lord Byron room; for something more cozy the Brahms room might be the ticket (only the jolly Dickinson room goes against the biographical grain). The bathrooms are as grand as the rooms.

🏠 202 C2 ⊠ 1315 22nd Street, Sacramento, CA 95816 ☎ (916) 444-8085 or (800) 755-6526; fax (916) 552-6529; email: info@amberhouse.com

▼▼▼ Murphys Historic Hotel and Lodge $–$$

With its historic section and saloon, this hotel offers a brush with the gold rush but also access to more current pastimes, such as shopping for art and antiques (though you can still pan for gold nearby if you wish). The hotel is also a good anchor for a Sierra Foothills winery tour: tasting rooms for the fine Black Sheep, Milliaire and Stevenot wineries are nearby. The nine rooms in the historic section have period antiques and share baths; past guests include Mark Twain and the bandit Black Bart (▶ 15). The rooms in the modern section have private baths and more modern furnishings.

🏠 20301 ⊠ 457 Main Street, Murphys, CA 95247 ☎ (209) 728-3444 or (800) 532-7684; fax: 209 728-1590; email: hotelmanager@murphyshotel.com

YOSEMITE

▼▼▼ Ahwahnee Lodge $$$

Opened in 1927, the Ahwahnee is one of the grandest lodges of America's national parks. The public rooms have enormous fireplaces and memorable views of the park; a highlight is afternoon tea in the Great Lounge. Guest rooms are on the small side, but tastefully decorated, with Native American accents. Seven cottages with 24 rooms are scattered in nearby woods.

🏠 203 E1 ⊠ Ahwahnee Road, Yosemite National Park, CA 95389 ☎ (559) 252-4848

▼▼▼ Best Western Yosemite Gateway Inn $

If you can't stay within the National Park, try this well-run motel on a woodsy hillside 15 miles (24 kilometers) from the parks southern entrance. The rooms are pleasing if nondescript. Some have mountain views, balconies, or patios, and some have kitchens. The units with two bedrooms and a kitchen are a great bargain for families (six-person maximum). There is a garden, heated indoor and outdoor pool, a hot tub, an exercise room and a coin-operated laundry.

🏠 203 E1 ⊠ 40530 Highway 41, Oakhurst, CA 93644 ☎ (559) 683-2378 or (800) 394-2799; fax (559) 683-3813

▼▼ Yosemite Lodge and Curry Village $–$$

Yosemite Lodge has 245 motel-like rooms, as well as restaurants, a bar and an Olympic-size pool, while rustic Curry Village has 183 cabins with and without baths, 427 canvas-walled tent cabins with shared bathrooms, a few motel rooms and eating facilities. Reservations are often easier to obtain here than at the Ahwahnee, but you'll still need to reserve well in advance.

🏠 203 E1 ⊠ Northside and Southside drives, Yosemite National Park, CA 95389 ☎ (559) 252-4848

LAKE TAHOE

▼▼▼ Lakeland Village Beach and Ski Resort $–$$$

This complex of modern units rests amid secluded forested grounds with its own stretch of sandy beach on the southern shores of Lake Tahoe. Nearby are Nevada casinos and ski resorts (free shuttles). Accommodations range from hotel-type rooms to four-bedroom town houses with sleeping lofts, but most units come with kitchens, fireplaces and balconies or decks. A pool, hot tub, sauna and tennis courts are among the facilities.

🏠 203 E2 ⊠ 3535 Lake Tahoe Boulevard, South Lake Tahoe, CA 96150 ☎ (530) 544-1685 or (800) 822-5969; fax: (530) 541-6278; email: stay@lakeland-village.com

Where to...
Shop

Arts and crafts, wines, gourmet foods, antiques and sporting gear are among shopping highlights of the region.

MENDOCINO

It's easy to wander Mendocino's compact streets and window shop for art, crafts and handmade jewelry. At the **Mendocino Art Center** (45200 Little Lake Street, tel: 707/937-5818), month-long shows highlight works of local artists.

SONOMA

On the main plaza in Sonoma, you'll find several specialty food shops and bakeries, including the **Sonoma Cheese Factory** (2 Spain Street, tel:

707/996-1931), which carries stocks of local cheeses.

SACRAMENTO

In Sacramento, the restored Old Sacramento district has a number of arts and crafts shops tucked among the historic riverfront buildings. At the **Huntington, Hopkins & Co. Store** (113 I Street, tel: 916/323-7234) you can shop for Victorian-era items in a replica of a mid-19th-century hardware store.

WINE COUNTRY

You can buy wines by the bottle or case at virtually any winery open for tastings or tours. Two branches of the historic **Oakville Grocery** carry outstanding selections of wines and gourmet foods. The original is in the **Napa Valley** (7856 St. Helena Highway, Oakville, tel: 707/944-8802); the second is in the **Russian River area** (124 Matheson Street, Healdsburg, tel: 707/433-3200).

Where to...
Be Entertained

Northern California is not known for its nightlife. Most entertainments in the region involve enjoying the rugged outdoors.

MUSIC

Northern California hosts several annual music festivals, among them **Mendocino Music Festival** (July; music ranges from classical to gospel, jazz to opera; tel: 707/937-2044), Lake Tahoe's **Summer Arts and Music Festival** (Valhalla – June to August), and the **Jazz on the River Festival** (September; casual weekend at Johnson's Beach on the Russian River; tel: 707/869-3940). In Sacramento you can check the entertainment listings in the

Sacramento Bee newspaper, or call Downtown Events Line (tel: 916/442-2500) for current happenings.

SPORT

Sacramento's National Basketball Association team, the **Kings**, plays at Arco Arena (1 Sports Parkway, tel: 916/928-6900).

Northern California is a wonderland for participant sports. During the warm months, hikers, mountain bikers and horseback riders can take to hundreds of miles of trails, while canoeists, kayakers and river rafters can test the region's many waterways. In winter, Northern California is a haven for skiers and snowboarders.

The Central Coast

In Three Days 102 – 103
Don't Miss 104 – 113
At Your Leisure 114 – 115
Where To 116 – 120

Getting Your Bearings

The revved-up pace of California's large cities relaxes considerably along the state's less populated Central Coast. Murky urban waters give way to aqua-blue clarity, powerful foamy-white waves crash against a mostly rocky shoreline and wildflowers sprout from steep slopes that plunge straight into the Pacific. You can bask in the windswept glory of it all from ocean-view bars and restaurants or hike the beaches and explore their tide pools. The best way to travel is by car, although buses serve parts of the area.

The Central Coast's highlights lie along winding, scenic Highway 1. The going can be slow in summer when traffic is at its heaviest, but fortunately you've got that fabulous view. Highway 1's vistas are half the fun of a Central Coast visit, but if you're the driver, pay attention: On the curvy sections, one false move and you'll turn your automobile into a submarine.

Previous page: Highway 1, near Big Sur

Below: Things smell a lot better in Monterey these days

Jellyfish glow at Monterey Aquarium

★ Don't Miss

2 The Monterey
Peninsula ➤ 104
3 Big Sur ➤ 107
4 Hearst Castle ➤ 108
9 Santa Barbara ➤ 110

At Your Leisure

1 Santa Cruz ➤ 114
5 Cambria ➤ 114
6 Harmony ➤ 114
7 Morro Bay ➤ 115
8 Avila Beach/Pismo
Beach ➤ 115
10 Ojai ➤ 115

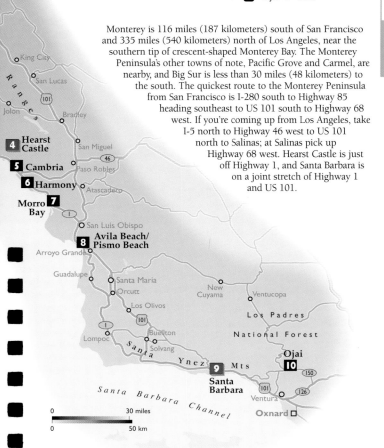

Monterey is 116 miles (187 kilometers) south of San Francisco and 335 miles (540 kilometers) north of Los Angeles, near the southern tip of crescent-shaped Monterey Bay. The Monterey Peninsula's other towns of note, Pacific Grove and Carmel, are nearby, and Big Sur is less than 30 miles (48 kilometers) to the south. The quickest route to the Monterey Peninsula from San Francisco is I-280 south to Highway 85 heading southeast to US 101 south to Highway 68 west. If you're coming up from Los Angeles, take I-5 north to Highway 46 west to US 101 north to Salinas; at Salinas pick up Highway 68 west. Hearst Castle is just off Highway 1, and Santa Barbara is on a joint stretch of Highway 1 and US 101.

King City
San Lucas
Jolon
Ranges
101
Bradley

4 Hearst Castle
San Miguel
5 Cambria
Paso Robles
46
6 Harmony
Atascadero
Morro **7** Bay
1
San Luis Obispo
8 Avila Beach/Pismo Beach
Arroyo Grande
Guadalupe
Santa Maria
Orcutt
New Cuyama
Ventucopa
Los Olivos
Los Padres
Lompoc
101
Buellton
National Forest
Santa
Solvang
Ynez Mts
9 Santa Barbara
Ojai
10
150
Santa Barbara Channel
101
Ventura
126
Oxnard

0 ___ 30 miles
0 ___ 50 km

Three days is just enough time to sample the Central Coast –
its sights and nautical attractions, but perhaps more important, its contributions to California cuisine.

The Central Coast in Three Days

Day 1

Morning
Begin on the **2 Monterey Peninsula** in Pacific Grove, where the bracing winds
at **Asilomar State Beach** (➤ 105) will surely rouse you. If you're visiting during
butterfly season, head over to the **Monarch Grove Sanctuary** (➤ 105), and
then cruise the spectacular **17-Mile Drive** (➤ 105) – and don't forget your
camera.

Afternoon
Lunch in Monterey on Euro-American bistro fare at sedate and tasteful
Montrio (414 Calle Principal, tel: 831/648-8880). Sea creatures await at
Monterey Bay Aquarium (➤ 105), where late-afternoon feedings always enter-
tain. From the aquarium, drive south on Highway 1 to Carmel to browse down-
town shops or walk through **Point Lobos State Reserve** (above, ➤ 106).

Evening
Return to Monterey for a romantic dinner at historic Stokes Adobe (➤ 116).

Day 2

Morning
Drive south on Highway 1 to **3 Big Sur** (➤ 107), stopping for coffee – and more importantly the view – at Café Kevah, part of the Nepenthe complex. Continue south on Highway 1, pulling into vista points.

Afternoon
Drop by the colony of northern elephant seals just north of Hearst Castle. Drive past the castle to **5 Cambria** (➤ 114) and have lunch with an ocean view at the Hamlet at Moonstone Gardens (off Highway 1, tel: 805/927-3535). Backtrack north to tour magnificent **4 Hearst Castle** (Roman Pool, left; ➤ 108). Later, check out tiny, intriguing **6 Harmony** (➤ 114), 5 miles (8 kilometers) south of Cambria.

Evening
Check into your lodgings in **7 Morro Bay** (➤ 114), walk a bit of the Embarcadero, before dinner.

Day 3

Morning
Highway 1 merges with US 101 at San Luis Obispo. Pause for a brief rest at **8 Pismo Beach** (➤ 115), strolling Pismo Pier or the beach, and then continue south on US 101 to **9 Santa Barbara**.

Afternoon
Settle into your Santa Barbara lodgings and have lunch at the raucous harborfront Brophy Bros. seafood restaurant (119 Harbor Way, tel: 805/966-4418). **Stearns Wharf** (➤ 110) juts into the Santa Barbara Channel off Cabrillo Boulevard not far from Brophy Bros. Park east of the wharf; after walking it, continue east to sandy, quintessentially Californian **East Beach** (➤ 111). Make a short drive to stately **Mission Santa Barbara** (➤ 112).

Evening
From the mission, head to one of the lots near the State Street shopping district (right, ➤ 120). Later, have dinner on State Street at Palazzo Trattoria Italiano (➤ 117).

The Monterey Peninsula

"Please don't tell anyone!" pleaded a 19th-century painter extolling the beauty of Monterey to a newly arrived friend. The artist's worst fears – that people would discover the town and overdevelop it – all came to pass, but the area's natural attributes are so compelling even the most egregious encroachments of civilization can't diminish them. The Monterey Peninsula's two must-sees are the Monterey Bay Aquarium and 17-Mile Drive.

Monterey

A good place to start a tour of Monterey is at the **Monterey State Historic Park Visitor Center** (Custom House Plaza), which has brochures for the 2-mile (3-kilometer) Path of History and sells tickets to the historic adobes and other sites along it. At touristy **Fisherman's Wharf,** a few hundred yards north of Custom House Plaza, you'll find T-shirt shops, seafood restaurants (some of them good) but precious few fishermen. They've all retreated to other piers.

The **Monterey Bay Recreational Trail** winds northwest for about a mile from Fisherman's Wharf to Cannery Row. You can walk the trail or take the bus. Many buildings that formerly housed smelly sardine-processing plants still line Cannery Row, whose

Monterey State Historic Park Visitor Center
✉ Foot of Alvarado Street ☎ (831) 649-7118 🕐 Path of History sites open daily; hours vary 🚌 Wave shuttle (summer only); Bus 1 💷 Inexpensive

Monterey Bay Recreational Trail
✉ Between Drake and David avenues 🚌 Wave shuttle (summer only); Bus 1

Monterey Bay Aquarium
✉ 886 Cannery Row ☎ (831) 648-4800 🕐 Daily 9:30–6, Jun–Aug; 10–6, rest of year 🚌 Wave shuttle (summer only); Bus 1 💷 Expensive

17-Mile Drive
✉ Five entrances, including Sunset Drive in Pacific Grove and Highway 1 in Carmel 🚌 Bus 1 💷 Moderate

Nature unfolds indoors at Monterey Bay Aquarium's kelp forest (below) and outdoors in Pacific Grove (right)

quirky habitués inspired John Steinbeck to write the novel of the same name. The street's been too gussied up with mostly unmemorable shops and restaurants to evoke the past. One shop that reflects current industry is **A Taste of Monterey** (700 Cannery Row), where you can sample wines by local vintners.

The **Monterey Bay Aquarium** sits at the western end of Cannery Row. This nearly complete survey of the bay's marine life merits a minimum two-hour visit. The highlights include the sea otter habitat, a three-story kelp forest and mesmerizing jellyfish displays, but the pièce de résistance is the vast tank filled with sharks and other denizens of the waters 50 miles (80 kilometers) offshore.

Pacific Grove

West of the aquarium, Cannery Row becomes Ocean View Boulevard, your signal you've entered **Pacific Grove.** The mellow town is known for its Victorian houses and bayside points of interest: among them sheltered Lovers Point Park Beach (a fine place to picnic) and Point Piños Lighthouse. **Asilomar State Beach**, south of the lighthouse, epitomizes the untamed splendor of this section of California's Pacific coast. Between October and March, migrating monarch butterflies inhabit the **Monarch Grove Sanctuary** (Lighthouse Avenue and Ridge Road, Bus 1).

17-Mile Drive

With all the eye-catching coastline to the north and south, it might seem absurd to pay to see the stretch named **17-Mile Drive**, but it really is special. Isolated and dramatic, the drive winds past breezy beaches battered by sometimes fierce waves. Rocks beneath the water create the peculiar phenomenon at the **Restless Sea,** where opposing ocean currents crash into each other and the waves appear to break in two directions. Other highlights along 17-Mile Drive include **Bird Rock,** a granite outcrop populated by seals, sea lions, gulls, cormorants and other wildlife, and the two-century-old **Lone Cypress,** sculpted by mighty winds that whip in from the sea. The booklet you receive at the entrance booth describes the key stops.

Above: Carmel Mission played a key role in 19th-century California

Other Attractions

Carmel is annoyingly quaint, flooded with boutiques, and a mob scene on sunny weekends, but once again the setting saves the day. You may find the Ocean Avenue shopping area west of Highway 1 too precious, but both **Carmel River State Beach** (Scenic Road, off Highway 1, tel: 831/649-2836) and **Point Lobos State Reserve** (Highway 1, tel: 831/624-4909) have great trails (pick up maps at the park entrances). At Point Lobos you can view sea lions from Sea Lion Point Trail or wander among the trees of Cypress Grove Trail. The handsome **Carmel Mission** (Rio Road and Lasuen Drive, tel: 831/624-3600) was command central for the 21 Franciscan missions established in California by Fra Junipero Serra.

Right: The waterfall at Julia Pfeiffer Burns State Park is justly one of California's most photographed sights

TAKING A BREAK

Sample the bounty of the bay at Monterey's casual **Café Fina** (Fisherman's Wharf, tel: 831/372-5200), a harbor-view Italian restaurant.

MONTEREY PENINSULA: INSIDE INFO

Top tips Bring a jacket in summer, when late-afternoon coastal fogs often roll in.
• From late May to early September, the **Wave shuttle bus** connects the major sights in historic Monterey. **Monterey-Salinas Transit** (tel: 831/899-2555) serves the area year-round. Take the company's Bus 1 from Fisherman's Wharf for an inexpensive scenic tour of Monterey and Pacific Grove.

Hidden gems You can taste local vintages, have a picnic or go on tour (call ahead to make necessary reservations) at two local wineries, **Chateau Julien** (8940 Carmel Valley Road, east of Highway 1, tel: 831/624-2600) and **Ventana Vineyards** (2999 Monterey-Salinas Highway, tel: 831/372-7415).

Big Sur

Nature rules in Big Sur, a land of fierce beauty immortalized in the photographs of Ansel Adams. The writer Henry Miller declared the terrain the "face of the earth as the Creator intended it to look." Almost every year winter floods wash out part of Highway 1, while in summer the winds howl and rocks tumble off steep cliffs onto the roadbed.

The Big Sur wilderness stretches from below Carmel nearly to Hearst Castle. **Bixby Bridge,** about 13 miles (21 kilometers) south of Carmel, is one of the world's highest single-span bridges. Park on the north side to view the structure's towering arches. South of Bixby, **Point Sur Lighthouse** (tel: 831/625-4419 for reservations) sits atop a sandstone outcrop. You can only visit it year-round on weekend tours (also on some weekdays from April through October).

Nine miles (14 kilometers) south of the lighthouse is Big Sur Station. Rangers here dispense maps and advice about area hiking and sights, including nearby Pfeiffer Beach, where waves crash through a tall, doughnut-shaped rock offshore. The station is at the west entrance to **Pfeiffer-Big Sur State Park** (tel: 831/667-2315). One of its trails passes through redwood groves to a 60-foot (18-meter) waterfall. Another heads up Pfeiffer Ridge to unparalleled coastal panoramas. About 12 miles (19 kilometers) south of Big Sur Station is **Julia Pfeiffer Burns State Park.** A .5-mile (.8-kilometer) trail here leads to a waterfall that flows out of a rocky cliff right onto the beach.

TAKING A BREAK

Dine or drink indoors or out at **Nepenthe** (Highway 1, tel: 831/667-2345), about 2.5 miles (4 kilometers) south of Big Sur Station. The adjacent **Café Kevah** is a good spot for brunch or lunch. (Bus 22 from Monterey heads to the town of Big Sur and Nepenthe twice daily.)

Hearst Castle

Party central for early Hollywood's elite and among the most elaborate private homes in America, Hearst Castle reposes in hazy majesty amid the Santa Lucia Mountains. The castle was indeed fit for a king – nearly what newspaper magnate William Randolph Hearst (1863–1951) had become by 1919, when he began building his fantasy house. When construction finally ceased in 1947, the place still wasn't complete, though by then the massive spread included 165 rooms, 127 acres (51 hectares) of gardens and two luxurious pools.

The pine, oak and walnut furnishings of the 115-room main house, Casa Grande, lend it a heavy feel but reflect both the California-Mediterranean style of the day and Hearst's memories of European castles he had visited as a youth and an adult. The guest cottages, by contrast, have an airier ambience.

"The Chief," as friends and employees called Hearst, was an avid collector of art and antiques. During a late-1930s financial crisis he sold off the cream of his holdings, though impressive pieces such as the tapestries in Casa Grande's entrance hall remain. While you take the tour, look up at the hand-carved

✚ 204 B4 **✉** Highway 1, San Simeon **☎** (916) 414-8400 **🕐** Daily 8:20–3:20 (sometimes later, Jun–Aug); evening tours (times vary) Mar–May and Sep–Dec. Closed Jan 1, Thanksgiving and Dec 25 **💲** Expensive

A Fine Collaboration
Hearst collaborated on his castle with Julia Morgan (1872–1957), whose knowledge of civil engineering came in handy building in earthquake country. The structure was built largely of reinforced concrete, a boon when the earth trembled, but a nightmare given Hearst's penchant for changing his mind. One example: Casa Grande originally had one bell tower. Hearst had it ripped out and replaced by the two seen today.

wooden ceilings Hearst acquired from European estates and monasteries. In the tour guides' commentary and the large-format film screened (for an additional charge) at the National Geographic Theater, Hearst comes off as an amiable visionary and arts lover, not the mercenary businessman who bullied civic leaders and annihilated people who crossed him. (*The Manchester Guardian* in England had this to say upon his death: "No man has ever done so much to debase the standards of journalism.") Hearst's professional tactics may be a matter of dispute, but there is no denying what he accomplished at San Simeon. He crowned an already regal landscape with a gem of an estate.

The Neptune Pool, with its marble statues and colonnades

TAKING A BREAK

The visitor center has a snack bar, but you're better off stopping to eat in nearby **Cambria** (➤ 114).

HEARST CASTLE: INSIDE INFO

Top tips You can only visit Hearst Castle on **one of four tours** (each just under 2 hours). All pass the outdoor Neptune Pool, made of marble, and the indoor Roman Pool, lined with blue Venetian glass and glittery gold tiles. For first-time visitors, the castle's staff recommends Tour 1, which takes in the gardens, a guest house and Casa Grande's ground floor. More interesting is Tour 2, which covers Casa Grande's upper floors, passing through the library, the Doge's Suite (a copy of a room in the Doge's Palace in Venice), four guest rooms and Hearst's private suite.
• **Make tour reservations** at least 48 hours ahead, especially in summer.

One to miss You can **skip the film** in the National Geographic Theater. You'll learn enough about Hearst on the tour and at the visitor center.

Santa Barbara

Santa Barbara bills itself as the American Riviera, but this city of about 90,000 residents sells itself short: The French Riviera should be this well manicured and have weather so consistently phenomenal. Billboard-free, discreet, mellow and a mere 90-minute drive from Los Angeles, Santa Barbara has for decades been a hideaway for Hollywood's moneyed elite – Ronald Colman and Ronald Reagan, Michael Douglas and Michael Jackson live or have lived here. Yet the city remains remarkably down-to-earth.

The county courthouse, Mission Santa Barbara and the waterfront are among the important sights to see – and you should see them – but if you find yourself adopting a casual rhythm, don't fight it. Linger over that harbor-view lunch, space out in the Santa Barbara Botanic Garden, or laze in the sand at East Beach or Butterfly Beach. This a place to relax and feel fabulous.

Unlike the beaches and waterfronts of most West Coast towns, Santa Barbara's face south, not west. Wood-plank **Stearns Wharf,** which extends several hundred yards into the Santa Barbara Channel, is a good place to start a

An ancient Roman temple inspired Mission Santa Barbara's façade

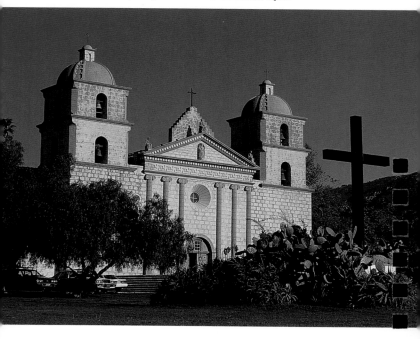

waterfront tour. Park along Cabrillo Boulevard, stroll to the end of the wharf, and you can sit on a bench and gaze out to sea or back at the city. The kids-oriented **Sea Lab** contains exhibits about area marine life, and restaurants, shops, and video and other amusements can also be found on the wharf.

From the wharf head east 2 miles (3 kilometers) on Cabrillo Boulevard to the **Andree Clark Bird Refuge.** Signs along the foot and bicycle path identify the native and migratory species that frequent this serene lagoon and gardens that are great to pedal around. You can see the grounds of the Santa Barbara Zoo (no great shakes but pleasant) from the refuge.

Across Cabrillo Boulevard from the refuge is always animated **East Beach.** Seeing those tanned, toned Santa Barbarans playing Frisbee or sand volleyball, you may chide yourself for not doing more abs and push-ups before departing on vacation (the beach sometimes looks like a "Baywatch" casting audition). The Cabrillo Pavilion Bathhouse has showers and lockers, but no towel concession.

Backtrack west on Cabrillo Boulevard past Stearns Wharf to the **Santa Barbara Yacht Harbor.** The fleet comes in with the day's catch – including thousands of sea urchins for import to Japan – at this long breakwater.

A pelican looking for lunch at Stearns Wharf

🚹 204 C3 🚌 Downtown Shuttle (waterfront to Sola Street)

Stearns Wharf
✉ E. Cabrillo Boulevard, southern end of State Street 🚌 Waterfront or Downtown Shuttle 🎟 Free

Sea Lab
✉ 211 Stearns Wharf 🕾 (805) 682-4711 🎟 Inexpensive

Andree Clark Bird Refuge
✉ 1400 E. Cabrillo Boulevard off US 101 🕾 (805) 564-5433 🚌 Waterfront Shuttle (to zoo; short walk to refuge or transfer at Milpas Street to Bus 14) 🎟 Free

East Beach
✉ E. Cabrillo Boulevard and Milpas Street 🚌 Waterfront Shuttle 🎟 Free

Santa Barbara Yacht Harbor
✉ West end of Cabrillo Boulevard 🚌 Waterfront Shuttle

County Courthouse
✉ 1100 block Anacapa Street 🕾 (805) 962-6464 🕐 Mon–Fri 8:30–4:45, Sat–Sun 10–4:45 (tours Mon–Sat at 2, also Mon, Tue and Fri at 10:30). Closed Dec 25 🚌 Downtown Shuttle (to Anapamu Street; walk one block east) 🎟 Free

Mission Santa Barbara
✉ 2201 Laguna Street 🕾 (805) 682-4149 🕐 Daily 9–5. Closed Easter, Thanksgiving and Dec 25 🚌 Bus 22 (from downtown transit center, Chapala and Carrillo streets) 🎟 Inexpensive

Santa Barbara Botanic Garden
✉ 1212 Mission Canyon Road (from the mission take E. Los Olivos Street north to Mission Canyon Road, make a right on Foothill Road and a left on Mission Canyon) 🕾 (805) 682-4726 🕐 Mon–Fri 9–5, Sat–Sun 9–6, Mar–Oct; Mon–Fri 9–4, Sat–Sun 9–5, rest of year. Closed Jan 1, Thanksgiving and Dec 25 🚌 No bus service 🎟 Inexpensive

Brophy Bros. Clam Bar and Restaurant (119 Harbor Way, tel: 805/966-4418) is a popular lunching and dining spot.

From the waterfront you can take the State Street Shuttle up State Street or drive up Chapala Street and park in any of the public lots north of Gutierrez Street. **State Street,** Santa Barbara's downtown spine, is so convivial that folks from as far away as Los Angeles come for shopping weekends, visiting

Mariachi musicians serenade at El Paseo

boutiques, antiques shops, outlet stores and other businesses. Two small malls are **El Paseo** (Cañon Perdido and State Street), whose core section dates from the early 20th century, and the newer **Paseo Nuevo** (700–800 blocks of State Street). Some of Santa Barbara's best restaurants and nightclubs are also on or near State.

A hint of silent-era Hollywood excess enlivens the interior of the **Santa Barbara County Courthouse,** one block east of State Street at the corner of Anapamu and Anacapa streets. The Spanish-Moorish-style structure was completed in 1929. Take a tour or poke around a bit, then ride the elevator to the rooftop for a 360-degree city view. The **Red Tile Tour** (➤ below) begins here.

You'll need to drive or take the bus to visit **Mission Santa Barbara.** If you're only going to visit one California mission, make it this one. The padre overseeing the design of this 1820 structure (the mission was established in 1786) based its façade on that of an ancient Roman temple. Santa Barbara's

1925 earthquake devastated the mission, but care was taken during reconstruction to preserve the original 1820 design. Among the rooms on view are the main church, a chapel, a bedroom and a kitchen. The grounds include two well-tended gardens with succulents and other indigenous plants.

You'll need a car to get to the splendid **Santa Barbara Botanic Garden,** whose

Spanish-Moorish architecture sets the tone in Santa Barbara

Red Tile Tour

This 12-block, self-guided tour of adobes, parks, museums and other historic downtown sights is named for the curved terra-cotta roof tiles of the many Spanish-style buildings along the way. Pick up a map at the Santa Barbara Visitor Center (Garden Street and Cabrillo Boulevard, tel: 805/965-3021), a few blocks east of Stearns Wharf. Then walk, drive or take the Downtown Shuttle to the tour's starting point (about .5 miles/.8 kilometers away), the **County Courthouse** (➤ above).

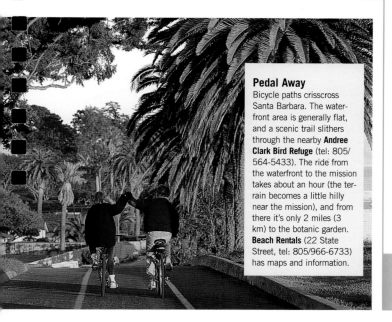

Pedal Away
Bicycle paths crisscross Santa Barbara. The waterfront area is generally flat, and a scenic trail slithers through the nearby **Andree Clark Bird Refuge** (tel: 805/564-5433). The ride from the waterfront to the mission takes about an hour (the terrain becomes a little hilly near the mission), and from there it's only 2 miles (3 km) to the botanic garden. **Beach Rentals** (22 State Street, tel: 805/966-6733) has maps and information.

65 acres (26 hectares) support plant life from California's varied regions – deserts, mountains, coastal areas and inland plains.

Palm trees tower over a Montecito cycle path

TAKING A BREAK

Stop by **D'Angelo Bread** (25 W. Gutierrez Street, tel: 805/962-5466) for pastries or a light snack.

SANTA BARBARA: INSIDE INFO

Top tips You can park easily in lots on either side of State Street or on city streets elsewhere.
• Downtown and the waterfront are **within walking distance of each other,** but during the day (until 9 on Friday and Saturday) inexpensive shuttles serve the waterfront and the main State Street shopping district. Another option is to rent a bicycle (➤ above).

Hidden gems Try for one of the limited number of slots that allows you to tour the lavishly eccentric gardens at **Lotusland** (695 Ashley Road, tel: 805/969-9990 in advance, expensive), the **Montecito estate** of the late Madame Ganna Walska, a Polish opera singer. You will need to make an appointment months in advance to see the Egyptian lotuses, water lilies, topiary and dragon trees in the gardens, which are open from mid-February to mid-November.
• The heart of the Santa Barbara County **wine country** lies about an hour's drive (➤ 183–185) north of the town.

At Your Leisure

❶ Santa Cruz

Surfer dudes, New Age types and students all rub shoulders in easy-going Santa Cruz. With a 1911 Looff carousel and the 1924 Giant Dipper, the only wooden roller-coaster on the West Coast, the Beach Boardwalk (Beach Street) retains a retro feel. Nearby is the wharf, good for a sunset stroll. Unlike elsewhere along the northern Central Coast, you can swim during summer at the main beach without freezing to death. To watch surfers in action, stand at Lighthouse Point (West Cliff Drive). The **Harley-Davidson Museum** (1148 Soquel Avenue, off Ocean Street, tel: 831/421-9600) dazzles with vintage motorcycles. Santa Cruz's best cafés, restaurants and boutiques are in the downtown Pacific Avenue business district.

🚩 204 A5 ✉ Highway 1 and Highway 17, 74 miles (119 km) south of San Francisco

❺ Cambria

The largest town near Hearst Castle contains shops, galleries, restaurants and lodgings, and beautiful beaches. Walk the paths at **San Simeon State Park** for close-up views of clear-blue ocean, white-cap waves and swaying patches of kelp; low tide at **Leffingwell's Landing** reveals the sea life that thrives offshore. From just south of Cambria you can detour on Highway 46 into the **wine region** centered around Paso Robles and Templeton. The area's oldest winery, **York Mountain** (7505 York Mountain Road, tel: 805/238-3925), established in 1882, is about 17 miles (27 kilometers) from Cambria. You can pick up wine-touring maps and brochures here. Other wineries of note include Turley, Justin, Wild Horse, Windward, Martin & Weyrich, and Mastantuono.

🚩 204 B4 ✉ Highway 1, 6 miles (10 km) south of Hearst Castle

❻ Harmony

With a name like Harmony, you could expect the two dozen or so residents of this tiny, artsy former dairy town to get along, and that they do. You can watch glassblowers at work, visit shops selling crafts, taste wine and sit in a brick-lined courtyard where flowers sprout from rusting farm implements. Harmony's cute, but too small to get too cute.

🚩 204 B4 ✉ Highway 1, 5 miles (8 km) south of Cambria

The Otter Limits

The **California Sea Otter Game Refuge** extends from Monterey to Cambria. The prime spots for otter viewing are near Hearst Castle at Santa Rosa State Beach, Hearst State Beach and Leffingwell's Landing, all right off Highway 1.

Four miles (6 km) north of Hearst Castle (just south of Mile Marker 63), a colony of northern elephant seals resides near the vista point parking lot.

7 Morro Bay

Meander along this fishing village's Embarcadero, and you may feel you have entered another era. Geologically speaking, you have: Morro Rock, the 576-foot (175-meter) town landmark, is one of several dormant volcanic peaks in the area. The estuary here shelters endangered species that include falcons and other birds and fish.

➕ 204 B3 ✉ Highway 1, 20 miles (32 km) south of Cambria

8 Avila Beach/ Pismo Beach

If you're driving south, these will be the first of the good Southern California-style beaches that you'll come to along the Central Coast, with wide swaths of sand and some surfside diversions. A walk along the beach and Pismo Pier will help you recover from the curves and swerves of Highway 1. (If you've an itch to spend

Wildlife thrives on Morro Rock, just offshore in Morro Bay

some time shopping, follow the signs to the Prime Outlets.)

➕ 204 C3 ✉ Highway 1, 47 miles (75 km) south of Cambria

10 Ojai

Frank Capra used Ojai as the setting for Shangri-La in his 1937 film "Lost Horizon," which should tell you everything you need to know about this captivating haven that's an easy 33-mile (53-kilometer) trip from Santa Barbara. The diversions are varied: You can challenge yourself hiking the trails through **Los Padres National Forest** or take things easy at the **Ojai Valley Inn & Spa** (1203 Highway 33, tel: 805/646-5511). **Libbey Park**, on Ojai Avenue (Highway 150), the town's main street, is eminently strollable. Many Ojai artists exhibit their works at the **Ojai Arts Center** (113 S. Montgomery Street). Large oaks shade **Bart's Books** (302 W. Matilija Street), an outdoor bookstore of local renown.

➕ 205 D3 ✉ Highway 150, east from US 101

Where to...
Eat and Drink

Prices

Expect to pay per person for a meal, excluding drinks and service
$ under $15 $$ $15–25 $$$ over $25

MONTEREY PENINSULA

Robert's Bistro $$–$$$

Chef-owner Robert Kincaid's rustic French food ranks with the best on the Monterey Peninsula. Highlights of his bistro cuisine include a long-simmering cassoulet that has white beans, grilled duck confit, rabbit sausage and garlic prawns. Desserts are creative and rich, while service is attentive without being overbearing. Exposed wood-beam ceilings mark the restaurant's country-style Provençal decor. Meals are prix fixe Sunday through Friday 4–5:30 pm.

➕ 204 A5 ⬜ 217 Crossroads Boulevard, Carmel ☎ (831) 375-9626
🕐 Sun–Fri 4–late, Sat 5:30–late. Closed Thanksgiving and Dec 24–25

Rio Grill $$

Rio Grill's creative California cooking, with Southwestern touches, helped pioneer New American cuisine in Carmel back in the early 1990s. The festive, relaxing surroundings include original artwork on the walls; butcher paper and crayons adorn the tables comes complete with crayons. Duck, pork ribs and chicken are all wood-smoked here, seafood is

grilled and produce is fresh and locally grown. A full bar and extensive wine list complement the food.

➕ 204 A5 ⬜ Highway 1 and Rio Road, Carmel ☎ (831) 625-5436
🕐 Daily lunch 11:30–4, dinner 5–10. Closed Thanksgiving and Dec 25

Stokes Adobe $$

Influences from Provence in France, northern Italy and Catalan Spain intermingle with California cuisine in this appropriately sun-drenched 19th-century adobe. Choose from both hot and cold dishes, on either small or large plates. The menu changes seasonally, but there are always creative pastas, vegetarian selections and seafood dishes. A specialty is chicken under a brick, which might be served with potato-corn risotto or garlic mashed potatoes.

➕ 204 A5 ⬜ 500 Hartnell Street, Monterey ☎ (831) 373-1110
🕐 Mon–Sat 11:30–10, dinner only Sun 5–9. Closed Dec 25

Tarpy's Roadhouse $$

A short drive outside Monterey is Tarpy's, set in a century-old stone-covered ranch house. On cool days you can sit inside by the fireplace, or, on warm days, outside in a flower-filled courtyard. The innovative roadhouse cuisine features sandwiches, salads and pasta dishes at lunch, and more complex offerings at dinner, such as duck, pork chops, steaks and seafood from a wood-burning grill.

➕ 204 A5 ⬜ 2999 Monterey-Salinas Highway (Highway 68), Monterey
☎ (831) 647-1444 🕐 Daily 11:30–10. Closed Thanksgiving and Dec 25

BIG SUR

Cielo at the Ventana $$$

Located in landmark Ventana Inn, about 28 miles (45 kilometers) south of Carmel, Cielo serves eclectic California cuisine – highlighted by fresh seafood, game, pastas and vegetarian dishes – with dramatic views of the ocean and mountains.

You can eat either indoors, with its picture windows and open-beam, vaulted ceiling, or on the year-round outdoor terrace, which regularly fills up with customers for lunch.

🛏 204 A4 ⊠ Highway 1, Big Sur ☎ (831) 667-4242 or (800) 628-6500 ⏰ Lunch daily noon–3; dinner daily 5:30–9 (8:30 in winter)

🍷🍷 Chad's on Chapala $-$$$

Seafood and steaks are the focus at this convivial bar and restaurant locals laud as much for its fruit-infused martinis as for its contemporary cuisine. The soup of the day is always a good choice, as is the caramelized halibut, which comes with highly addictive mashed sweet potatoes.

🛏 204 C3 ⊠ 625 Chapala Street, Santa Barbara ☎ (805) 568-1876 ⏰ Dinner Mon–Sat 5:30–closing (happy hour starts at 4:30). Closed Thanksgiving and Dec 25

La Super-Rica $

This modest little taco joint has a reputation that extends up and down the coast – the soft-sided steak, chorizo or chicken tacos, made with fresh corn tortillas, are legendary. Unless you arrive at an off hour, you'll probably have to wait in line before placing your order at the window and grabbing a seat at one of the picnic tables on the semi-enclosed garden patio. When your tacos are ready, help yourself to the spicy salsas and dig in.

🛏 204 C3 ⊠ 622 N. Milpas Street, Santa Barbara ☎ (805) 963-4940 ⏰ Daily 11–9:30. Closed Jan 1, Thanksgiving and Dec 25

Montecito Café $$

For a quick bite or a full meal – you will find that the pastas and fish dishes are consistently excellent – try this airy establishment in the Montecito Inn.

🛏 204 C3 ⊠ 1295 Village Coast Road, Montecito ☎ (805) 969-3392 ⏰ Daily 11:30–2:30, 5–11

🍷🍷 Palazzio Trattoria Italiano $$

This often crowded Italian trattoria is one of the best bargains in the Santa Barbara area. Portions are huge – a single order of pasta, such as a delicious mound of cappellini with shrimp, can usually be split into two meal-sized portions. It's also fun to eat here: Waiters unexpectedly break into song, and wine self-service is by the honor system.

🛏 204 C3 ⊠ 1026 State Street, Santa Barbara ☎ (805) 564-1985 ⏰ Lunch Mon–Fri 11:30–3; dinner daily 5:30–10.30. Closed Thanksgiving and Dec 25

Santa Barbara Shellfish Company $-$$

The harbor views from this modest-looking Stearns Wharf restaurant alone rate a visit, but even though the chefs here don't strive for attention the way their counterparts in the city's snazzier restaurants do, the preparations here are quite fine. Ask what's freshest and go with that. The clam chowder, steamed mussels, steamed clams and cioppino (seafood stew) are among the best in town.

🛏 204 C3 ⊠ 230A Stearns Wharf, Santa Barbara ☎ (805) 966-6676 ⏰ Daily 11–9. Closed Thanksgiving and Dec 25

🍷🍷 Sea Chest Restaurant and Oyster Bar $$-$$$

The Sea Chest turns out food worthy of the great ocean views from its cliff-top perch. You won't find better seafood this close to Hearst Castle; fresh oysters and locally caught ocean fish are the highlights. Since the restaurant doesn't take reservations, it's a good idea to arrive early – you'll also have a better chance of catching the sunset. Bring plenty of cash; credit cards aren't accepted.

🛏 204 B4 ⊠ 6216 Moonstone Beach Drive, Cambria ☎ (805) 927-4514 ⏰ Dinner daily 5:30–closing. Closed Tue, Sep–May, and Thanksgiving and Dec 25

Where to... Stay

Prices

Expect to pay per room

$ under $100 per night **$$** $100–175 per night **$$$** over $175 per night

▾▾ Green Gables Inn $$

Of Pacific Grove's landmark mansions, the Green Gables Inn, an 1888 green-and-white Queen Anne that overlooks the rocky coastline, is one of the most dramatic to behold. Its interior details – original woodwork, moldings, fixtures, arches, stained glass – are equally compelling. Most rooms have bay windows with breathtaking water views. The rear carriage house has larger, more modern rooms, all with private bath (four rooms in the main house share baths). A generous buffet breakfast and afternoon wine and hors d'oeuvres are included.

🏠 204 A5 ⊠ 104 5th Street, Pacific Grove, CA 93950 ☎ (831) 375-2095 or (800) 722-1774; fax: (831) 375-5437; email: info@foursisters.com

▾▾▾ Monterey Plaza Hotel and Spa $$$

A rooftop luxury spa and other amenities reinforce the reputation of this attractive four-story Cannery Row hotel as Monterey's finest full-service lodging. The bay views are dramatic not only from the spa, but also from the many room balconies and the big outdoor patio, where you can spot sea lions and sea otters in the waters below. On a site once occupied by a cannery, the hotel now draws its design from early California and Mediterranean influences. Rooms are spacious. The Duck Club restaurant serves breakfast and elegant dinner with a view.

🏠 204 A5 ⊠ 400 Cannery Row, Monterey, CA 93940 ☎ (831) 646-1700 or (800) 368-2468; fax: (831) 646-0285; email: reservations@montereyplazahotel.com

▾▾▾ Old Monterey Inn $$$

Innkeepers Gene and Ann Swett restored this historic Tudor-style home in a quiet residential section of Monterey and have turned it into one of the finest bed-and-breakfasts in California. No detail is left unattended, and service is legendary. The rooms are themed – the Library, for instance, contains shelves of books – and stocked with featherbeds and down comforters. You can take your breakfast in a formal dining room, the rose garden or in your room, perhaps on your sundeck, in front of your fireplace or even in your whirlpool bath.

🏠 204 A5 ⊠ 500 Martin Street, Monterey, CA 93940 ☎ (831) 375-8284 or (800) 350-2344; email: omi@oldmontereyinn.com; fax: (831) 375-6730 ⊙ Closed Dec 21–25

▾▾ Pine Inn $$-$$$

The three-story Pine Inn dates from 1889. Today, it offers convenience – right on one of Carmel's main shopping and strolling streets, about four blocks from the beach – and a hint of elegance at comparatively reasonable prices for the standard rooms. The decor leans heavily toward the Victorian, with antiques and padded wall fabrics. The in-house restaurant, Il Fornaio, known for its outstanding breads, good Italian food and pleasant dining patio, is a big plus.

🏠 204 A5 ⊠ Ocean Avenue and Monte Verde, Box 250, Carmel, CA 93921 ☎ (831) 624-3851 or (800) 228-3851; fax: (831) 624-3030; email: info@pine-inn.com

BIG SUR

☞☞☞ Ventana Inn & Spa $$$

Ventana Inn, the quintessential Big Sur retreat, rests serenely atop a wooded ridge overlooking the Pacific Ocean in one of the most spectacular stretches of the California coastline. Rooms are clustered within small buildings. (For maximum romance, ask for a room with a fireplace and ocean view.) The service is efficient, and the pools are oh-so-relaxing. Spa treatments include thalassotherapy (using algae and seaweed), pelotherapy (muds and clays), and aromatherapy (scents). If you opt for a basic massage or other dry treatment, you can enjoy the experience in your room. Cielo, the very fine restaurant (▲ 116), emphasizes California foods and wines. Room rates include a full breakfast and afternoon wine and cheese.

✠ 204 A4 ☒ Highway 1, Big Sur, CA 93920 ☎ (831) 667-2331 or (800) 628-6500; fax: (831) 667-0573; email: reservations@ventanainn.com

CAMBRIA

☞☞☞ Pelican Suites $-$$$

Pelican Suites offers proximity to sea, sand and Hearst Castle, as well as dynamite ocean views. This two-story hotel, right on the beach, has 24 suites with private balconies or patios facing the water. The custom-designed furniture includes king-size beds. Larger rooms with whirlpool tubs, full ocean views and more space are more expensive. All rooms have fireplaces and kitchenettes. Full breakfast and afternoon tea and snacks included.

✠ 204 B4 ☒ 6316 Moonstone Beach Drive, Cambria, CA 93428 ☎ (805) 927-1500; fax: (805) 927 0218; email: timm@pelicansuites.com

SANTA BARBARA

☞☞☞☞ Four Seasons Biltmore $$$

Overlooking the Pacific, surrounded by gardens and lawns, this grand Spanish colonial-style resort has attracted celebrities since the late 1920s. Though all rooms are luxurious, the choicest are the airy cottage suites behind the main building, which have fireplaces and patios. With swimming pools, hot tubs, saunas, exercise facilities, lighted tennis courts, two restaurants (one indoor, one outdoor) a bar and a DVD player in every room, you never really have to leave, except perhaps to ride on your complimentary bicycle.

✠ 204 C3 ☒ 1260 Channel Drive, Montecito, CA 93108 ☎ (805) 969-2261 or (888) 424-5866; fax: (805) 565-8321; email: res@fourseasons.com

☞☞☞ Glenborough Inn $$-$$$

Five Victorian and Craftsman houses along prim Bath Street make up this delightful bed-and-breakfast inn, where breakfast is delivered in a picnic basket to your room or may be taken on the outdoor patio. The understated room decor varies but conforms to each house's architectural style – expect a few well-chosen lamps or other accessories rather than knick-knacks. Several rooms and suites have private hot tubs, fireplaces or patios.

✠ 204 C3 ☒ 1327 Bath Street, Santa Barbara, CA 93101 ☎ (805) 966-0589 or (800) 962-0589; fax: (805) 564 8610; email: santabarbara@glenboroughinn.com

☞☞☞ Inn by the Harbor $-$$

A number of hotels and motor inns line Santa Barbara's waterfront, but, while delivering great views, they charge you dearly for them. By staying three blocks away from the harbor, you can save money at this almost accurately named motel that nonetheless offers comfort and value. The majority of rooms, done in French country decor, have kitchenettes, and there's an outdoor pool and hot tub in a garden setting.

✠ 204 C3 ☒ 433 W. Montecito Street, Santa Barbara, CA 93101 ☎ (805) 963-7851 or (800) 626-1986; fax: (805) 962-9428; email: tropicana@sbhotels.com

Where to... Shop

Two affluent resort towns, Carmel and Santa Barbara, dominate the Central Coast shopping scene. Each is known for its upscale boutiques, art galleries and specialty shops, though you can dig up some bargains amid the high-end merchandise. You can also find good wines for sale among vineyards in the areas around Monterey and Santa Barbara.

Carmel has a wealth of art galleries, especially along Dolores Street. For the works of local artists, check out the **Carmel Art Association** (Dolores Street between 5th and 6th avenues; tel: 831/624-6176). The town is also known for a plethora of trinket and gift shops,

ranging from the tacky to the tasteful.

For bargains on brand-name merchandise, head to Pacific Grove and the **American Tin Cannery Outlet Center** (125 Ocean View Boulevard, tel: 831/372-1442) near Monterey's Cannery Row, where you'll find some 50 stores offering substantial discounts on designer clothing, jewelry and other items.

In Santa Barbara, the prime shopping territory is along **State Street**, where the shops range from elegant to funky. The **Paseo Nuevo** (State and de la Guerra streets, tel: 805/963-2202) is an attractive open-air mall showcasing several department stores and interesting specialty shops. Nearby is **El Paseo**, an older arcade whose boutiques, art galleries and courtyards lie along Cañon Perdido Street between State and Anacapa streets. Two blocks west of State Street on Brinkerhoff Avenue is a row of Victorians housing antiques and gift shops.

Where to... Be Entertained

In the Monterey area, check weekend editions of the *Monterey Herald* newspaper, or call the Monterey Peninsula Visitors and Convention Bureau's 24-hour recorded events hotline (tel: 831/649-1770). In Santa Cruz, try the free newspaper *Good Times*, and *The Independent*, a free weekly in Santa Barbara.

MUSIC AND THEATER

The **Cabrillo Music Festival** (orchestral music, tel: 831/426-6966) and **Shakespeare Santa Cruz** (tel: 831/459-2121) are among annual summertime arts events in Santa Cruz.

The Monterey Peninsula hosts a number of summertime arts festivals, including the **Carmel Bach Festival** (tel: 831/624-2046), the **Monterey Bay Blues Festival** (tel: 831/394-2652) and **Monterey Bay Theatrefest** (tel: 831/622-0700). The famous **Monterey Jazz Festival** (tel: 831/373-3366) is held each September.

NIGHTLIFE

In **Santa Cruz**, clubs along Pacific Avenue often feature rock and blues acts. In **Monterey**, much of the action is in the Cannery Row area. In **Santa Barbara**, nightlife is centered in the bars on Lower State Street that present live music.

Los Angeles Area

In Three Days 124 – 125
Don't Miss 126 – 135
At Your Leisure 136 – 143
Where To 144 – 150

Getting Your Bearings

"Seventy-two suburbs in search of a city," goes the famous crack from writer Dorothy Parker about Los Angeles, a city that's seriously big. The five-county (Los Angeles, Orange, Riverside, San Bernardino and Ventura) metropolitan area contains 16.4 million people, more than every U.S. state except New York, Texas and California itself.

What binds this seemingly boundless region? Freeways, of course. You needn't memorize all the roads, but it's good to know some key routes. The San Diego Freeway (I-405), Hollywood Freeway (US 101 near Hollywood and Downtown; Highway 170 north of Hollywood), Golden State Freeway (I-5 in Los Angeles) and the Santa Ana Freeway (I-5 in East Los Angeles and Orange County) travel more or less north–south through the area. The Foothill Freeway (I-210), Ventura Freeway (Highway 134/US 101 in the San Fernando Valley), Santa Monica Freeway (I-10) and Century Freeway (I-105) are major east–west routes. Sunset, Santa Monica and Wilshire boulevards are key east–west surface streets.

Its impressive thoroughfares keep this Pacific Rim hub – home to America's largest Hispanic and Asian/Pacific Islander populations – in seemingly perpetual motion, at once isolating the citizenry in their autos and providing them with a common identity as commuters. These disparate souls, though, whiz around not in search of a city, for Los Angeles already has one of the most coherent, if occasionally daffy, personalities of any metropolis in the world. Rather, they're chasing dreams that range from renewal and self-determination to glamour and glory. Because they do it with style and a sense of adventure, their city has captured the world's imagination, if not always its admiration.

Previous page: Los Angeles at dusk

★ Don't Miss
3 Hollywood ➤ 126
5 Beverly Hills ➤ 130
6 The Getty Center ➤ 132
14 Disneyland® Park ➤ 134

At Your Leisure
1 Pasadena ➤ 136
2 Universal Studios ➤ 137
4 Sunset Strip ➤ 137
7 Museum of Tolerance ➤ 138

8 Downtown Los Angeles ➤ 138
9 Downtown Museums ➤ 139
10 Malibu ➤ 140
11 Santa Monica ➤ 141
12 Venice Beach ➤ 141
13 *Queen Mary* ➤ 141

Farther Afield
15 Catalina Island ➤ 142
16 Newport Beach ➤ 142
17 Laguna Beach ➤ 143

While touring Los Angeles it's important to remember one thing: You're fabulous. In fact, everybody's fabulous in this on-the-make city, which is why it's so great to visit.

Los Angeles Area in Three Days

Day 1

Morning
Hooray for **3 Hollywood** (► 126–129), where you'll have your first brush with the stars (well, the ones along the Walk of Fame anyway). Then it's off to the **Griffith Observatory** (► 129) for a lofty perspective on a great city.

Afternoon
Have lunch at jolly Fred 62 (► 145) diner in Los Feliz, then either tour **Warner Bros.** or check out **2 Universal Studios** (► 137). If you've gone to Warner's, you'll have time in the late afternoon to explore a little of **5 Beverly Hills** (► 130–131).

Evening
Drive or walk the **4 Sunset Strip** (► 137), stopping at the Virgin Megastore complex (► 137) for dinner at Wolfgang Puck's Café or continuing on to Puck's ritzier venture, Spago Beverly Hills (► 146).

Day 2

Morning
Have breakfast at Du-par's or Kokomo Café (► 129) in Farmers Market, then continue south on Fairfax Avenue to Wilshire Boulevard and make a left. Check out **La Brea Tar Pits** (► 138) and perhaps the **Petersen Automotive Museum** (► 138). By late morning make your way to the **6 Getty Center** (right, ► 132–133).

Afternoon
Wander through the Getty's galleries and gardens, interrupting your tour with lunch at the café or restaurant. Work off your meal on a half-hour, guided architectural walk. When you depart the Getty, head south on Sepulveda Boulevard and west on Wilshire Boulevard to **11 Santa Monica** (➤ 141). Walk the beach (above) and check out Santa Monica Pier.

Evening
Catch a little of the action along the 3rd Street Promenade (➤ 141). Enjoy inventive Mexican cuisine at the convivial Border Grill (1445 4th Street, tel: 310/451-1655) or try the zippily contemporary Asian selections at the pricier Chinois Santa Monica (2709 Main Street, tel: 310/392-9025).

Day 3

Morning/afternoon
Give the day over to fantasy at **14 Disneyland Park** (right, ➤ 134–135) or, if you didn't head there on Day 1, north to **2 Universal Studios** (➤ 137).

Evening
After the evening traffic has died down (7:30 or so), head north to The Ivy (113 N. Robertson Boulevard, tel: 310/274-8303) for dinner and perhaps some last-minute celebrity sighting.

Hollywood

Pity poor Hollywood – but perhaps not for long. Once the quintessence of glamour, it deteriorated after several movie studios moved to the San Fernando Valley. But the town's making a comeback, the most potent symbol of this being the return of the Academy Awards ceremony to Hollywood Boulevard, where the event first took place.

The must-see along Hollywood Boulevard is **Mann's Chinese Theatre**, and there are a few other points of interest within walking distance. Hollywood showman Sid Grauman erected the Chinese Theatre, then named for him, in 1927. For years the scene of chic Hollywood premieres, the whimsical pagoda-style structure has a frenetic, dragon-festooned exterior. Stars of the past and present have left their prints – hand, foot or otherwise (Jimmy Durante's nose, Lassie's paw) – in the cement courtyard. Legend has it that an actress (Norma Talmadge in some versions, Mary Pickford in others) accidentally stepped in wet cement during construction and that Grauman immediately grasped the promotional possibilities. (According to Grauman's biographer, the impresario came up with the idea on his own.) With another tourist bus pulling up nearly every minute, pandemonium reigns, but in this case it's a plus – every day seems like a major motion-picture event. In the 1940s, the theater hosted the Academy Awards ceremony, but since 2002 the event has been held a few doors east at the

Celebrity star on the Walk of Fame

Kodak Theatre, part of the Hollywood and Highland entertainment-and-retail complex (that also includes Mann's).

Though it's not as glamorous as it was in the 1920s, the **Hollywood Roosevelt Hotel** (7000 Hollywood Boulevard, tel: 323/466-7000), across the street, retains its Spanish-Moorish arches and painted ceramic tiles. An informative mezzanine-level exhibit surveys Hollywood's glory days.

The Chinese Theatre and Hollywood Roosevelt Hotel are near the western end of the **Hollywood Walk of Fame** (Hollywood Boulevard from Vine Street west to La Brea Avenue; Vine Street from Yucca to Sunset). Along the walk, the names of entertainment figures stand out in brass letters amid a pink terrazzo star surrounded by charcoal-gray terrazzo. One of five logos – a motion-picture camera, radio microphone, TV set, theatrical mask or record – indicates the honoree's profession. Barbra Streisand, Elton John and Jack Nicholson are among those with stars near the Chinese.

Mann's Chinese Theatre, with its fire-breathing dragon

As you stroll east on Hollywood Boulevard, you'll shortly pass one of the street's most ornate structures, the Spanish Colonial Revival **El Capitan Theatre** (6838 Hollywood Boulevard, tel: 323/467-7674), a veritable riot of carved terracotta patterns and figures. The Disney Company showcases its animation pictures here.

A little east of the El Capitan is the **Egyptian Theatre** (6712 Hollywood Boulevard, tel: 323/466–3456). Things Egyptian were all the rage following the discovery of King Tut's tomb in the 1920s, and Sid Grauman capitalized on the fad with the theater's design. Rows of palm trees line the long exterior courtyard of this exquisitely restored movie palace.

Hollywood
➕ 205 E2 🔵 Metro Red Line (Hollywood and Highland) 🚌 MTA Bus 2, 26, 163, 180, 181, 210, 212, 217, 310, 429; DASH buses loop north and south of Hollywood Boulevard

Mann's Chinese Theatre
✉ 6925 Hollywood Boulevard ☎ (323) 464-8111 ✋ Free (to courtyard; interior open only to movie attendees)

Griffith Park
✉ 2800 East Observatory Road (south entrance to park is at Los Feliz Boulevard and Vermont; follow signs) ☎ (323) 664-1191 🕐 Park grounds: daily 6 am–10 pm. Planetarium: reopens in late 2005; call for opening times. Closed 2nd Mon in Oct, Thanksgiving and Dec 25 🚌 MTA Bus 180 ✋ Free

Vital Statistics

• Some dispute the claim, but **Cecil B. DeMille** generally receives credit for producing the first feature-length film in Hollywood. The converted barn that served as DeMille's studio in 1913 for the production of "The Squaw Man" still exists (at 2100 N. Highland Avenue), several blocks from its original location.

• Billions of people watch the **Academy Awards** ceremony these days, but a mere 270 people attended the first event, in the Blossom Room of the Hollywood Roosevelt Hotel. The private dinner was held in 1929 to honor the films of 1927 and 1928.

• Fame doesn't come cheap. Getting a star on the **Walk of Fame** costs $15,000, which is usually paid by the entertainment company promoting the honoree's project at the time of the unveiling.

Across the street and east of the Egyptian is **Musso & Frank Grill** (6667 Hollywood Boulevard, tel: 323/467-5123), which opened in 1919 and evolved into the hangout of screenwriters such as Lillian Hellman, Dashiell Hammett and William Faulkner. Hoist one of the textbook martinis in their honor. The food's nothing special, but the atmosphere's great.

Stars bustled in and out of nightclubs and eateries at the intersection of Hollywood and Vine, and newcomers were discovered (or so the planted publicity went) right on the street. Two period theaters, the **Pantages** (6233 Hollywood Boulevard) and the **Palace** (1735 N. Vine Street) have survived more or less intact.

The circular **Capitol Records Building** (1750 N. Vine Street), erected in the 1950s north of Hollywood and Vine, is said to have been designed to resemble a stack of records.

East on Hollywood Boulevard and north on Vermont Avenue lies 4,107-acre (1,662-hectare) **Griffith Park.** A bust of the actor James Dean outside the **Griffith Observatory** (inside the park, follow signs; closed until late 2005 for renovation of the planetarium and other facilities) commemorates several pivotal scenes in his picture "Rebel Without a Cause" that took place at the hillside facility. The on-site planetarium puts on enjoyable shows about the galaxies, but the (free) views of this world – Hollywood in particular – and the building's Mayan-deco exterior design are other reasons to visit. Because you're often above the smog level, you may even see blue sky. Also within Griffith Park are a zoo, the **Autry Museum of Western Heritage** (a celebration of the American West in movies and for real), and the outdoor Greek Theatre concert venue.

Boop-oop-a-doop: Betty Boop at Universal Studios

The observatory is one of many places (the Hollywood Freeway's another) with a good vantage point on the famous **HOLLYWOOD** sign. From the 1920s to the 1940s letters on the slope of Mt. Lee spelled out "Hollywoodland," to advertise a real-estate development. The letters are 50 feet (15 meters) high.

If you're driving, leave the observatory via West Observatory Drive (if you followed the above directions, you got here via East Observatory Drive). Make a left on Canyon Drive, which eventually becomes Western Avenue and leads you south out of the park. Continue south to Santa Monica Boulevard and make a right. **Hollywood Forever** (6000 Santa Monica Boulevard, tel: 323/469-1181, daily 8–5) is the current name of the former Hollywood Memorial Park Cemetery, final resting place of directors Cecil B. DeMille and John Huston, actors Rudolph Valentino, Marion Davies and Tyrone Power, the gangster Bugsy Siegel and even the notorious Virginia Rappe (➤ 19). Douglas Fairbanks Sr. has a memorial that includes a long, lotus-filled reflecting pool. Unlike at Forest Lawn and other famous burial grounds, the employees encourage visitors to seek out star graves – pick up a map at the gift shop (it closes an hour before the cemetery), just inside the entrance.

TAKING A BREAK

Farmers Market (6333 W. 3rd Avenue, tel: 323/933-9211) began as an open-air market in the 1930s and expanded into the present warren of hot-food and souvenir stalls. Two long-time favorites are **Kokomo Café** and **Magee's Kitchen and Deli,** both in the open-air section, and **Du-par's,** a diner.

HOLLYWOOD: INSIDE INFO

Top tip For a quick taste of Hollywood's golden age, **park your car in one of the lots near the Chinese Theatre** and check out the immediate area.

Hidden gem The museum-like attractions in Hollywood tend to be tacky – they're best visited when you're in a silly mood. The one essential stop is the **Hollywood Museum** (1666 N. Highland Avenue, tel: 323/464-7776, moderate) in the art-deco Max Factor Building. The marvelous artifacts here tell the story of the movies from the silent era to the present.

Beverly Hills

Few words connote wealth and glamour more succinctly than "Beverly Hills," where movie-star mansions have captured the world's imagination since the days of silent pictures. A visit to Beverly Hills provides you with a chance to take a peak at the lifestyles of the rich and famous, along residential streets and the renowned Rodeo Drive shopping area.

"I Love Lucy" episodes notwithstanding, stars, movie execs and TV titans don't find it charming when fans drop in – a sign on Barbra Streisand's property, just west of Beverly Hills in Holmby Hills, warns of an armed guard on duty. But you can often glimpse façades and gardens from the street. Sunset Boulevard, Roxbury (where Lucy's daughter lives in her mom's old house) and Summit Drive are good places to start.

The most lavish homes are actually just outside the city limits. In the 1990s, Aaron Spelling, the producer of "Beverly Hills 90210," "Melrose Place" and other such fare, built a 123-room, 56,550-square-foot (5,253-sq-meter) abode – "bigger than the Taj Mahal" gushed one newspaper account – in Holmby Hills. (Proving that all things are – pardon the pun – relative, daughter Tori, a star of "90210," reportedly flew the coop because she needed "space.") And media mogul David Geffen spent about $47.5 million on his nearby manse.

To get closer to the good life, dress up and have a drink or breakfast in the Polo Lounge at the **Beverly Hills Hotel** (9641 Sunset Boulevard, tel: 310/276-2251). The hotel, which opened in 1912, was swank even before the city was.

Southern California's most chic boutiques do business south of Sunset along **Rodeo Drive**. The street's not quite as exclusive as it was in past days, though the wealthy still

Chic boutiques line famous Rodeo Drive

Beverly Hills
✚ 205 E2 ⊠ Sunset, Santa Monica and Wilshire boulevards, west of Doheny Drive 🚌 MTA Bus 2, 302 (Sunset Boulevard); MTA Bus 4, 304 (Santa Monica Boulevard); MTA Bus 20, 21 (Wilshire Boulevard) and many others

Museum of Television and Radio
⊠ 465 N. Beverly Drive ☎ (310) 786-1000 🕐 Wed–Sun noon–5. Closed Jan 1, Jul 4, Thanksgiving and Dec 25 🚌 MTA Bus 4, 14 💵 Moderate

shop by appointment and the rents are among the world's highest. Frank Lloyd Wright designed the mini-mall at 332 N. Rodeo Drive, whose ramp zigzags to the upper floors (be careful walking up it if you've just had a cocktail). At Rodeo Drive and Wilshire Boulevard are the chichi Via Rodeo shopping lane – Versace, Gucci, et al. – and the posh Regent Beverly Wilshire Hotel.

This house was a B-movie studio headquarters in Culver City before being moved to Beverly Hills

Richard Meier, architect of the Getty Center (➤ 132–133), designed the stylish digs of the **Museum of Television and Radio**. You can view tapes of TV shows and listen to radio shows in private booths or attend screenings in various theaters.

TAKING A BREAK

Perch yourself at a view table above Wilshire Boulevard and Rodeo Drive and have a snack or a meal at **Piazza Rodeo** (208 N. Rodeo Drive, tel: 310/275-2428).

BEVERLY HILLS: INSIDE INFO

Top tip Parking is **free for the first two hours** in lots on and just off Beverly Drive. Look for public-parking signs.

Hidden gem West of Beverly Hills is even more exclusive **Bel-Air,** home to Jack Nicholson and other superstars.

One to miss Maps to **stars' houses** are often inaccurate or out of date.

The Getty Center

"Nothing succeeds like excess," wrote Oscar Wilde, some-thing the Getty Center proves in spades. With striking build-ings, sleek galleries and the Santa Monica Mountains setting competing for your attention, you may occasionally have to remind yourself to look at the art, though the architecture was intended as a work of art in itself.

Richard Meier designed the light-beige, rough-hewn travertine buildings, whose overall effect is of a suave, modernist varia-tion on the Acropolis of Athens. Artist Robert Irwin groomed the controversial Central Garden, which Meier is said to have hated for its darker colors and unruly foliage (notice Meier's more orderly cactus garden and tree arrangements closer to the main buildings). The French architect Thierry Despont designed the cases and chose the colors and finishes for the 14 decorative arts galleries (again with some reported grumbling from Meier). The Getty's few architectural incongruities aside – that garden really does clash with Meier's aesthetic – the Center (plan to visit for at least 2 hours) is truly a sight to behold. A tram (to be precise, a horizontal Otis elevator) whisks you from

Meier imported 16,000 tons of Italian traver-tine limestone for the Getty

🔲 205 E2 ✉ 1200 Getty Center Drive off I-405, Brentwood ☎ (310) 440-7300 ⏰ Tue–Thu and Sun 10–6, Fri–Sat 10–9. Closed Mon, Jan 1, Jul 4, Thanksgiving and Dec 25 🍴 $–$$$ 🚌 MTA Bus 761 💵 Inexpensive

What's Where
North Pavilion Before 1600
East Pavilion 1600–1800
South Pavilion 1600–1800
West Pavilion After 1800
Exhibition Pavilion (between
the museum entrance and
the West Pavilion).
Temporary exhibitions

The Getty's permanent collection includes *Adoration of the Magi* by Andrea Mantgena

the parking area to an arrival plaza. Stairs sweep up from here to the Main Plaza, off which are five two-story pavilions. Four house the permanent collection; the fifth hosts temporary exhibitions. Paintings are on the upper levels; decorative arts, drawings, manuscripts and photographs on the lower.

The particular loves of collector and oil magnate J. Paul Getty were antiquities and medieval illuminated manuscripts. Over the years the curators have filled in the gaps in the museum's largely European holdings, which include paintings, drawings, sculpture, decorative arts and 19th- and 20th-century American and European photographs. Titian, Gainsborough, Rembrandt, Turner, Monet and Cézanne are among the painters represented. Van Gogh's *Irises* is the most popular of the Getty's post-Impressionist works.

Light and color are the two key elements of the Central Garden, which Irwin designed as a fluctuating work of art, varying with the time of day or year. Waterfalls and streams reflect the ever-changing colors.

TAKING A BREAK

The Getty operates a full-service restaurant and two cafés, one with table service, the other self-service. You can dine indoors or out. The food's quite good.

THE GETTY CENTER: INSIDE INFO

Top tip You can explore the artworks in chronological order or at random. A good strategy is to **watch the 10-minute introductory film** shown in the entrance hall and then proceed to the areas that most interest you. The audio guide available at the entrance is worth the small fee.

Hidden gem If you're traveling with children, **check out the family room,** where displays and hands-on activities, such as a set-up for portraiture, help kids make sense of the artistic process.

One to miss J. Paul Getty wasn't much interested in **20th-century art,** something the museum's so-so modern collection bears out.

Disneyland® Park

© Disney Enterprises, Inc.

A sign at the entrance to the famed Disneyland Theme Park proclaims that you're leaving the world of reality and entering a place where fantasy reigns. And aside from the rampant, if discreet, commercialism and the occasional views of Orange County's smog from the park's loftier points, you *have* stepped into another world.

Main Street, U.S.A. leads into the Central Plaza, off which are several themed areas – including Fantasyland, Tomorrowland, Frontierland, Critter Country and New Orleans Square. Tyke-sized amusements enchant the kiddies at **Mickey's Toontown.**

The absolute don't-miss attraction is the **Indiana Jones™ Adventure,** which puts you inside re-created scenes from the Indiana Jones movies. You'll face untold "dangers," from boulders to snakes, in this daffy living cartoon that's the highlight of Adventureland. **Matterhorn Bobsleds,** a ¹⁄₁₀₀th-scale re-creation of a Swiss mountain, is Disneyland Park's oldest roller-coaster and still one of its best. **Space Mountain**, an indoor roller-coaster in Tomorrowland, is deliriously disorienting. The **Splash Mountain** flume ride, found in Critter Country, climaxes with a drenching five-story drop in a floating ride – stimulating and refreshing.

➕ 205 E2 ✉ 1313 Harbor Boulevard (off I-5), Anaheim ☎ (714) 781-4565 🕐 Hours vary (open as early as 8 am or as late as 10 am; closed as early as 6 pm or as late as 3 am). Call (714) 781-7290 for particular dates or log on to www.disneyland.com 🚌 MTA Bus 460 (from downtown); Orange County Transit (OCTA) 43 🍴 $–$$$ 💰 Expensive

© Disney Enterprises, Inc.

Something for every mood: Sleeping Beauty Castle, left, and the Pirates of the Caribbean, above

You'll get less wet on a **Jungle Cruise**, an Adventureland attraction that passes through re-creations of the rivers of four continents. The other great boat attraction is **Pirates of the Caribbean**, in New Orleans Square. The **Mad Tea Party** ride and **Mickey's House** are two perennial favorites of younger kids. **Disney's California Adventure Park**, an adjacent theme park (separate admission), is a fantasy version of the state, which has some engaging attractions.

TAKING A BREAK

Cafés, restaurants and take-out stands abound. Three good choices: **Blue Bayou** (New Orleans Square), **Carnation Café** (Main Street), **Redd Rockett's Pizza Port** (Tomorrowland).

DISNEYLAND: INSIDE INFO

Top tips Arrive early and head immediately to one of the popular rides/attractions such as **Indiana Jones™ Adventure** or **Splash Mountain**. Then take a ride on the **Disneyland Railroad**, which will orient you to the rest of the park.
• Disneyland is **more fun during off-peak times**, especially on weekdays just before and after summer, when the weather's still fine but lines are shorter.
• If you've arrived during a busy period, **go on the rides/attractions in the morning** or the evening and hit the shows during the afternoon.
• **Check into Annual Passports** (available online at www.disney.com/disneyland and through travel agents but not at the park) if you'll be spending more than a day at the park. The passes allow three or five visits within 14 consecutive days.

Hidden gems Try to catch at least **one of the live shows**, whose production numbers rival those of many a Broadway presentation. And stick around for the parade (and accompanying fireworks some nights) that closes each day.

Don't miss Fantasmic!, an evening show in which Mickey Mouse battles villains galore. It's a dazzling multimedia extravaganza (lasers, pyrotechnics, flashing lights, lit-up dancing fountains), but you need to snag a good spot two or three hours ahead of time or your sight lines will be blocked.

At Your Leisure

❶ Pasadena
This San Gabriel Valley town hosts the Tournament of Roses Parade each New Year's Day. The entire **Old Pasadena** district, much of it built in the 1920s and 1930s, is on the National Register of Historic Places. Chain clothing stores, boutiques, and restaurants and cafés line Old Pasadena's main drag, Colorado Boulevard, and nearby streets and alleys from Pasadena Avenue east to Arroyo Parkway.

➕ 205 E2 ✉ **Northeast of downtown Los Angeles, off the 110 freeway**
🚇 **Metro Gold Line (various stations)**
🚌 **MTA Bus 180, 181, 380**

Gamble House
The three-story Gamble House, the handiwork of Charles and Henry Greene, is a superb example of early 20th-century Craftsman architecture. The brothers incorporated many natural woods into a meticulous design that's pragmatic yet exudes a joie de vivre and a subtle appreciation of nature. The stained-glass entry doors, which depict coastal live oaks, are among the highlights.

✉ **4 Westmoreland Place, off Orange Grove Boulevard (west side, north of Walnut Street)** ☎ **(626) 793-3334**
🕐 **Thu–Sun noon–3. Closed Jan 1, Easter, Jul 4, Thanksgiving and Dec 25**
🚌 **MTA 180** 💲 **Moderate**

Norton Simon Museum
"Visit the Getty for the architecture and the Norton Simon Museum for the art." This tip from LA's cultural cognoscenti acknowledges the discriminating taste of the financier Norton Simon, who assembled one of America's finest private collections of European art from the Renaissance to the early 20th century. Pivotal works by Raphael, Rubens, Goya, Rembrandt, Renoir, Manet, Degas, Picasso and Kandinksy attest to Simon's preference: quality over quantity. The slate floors and columns designed by architect Frank Gehry for the South Asian galleries create a stunningly contemporary yet reverent, temple-like setting for the mostly religious-oriented artworks. Impressionist Claude Monet's beloved garden in Giverny, France, inspired the sculpture garden.

✉ **411 W. Colorado Boulevard**
☎ **(626) 449-6840** 🕐 **Wed–Thu and Sat–Mon noon–6, Fri noon–9. Closed Jan 1, Thanksgiving and Dec 25**
🚌 **MTA Bus 180, 181** 💲 **Inexpensive**

Huntington Library, Art Collections and Botanical Gardens
You may have a hard time deciding whether to spend your time indoors or outdoors at the Huntington Library, Art Collections and Botanical Gardens, southeast of Pasadena in the town of San Marino. Significant holdings include a rare copy of the Gutenburg Bible on vellum, the Ellesmere manuscript of Geoffrey Chaucer's *Canterbury Tales*, Thomas Gainsborough's *The Blue Boy* and Sir Thomas Lawrence's *Pinkie*. The Japanese, rose and desert gardens are three standouts of the 150-acre (60-hectare) botanical gardens. On most days, reservations are required for

English tea in the Rose Garden
Tea Room.

✉ 1151 Oxford Road, off San Marino
Avenue (south of I-210) ☎ (626) 405-
2100 (info); (626) 683-8131 (tea room)
🕐 Tue–Sun 10:30–4:30, Jun–Aug;
Tue–Fri noon–4:30, Sat–Sun 10:30–
4:30, Sep–May. Closed Jan 1, Jul 4,
Thanksgiving and Dec 24–25 🚌 MTA
Bus 79 (from downtown LA; exit at San
Marino Avenue and walk about
¼ mile/.4 km) 🎟 Moderate (free first
Thu of the month)

2 Universal Studios

The emphasis at this theme park is
on entertainment, not moviemaking.
The highlights include the
"Terminator 2" production number,
which mixes live action and filmed 3-
D effects, and **Revenge of the
Mummy: The Ride**, a superfast,
superscary rollercoaster. On a hot
day, along with thrills (among them
an eight-story drop), **Jurassic Park –
The Ride** provides much-needed
chills as your boat plunges into rag-
ing waters. The **back-lot tram tour**
passes sites from "Jaws," "Psycho"
(the infamous Bates Motel) and other
notable films before subjecting riders
to a simulated 8.3 earthquake.

🚩 205 E2 ✉ Universal Center Drive,
off Hollywood Freeway (US 101),
Universal City ☎ (818) 622-3801
🕐 Daily 8 am–10 pm, late May to early
Sep; 9–7, rest of year. Closed
Thanksgiving and Dec 25 🚇 Metro Red
Line (Universal City) 🚌 MTA Bus 96
🎟 Expensive

4 Sunset Strip/West Hollywood

Sunset Boulevard in West Hollywood
is known as the Sunset Strip. Huge
billboards on Sunset tout the latest
stars and wannabes, and nearly
everyone's tanned and toned (you
never know when a casting director
might materialize). The Strip has
been party central for entertainment
folk since Hollywood's golden age.
The action continues these days at
nightclubs such as the **Key Club** and
the **Viper Room** (► 150). Drive the

Marilyn's all oohs and ahs at Universal

How Do They Do It?
To see how television shows and
movies are really made, head to
Warner Bros. (tel: 818/972-8687) or
Universal Studios (tel: 818/622-3801),
where the two-hour tours pass by
working sets, technical departments
and the back lots. The tour at
Warners focuses more on the nuts
and bolts of moviemaking than does
Universal's, but you'll learn a lot on
either one.

Strip and then walk south for a bit
from the 880 block of Sunset
Boulevard, at Horn Avenue. The
Virgin Megastore complex (8000
Sunset Boulevard, at Crescent
Heights Boulevard) encompasses the
former site of Schwab's Pharmacy, at
whose soda fountain celebrities such
as Charlie Chaplin and James Dean
hung out and future stars and starlets
were supposedly discovered.

🚩 205 E2 ✉ Sunset Boulevard,
west from Crescent
Heights Boulevard
to Doheny Drive
🚌 MTA Bus 2

Museum Row

The delightful **Petersen Automotive Museum** displays roadsters, coupés, touring cars, sedans, trucks and motorcycles, many of them in amusing and innovative settings. The historical displays include gas pumps through the ages and show the automobile's influence in city planning and other areas. (6060 Wilshire Boulevard; tel: 323/930-2277, open: Tue–Sun 10–6. Closed Jan 1, Jul 4, Thanksgiving and Dec 25. Admission: moderate.)

Key holdings at the comprehensive **Los Angeles County Museum of Art** include European, Chinese and contemporary American and European art. A separate pavilion holds the superlative Japanese collection. Sunday is family day, with various themed projects for kids and their parents. (5905 Wilshire Boulevard, tel: 323/857-6000, open: Mon, Tue, Thu noon–8, Fri noon–9, Sat–Sun 11–8. Closed Thanksgiving and Dec 25. Admission: moderate; free second Tue of month; full admission for ticketed exhibitions.)

Primordial ooze – well, to be more precise, prehistoric asphalt – still bubbles up from **La Brea Tar Pits**, which you can view for free (until 10 pm) along outdoor pathways. The **George C. Page Museum of La Brea Discoveries** contains dinosaur bones and other fossils recovered from the pits. (Hancock Park, 5801 Wilshire Boulevard, tel: 323/934-7243, open: Mon–Fri 9:30–5, Sat–Sun 10–5. Closed Jan 1, Jul 4, Thanksgiving and Dec 25. Admission: moderate.)

7 Museum of Tolerance

The museum of the Simon Wiesenthal Center provides a vivid introduction to bigotry in action. The Holocaust Section, which alone takes about an hour to tour, skillfully dissects the conditions that enabled the German Nazi leader Adolf Hitler to carry out his plan to exterminate Jews and other so-called undesirables.

205 E2 9786 W. Pico Boulevard (310) 553-8403 Mon–Thu 11:30–6:30, Fri 11:30–3, Sun 11:30–7:30 (last entry 2–2½ hours before closing time. Closed Jewish holidays, Jan 1, last Mon in May, Jul 4, first Mon in Sep, Thanksgiving and Dec 25 Santa Monica Big Blue Bus 7 Moderate

Sombreros for sale on Olvera Street

8 Downtown Los Angeles

Walt Disney Concert Hall

Many years in the making, the stunning $274 million home of the Los Angeles Philharmonic, designed by architect Frank Gehry, has a wavy, shiplike façade that stuns from every angle. Early reports on the acoustics of the hall have also been favourable.

205 E2 111 S. Grand Avenue (323) 850-2000 for event information Metro Red Line (Civic Center) MTA Bus 2, 60, 460 DASH Route A (weekdays), DD (weekends)

Cathedral of Our Lady of the Angels

Controversy surrounded Downtown's other grand edifice of recent vintage, the Roman Catholic cathedral designed by Spanish architect José Rafael Moneo. But his supposed sins – some of the faithful (and a few

Multiple architectural styles rarely blend as pleasingly as they do in Union Station

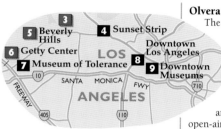

architecture critics) initially found the ambience unsettlingly futuristic – seem to have been forgiven, and the austere building is a marvel to visit. Free tours (1 pm on weekdays) leave from the entrance fountain.

➕ 205 E2 ✉ 555 W. Temple Street
☎ (213) 680-5200 🕐 Mon–Fri 6 am–8 pm, Sat 9–7, Sun 7–7 🚇 Metro Red Line (Civic Center) 🚌 MTA Bus 2, 78, 81 (and others) 🚌 DASH Route B (weekdays), DD (weekends)

Union Station
Fanciful Union Station is one of Los Angeles' great public spaces. With its Spanish-Moorish and late art-deco flourishes, the station radiates subdued whimsy yet also has a vaguely cathedral-like feel. Union Station has appeared in "Bugsy," "Blade Runner," "Sunset Boulevard" and other films.

➕ 205 E2 ✉ 800 N. Alameda Street
🚇 Metro Red and Gold Lines (Union Station) 🚌 MTA 33, 42; DASH Route B (weekdays), DD (weekends)

Olvera Street/Chinatown
The best time to visit downtown is on weekends, when parking is easy everywhere but near Olvera Street, a Mexican-style plaza often aflutter with mariachi music, *folklorica* dancing and the chatter of patrons at open-air restaurants. Spanish and Mexican settlers established the pueblo that became Los Angeles in this area in 1781. North of Olvera, LA's workaday Chinatown contains gift shops and restaurants though the area is less of a tourist attraction than its counterparts in other cities.

➕ 205 E2 ✉ West of Alameda Street, between Aliso Street and Cesar E. Chavez Avenue (Union Station) 🚌 MTA Bus 2, 4, 81, 94 🚌 DASH Route B (weekdays), DD (weekends)

⑨ Downtown Museums

Museum of Contemporary Art
The Museum of Contemporary Art has two Downtown branches. The main **MOCA at California Plaza** location is known for its international collection of post-1940s art. Works by Rauschenberg, Johns, Beuys, Rothko and Serra are among the key holdings.

➕ 205 E2 ✉ 250 S. Grand Avenue
☎ (213) 626-6222 🕐 Mon and Fri 11–5, Sat–Sun 11–6, Thu 11–8. Closed

Jan 1, Jul 4, Thanksgiving and Dec 25
🚇 Metro Red Line (Pershing Square)
🚌 DASH Route B (weekdays), DD
(weekends); or shuttle from Geffen
Contemporary) 💰 Moderate (free Thu
and with same-day Geffen
Contemporary admission ticket)

MOCA at The Geffen Contemporary

The warehouse-like MOCA at The
Geffen Contemporary often presents
huge installations – large sculptures,
billboard art and the like.
➕ 205 E2 ✉ 152 N. Central Avenue
☎ (213) 626-6222 🕐 Mon and Fri
11–5, Sat–Sun 11–6, Thu 11–8. Closed
Jan 1, Jul 4, Thanksgiving and Dec 25
🚇 Metro Red Line (Civic Center)
🚌 MTA Bus 30, 40, 439 🚌 DASH Route
A (weekdays), DD (weekends)
💰 Moderate (free on Thu and with
same-day MOCA admission ticket)

Japanese American National Museum

An old Buddhist temple and a modernist structure house this museum,
whose exhibits shed light on the lives
and contributions of Americans of
Japanese descent, and their struggle
for acceptance in their adopted home.
➕ 205 E2 ✉ 369 E. 1st Street, at
Central Avenue ☎ (213) 625-0414
🕐 Tue–Wed and Fri–Sun 10–5, Thu
10–8 (free after 5 and third Thu of
month). Closed Jan 1, Thanksgiving and
Dec 25 🚌 MTA Bus 30, 40, 439; DASH
Route A (weekdays), DD (weekends)
💰 Inexpensive

More Than a Façade

Broadway, downtown's main street a
century ago, contains several architectural gems, among them the 1893
Bradbury Building (304 S. Broadway,
at 3rd Street), whose designer was
inspired in part by a popular novel
about a utopian society *circa* 2000.
Natural overhead light floods the
lobby (open weekdays 9–6) and its
tile floors, marble and exposed
wrought-iron staircases. Scenes from
"Blade Runner" were shot here
before the structure was restored;
"Wolf" shows the refurbished interior.
Sid Grauman, of Chinese Theatre
fame, built the **Million Dollar Theater**
(307 S. Broadway), one of several
silent and early-talkie movie palaces
still standing between 3rd and 9th
streets. Broadway is best visited by
car or bus. The street is busy during
the day and safe enough to walk, but
be advised this is not Beverly Hills.
🚌 MTA Bus 45, 46

🔟 Malibu

Upscale Malibu is famous for its
celebrity palaces and occasional mud-
slides and firestorms. For all the star
wattage, the scene is remarkably subdued, with the shoreline along the
Pacific Coast Highway (PCH) the
main draw. Surfers head to **Leo
Carrillo State Beach** (35000 PCH),
whose tide pools teem with sea creatures. A stairway leads down the cliffs
to secluded **El Matador State Beach**

Impromptu
performances
enliven Santa
Monica's
3rd Street
Promenade

(32350 PCH). Tanned babes and pumped-up Adonises frolic along **Zuma Beach** (30000 PCH), a quintessentially SoCal strand. Overlooking **Malibu Lagoon State Beach** (23200 PCH at Serra Road), whose namesake waterway shelters many migratory birds, is the **Adamson House**. Locally produced ceramic tiles decorate the fetching 1929 Spanish Colonial Revival structure.

➕ 205 D2 ✉ Pacific Coast Highway north of Santa Monica and Pacific Palisades 🚌 Santa Monica Big Blue Bus 434 (along PCH)

🔟 Santa Monica

Appealing, independent-minded Santa Monica has a slightly bohemian style. Though heavily gentrified, the town attracts yuppies, tourists, the homeless, street artists, beachgoers, teens, older people. All these and more head to the beach and the **3rd Street Promenade**, the pedestrians-only stretch of 3rd Street between Broadway and Wilshire Boulevard.

(There are plenty of public parking lots.) Continue west on Wilshire and you'll run into **Santa Monica State Beach**, where the sand is clean, the views are great and there is plenty to entertain you on the **Santa Monica Pier**. To the south on Main Street, trendy boutiques and restaurants line the blocks from Hollister Avenue south to the town of Venice.

➕ 205 E2 ✉ West end of I-10 🚌 MTA Bus 4, 6, 33 (and others)

🔟 Venice Beach

A carnival atmosphere prevails along **Ocean Front Walk**, the paved promenade that straddles exuberant Venice Beach. Stroll Ocean Front south of Rose Avenue and you're liable to encounter trained parrots, skilled and unskilled musicians, and proselytizers for all sorts of religious and social movements. On a sunny day the pièce de résistance, at 18th Street, is **Muscle Beach**, an outdoor pavilion where guys and gals pump iron and chat up the crowd. Vendors sell sunglasses, clothing, records and more, and you can dine on anything from focaccio to foie gras. **Figtree's Café** (429 Ocean Front Walk) is a good quick stop.

➕ 205 E2 ✉ Ocean Front Walk (main action between Rose Avenue and Venice Boulevard) 🚌 MTA Bus 33 (and others)

🔟 Queen Mary

The era of plush luxury liners peaked with the construction of the art-deco-style *Queen Mary*, built in the mid-1930s. The ship's speed was renowned – she set a world record by sailing from Europe to New York in four days – but opulence was her true calling card. The ship transported troops during World War II – the pool was turned into barracks, and soldiers slept in shifts. The Behind the Scenes Tour takes you to the ballroom and some private staterooms. You can dine on board, café-style or in fancier restaurants. Long Beach's number-two draw, the **Aquarium of the Pacific**, sits across Rainbow Harbor from the ship.

➕ 205 E2 ✉ 1126 Queens Highway (follow signs at southern end of I-710), Long Beach ☎ (562) 435-3511 🕐 Daily 10–6 🚇 Metro Blue Line (Transit Mall station; transfer to free Passport Shuttle C: "Aquarium/*Queen Mary*") 💲 Expensive

Farther Afield

🅖 Catalina Island

Pristine natural settings can be hard to come by in overbuilt Southern California, but Catalina Island (officially Santa Catalina Island), most of which is owned by a nature conservancy, is a marvelous exception. On a clear day you can see the island from the mainland – Catalina's just 22 miles (35 kilometers) offshore.

Resort activities center around the town of **Avalon.** You could spend an enjoyable day just hanging out in town or at nearby Descanso Beach or Lover's Cove, but natural and man-made pleasures await elsewhere.

If you're making a day trip, maximize your time by taking a guided sightseeing tour on land, sea or both. **Discovery Tours** (tel: 310/510-2500) conducts some of its outings aboard a submarine-like "semisubmersible" that's the next best thing to snorkeling for seeing the abundant marine life – anything from moray eels to colorful fish. If you're up for something more strenuous than touring, you can go snorkeling or horseback riding or play golf, tennis or other outdoor sports.

Popular sights include the island's most visible landmark, the 12-story-high **Casino,** said to be the world's largest circular ballroom. Within the Casino is an art deco-style movie palace, the **Avalon Theatre,** adorned inside and out with stunning murals on aquatic and American West themes. The main artists also decorated the Chinese Theatre in Hollywood.

To get to the island from San Pedro, Long Beach or Dana Point, take the **Catalina Express** ferry (tel: 310/519-1212 or 800/805-9201) or the **Catalina Flyer** (tel: 949/673-5245) from Newport Beach's **Balboa Pavilion** (▶ opposite). If you get seasick, take the appropriate medication before boarding the boats. For further information call the **Catalina Island Visitors Bureau** (Green Pleasure Pier, Avalon, tel: 310/510-1520).

🅗 Newport Beach

With mansions, yachts, fancy cars and plush hotels, Newport Beach is one of California's ritziest communities, but it manages to retain the homey beachside flavor that has drawn vacationers for more than a century. Wide, white-sand beaches stretch from the Santa Ana River south several miles to the tip of **Balboa Peninsula,** which separates Newport Bay from the ocean.

Newport Boulevard heads south and then east into Balboa Peninsula from the Coast Highway (the Pacific Coast Highway's name in most of Orange County). Park when you see signs for the **Newport Pier,** which like **Balboa Pier,** 2 miles (3 kilometers) farther along, stretches several

Dory fisherman on the dock in Newport Beach

Relaxation is a top priority at Main Beach in Avalon

hundred yards into the ocean and makes for a pleasant stroll. Near each you can rent bicycles or in-line skates, an ideal way to see the peninsula.

Two short blocks across east of the harbor pier stands the **Balboa Pavilion,** a large Edwardian building that houses a restaurant with a superb view of the harbor.

Nearby are the **Balboa Fun Zone** amusement park and booths where you can buy tickets to 45-minute **Newport Harbor cruises,** which sail past palatial homes (some owned by celebrities) and other sights unseen by landlubbers. Another fun excursion is the seven-minute ferry ride to **Balboa Island.** Catch the ferry two blocks west of the pavilion at Palm Street. The island has some nice shops and cafés along Marine Avenue.

➕ 205 E2 ✉ Coast Highway at Highway 55 (Newport Boulevard) ☎ (949) 719-6100 or (800) 942-6278 (tourist information) 🚌 OCTA Bus 47, 71

🔢 Laguna Beach

The foliage that adorns Newport Beach along the Coast Highway becomes even greener and lusher as the road snakes southward to Laguna Beach. Park in one of the public lots off Broadway and head to **Main Beach** (Coast Highway and Broadway), a protected sandy cove

fronted by a grassy lawn with shade trees and picnic tables. After spending time at the beach, you can stroll **Forest and Ocean avenues,** which contain boutiques, art galleries, restaurants and cafés. Stop into the visitor bureau at 252 Broadway to pick up brochures with self-guiding tours of Laguna's historic bungalows and cottages and to find out what's happening in town during your stay. Laguna Beach's deservedly celebrated **Festival of Arts** (650 Laguna Canyon Road, tel: 949/494-1145) takes place each July and August.

North of Main Beach, close enough to walk, is **Heisler Park** (Cliff Drive, off Coast Highway), whose bluff-top trail yields stunning ocean views. Sharing those vistas is **Las Brisas** (361 Cliff Drive), a Mexican seafood restaurant open for breakfast, lunch and dinner. At the north end of Heisler Park lies **Diver's Cove,** a great place to snorkel.

Among the less crowded beaches are **Crescent Bay** (to the north of downtown, off Coast Highway) and **Victoria Beach** (to the south). Seals and other wildlife congregate on **Seal Rock,** in the waters of Crescent Bay. Just north of town at **Crystal Cove State Park,** which encompasses 3.5 miles (5.5 kilometers) of coastline, you can hike, swim, surf, fish and more.

➕ 205 E2 ✉ Coast Highway at Highway 133 (Broadway) ☎ (949) 497-9229 or (800) 877-1115 (tourist information) 🚌 OCTA Bus 1 (connects with Laguna Beach Transit)

Where to...
Eat and Drink

Prices

Expect to pay per person for a meal, excluding drinks and service

$ under $15 $$ $15-25 $$$ over $25

Asia de Cuba $$$

You might not expect the food in a place that's as groovy as Asia de Cuba to be as good as it is, but the Philippe Starck-designed restaurant pleases as much with its stunning look and city views (you can dine indoors or out), as it does with its "Asian-Latino" fare. Among the standout dishes are the calamari salad and the wok-fried crispy fish. This restaurant is a bit of a splurge, but because portions are large you can keep the cost down by sharing.

🚹 205 E2 ⊠ 8440 Sunset Boulevard, West Hollywood ☎ (323) 848-6000

🕐 Breakfast Mon–Fri 7–11, lunch Mon–Fri 11–3:30, brunch Sat–Sun 11:30–3:30, dinner Mon–Thu 5–11, Fri–Sat 5–midnight, Sun 5–10:30

Authentic Café $$

This hip West Hollywood Southwestern-Asian fusion restaurant draws crowds who go for the eclectic, reasonably priced dishes, typified by the yin and yang salad of roasted chicken, red cabbage, wontons and rice noodles in a red ginger dressing. The café has faux adobe walls and soft music and lighting. Prepare to wait in line for a table at peak times,

or grab a seat at the counter and watch the cooks at work.

🚹 205 E2 ⊠ 7605 Beverly Boulevard, Los Angeles ☎ (323) 939-4626 🕐 Mon–Thu 11:30–10, Fri–Sun 11:30–10:45. Closed Thanksgiving and Dec 25

Broadway Deli $-$$

The Broadway Deli is a handy restaurant to know about. It's open for three meals a day and snacks in between and until late night. You can find just about any kind of tasty food you want here, from diner-style blue-plate specials and comfort food to more upscale grilled fish and beef entrées. And it's located along Santa Monica's always lively 3rd Street Promenade, so it's great for people-watching. The downside is that it gets crowded and doesn't take reservations.

🚹 205 E2 ⊠ 1457 3rd Street Promenade, Santa Monica ☎ (310) 451-0616 🕐 Sun–Thu 7 am–midnight, Fri–Sat 8 am–1 am; limited hours on major holidays

⬤⬤⬤ Campanile $$$

Campanile draws consistent raves for its great food, romantic atmosphere and lively bar pouring wine by the glass. If the weather's nice, sit on the outdoor patio and dine on rustic, flavorful California-Mediterranean dishes dispensed from the open kitchen. The fresh-baked breads and the extraordinary pastries, featured at Sunday brunch, come from the adjacent La Brea Bakery, run by the chef-owner's wife. Monday nights are devoted to family-style meals.

🚹 205 E2 ⊠ 624 S. La Brea, Los Angeles ☎ (323) 938-1447 🕐 Lunch Mon–Fri 11:30–2; brunch Sat–Sun 9:30–1:30; dinner Mon–Thu 6–10, Fri–Sat 5:30–11. Closed Jan 1, Labor Day and Dec 25

⬤⬤ El Cholo $

You can find cheaper, and probably more authentic, Mexican food in LA, but El Cholo, the city's oldest Mexican restaurant, is both a landmark and a festive place to chow down on Tex-Mex favorites washed down with dynamite margaritas. You can make your own tacos from tortillas, beef, chicken, beans and salsas. Or, from May through October only, order El Cholo's famous homemade green corn tamales. El Cholo also has a newer branch in Santa Monica (1025 Wilshire Boulevard, tel: 310/899-1106).

➕ 205 E2 ⊠ 1121 S. Western Avenue, Los Angeles ☎ (323) 734-2773 ⓦ Mon–Thu 11–10, Fri–Sat 11–11, Sun 11–9. Closed Thanksgiving and Dec 25

Fred 62 $

The gaudy lime-green exterior, funky interior decor and even the slogan at this hip diner – "Eat Now, Dine Later" – sum up chef-owner Fred Eric's approach: Don't take yourself too seriously. But the food – an eclectic combo of retro diner favorites such as corn dogs and "punk tarts," and health-conscious choices such as Asian-style noodle

dishes and tofu scrambles – is good, and available 24/7/365, which is handy if you're planning to do some late-night club-hopping in trendy Los Feliz. Sit inside or at one of the sidewalk tables.

➕ 205 E2 ⊠ 1850 N. Vermont Avenue, Los Feliz ☎ (323) 667-0062 ⓦ Daily 24 hours

Hollywood Hills Coffee Shop $

Keep your eyes open at this quirky coffee shop housed in one corner of a Best Western motel in the Hollywood Hills – that might be Quentin Tarantino or Vince Vaughn in the next booth, loading up on tasty huevos rancheros, grilled trout and eggs, or chicken-fried steak. Used as a setting in the film "Swingers," it's a strictly dress-down Hollywood scene. Reservations aren't accepted, so prepare to wait in line at peak times, such as Sunday morning.

➕ 205 E2 ⊠ 6145 Franklin Avenue, Hollywood ☎ (323) 467-7678 ⓦ Daily 7 am–10 pm. Closed Dec 25

I Cugini $$

With a plant-filled patio right across Ocean Avenue from Santa Monica Beach, as well as a handsome interior, I Cugini cuts a dashing figure. It's also one of the rare restaurants that combine a sophisticated, romantic atmosphere, including a great bar, with child-friendly attitudes. But its charms go well beyond surface glitter. Specializing in Italian seafood – the whole fish roasted in a rock-salt crust is a signature dish – I Cugini can also be counted on for its pastas, pizzas and antipasti platters.

➕ 205 E2 ⊠ 1501 Ocean Avenue, Santa Monica ☎ (310) 451-4595 ⓦ Mon–Thu 11:30–10, Fri–Sat 11:30–11, Sun 10–10. Closed Dec 25

▼▼▼ Matsuhisa $$$

This upscale Japanese restaurant is a hit with LA residents who are willing to pay mightily for a memorable meal that often makes more standard Japanese dishes seem lame. Named for star chef Nobu

Matsuhisa, the restaurant turns out supremely fresh, imaginative and often dazzling seafood creations that range from sushi to sea scallops with black truffles and caviar.

➕ 205 E2 ⊠ 129 N. La Cienega Boulevard, West Hollywood ☎ (310) 659-9639 ⓦ Lunch Mon–Fri 11:45–2:15; dinner daily 5:45–10:15. Closed Thanksgiving and Dec 25

Nic's $$–$$$

Come for the sophisticated martini lounge and the nightly live music, but don't overlook the chance to have dinner at this newish restaurant run by owner-chef Larry Nicola, one of the local maestros of California cuisine. Service is as smooth as the martinis, the decor is as California as the food, and the dishes have many creative touches, such as oysters sautéed with spinach, garlic and walnuts.

➕ 205 E2 ⊠ 453 N. Cañon Drive, Beverly Hills ☎ (310) 550-5707 ⓦ Mon–Thu 5–10, Fri–Sat 5–10:30. Closed Thanksgiving and Dec 25

Oysters $–$$$

To sample the Orange County good life, slip up Pacific Coast Highway for oysters and California-Asian cuisine at this restaurant that consistently wins awards for its menu and its wine list. Ahi tuna, kung pao calamari, and wok-fried ginger rice bowls are among the stars, but you can stick to meat and potatoes if you wish. (The chefs even do the all-American cheeseburger proud.) The desserts include a zesty ginger and five-spice shortcake with wild berries, lemon curd, and ginger whipped cream. The ambience here is cosmopolitan, and jazz music is performed on most nights.

✚ 205 E2 ⊠ 2515 E. Pacific Coast Highway, Corona Del Mar ☎ (949) 675-7411 ⓦ Dinner 4–10 (late-night bar menu from 10 until closing). Closed Jan 1, Thanksgiving and Dec 25

▼▼▼ Patina $$$

Patina, relocated in late 2003 to a space in the Walt Disney Concert Hall (▶ 138), is one of the city's

most beloved restaurants. And chef-owner Joachim Splichal still produces food that people adore, creative California-French cuisine that includes German and Austrian touches. His specialty is potatoes, cooked in a variety of innovative ways, ranging from horseradish-glazed to potato truffle chips. Try one of the five-course tasting menus, which may feature all-vegetarian dishes or all-shellfish variations, including a chocolate sea-shell dessert.

✚ 205 E2 ⊠ 145 S. Grand Avenue, Los Angeles ☎ (213) 972-3331 ⓦ Lunch Mon–Fri 11:30–1:30, dinner daily 5–10:45. Closed Jan 1 and Dec 25

Philippe the Original $

You might find yourself sitting next to a business executive, a cop or a street person at the long communal tables in this old-time downtown restaurant, where everyone comes for the French dip sandwiches: roast beef, lamb, pork or turkey on a French roll, dipped in natural juices, which the founder invented

in 1908. Philippe isn't much for aesthetics, with sawdust on the floor and lines of customers waiting to order at the counter. But prices are rock bottom – coffee is all of nine cents – and it's a classic LA experience.

✚ 205 E2 ⊠ 1001 N. Alameda Street, Los Angeles ☎ (213) 628-3781 ⓦ Daily 6 am–10 pm. Closed Thanksgiving and Dec 25

▼▼▼ Spago Beverly Hills $$$

This spin-off from the original Spago Hollywood (now closed) is the most glamorous of Wolfgang Puck's fleet of restaurants. You may well spot movie stars or studio heads here – possibly as they're being led to that prized open-air patio table ahead of you. Expect a wait, even with a reservation, and prepare for a high-decibel experience. But the California cuisine, which sports Asian, Mediterranean and Austrian accents – tempura soft-shell crab with black bean sauce is one winner – seldom

disappoints. A more informal bar menu includes Puck's trademark designer pizzas.

✚ 205 E2 ⊠ 176 N. Cañon Drive, Beverly Hills ☎ (310) 385-0880 ⓦ Lunch Mon–Fri 11:30–2:15, Sat 11:30–2:30; dinner Sun–Thu 6–10:30, Fri–Sat 5:30–11:30. Closed Thanksgiving and Dec 25

Twin Palms $–$$$

A converted warehouse, this huge, boisterous Pasadena restaurant, capable of seating hundreds, has an indoor dining room, an outdoor patio open to the sky, and two bars, with live music most nights. The French-influenced California cuisine is as rich and lively as the setting; soups, salads and desserts are strong points, but all the food here pleases. An all-around good experience, unless crowds bother you.

✚ 205 E2 ⊠ 101 W. Green Street, Pasadena ☎ (626) 577-2567 ⓦ Mon–Thu 11:30–10, Fri–Sat 11:30 am–midnight; Sun 10:30–3. Closed Dec 25

Where to... Stay

Prices

Expect to pay per room

$ under $100 per night **$$** $100–175 per night **$$$** over $175 per night

⊕⊕⊕ The Ambrose $$–$$$

The creators of this boutique hotel drew on sources such as feng shui principles and Asian art to produce an instant hit in Santa Monica. With its soothing colors, Italian bed linens, Aveda bath products and high-tech Internet hookups, there's plenty to like. You may not need all the amenities – room service is available 24 hours and a Pilates trainer is on call – but their presence typifies the attention to detail.

⊞ 205 E2 ⊠ **1255 20th Street, Santa Monica, CA 90404** ☎ **(310) 315-1555 or (877) 262-7673; fax: (310) 315-1556; email: info@ambrosehotel.com**

⊕⊕⊕⊕ Beverly Hills Hotel and Bungalows $$$

Opened in 1912, predating the city of Beverly Hills itself, this classic hotel has hosted the likes of Marilyn Monroe and Charlie Chaplin, and its famed Polo Lounge is the film industry's original power dining spot. The hotel is a shimmering pink beauty, set in a ritzy residential area. Rooms have marble bathrooms and stereos; the bungalows have wood-burning fireplaces.

⊞ 205 E2 ⊠ **9641 Sunset Boulevard, Beverly Hills, CA 90210** ☎ **(310) 276-2251 or (800) 283-8885; fax: (310) 887-2887; email: reservations@beverlyhillshotel.com**

⊕⊕⊕ Carlyle Inn $$

If you're looking for good value near Beverly Hills, try this 32-room, four-story European-style hotel. Amenities include in-room bathrobes, VCRs, coffee makers, ironing boards and irons, and safes; a hot tub and fitness room are on a sundeck available to all guests. Rates include a big buffet breakfast and afternoon wine and cheese. The hotel also operates a free daytime shuttle service within a 5-mile (8-kilometer) radius.

⊞ 205 E2 ⊠ **1119 S. Robertson Boulevard, West Los Angeles, CA 90035** ☎ **(310) 275-4445 or (800) 322-7595; fax: (310) 859-0496**

Disneyland® Resort $$–$$$

The three hotels in the Disney complex represent a universe unto themselves: they are conveniently located, the rooms are perfectly fine, and you have privileges – chief among them early admission to the two theme parks. There are plenty of distractions, from pools to video arcades to shops, and the many

restaurants serve everything from burgers to haute cuisine. **Disney's Grand Californian** (⊕⊕ ⊕⊕) is the nicest (and priciest) of the properties, but the **Disneyland Hotel** (⊕⊕⊕) and **Disney's Paradise Pier Hotel** (⊕⊕⊕) are more than suitable.

⊞ 205 E2 ⊠ **Disneyland Hotel: 1150 Magic Way, Anaheim, CA 92802; Disney's Grand Californian: 1600 S. Disneyland Drive, Anaheim, CA 92802; Disney's Paradise Pier Hotel: 1717 S. Disneyland Drives, Anaheim, CA 92802.** ☎ **(714) 956-6425 (all three hotels); fax: (714) 956-6582 (Disneyland Hotel), (714) 300-7701 (Disney's Grand Californian), (714) 776-5763 (Disney's Paradise Pier Hotel)**

⊕⊕⊕ The Georgian Hotel $$–$$$

This historic hotel with a turquoise and gold art-deco exterior will catch your eye on Santa Monica's Ocean Avenue. The architecture is right out of the 1930s, but the recently renovated rooms are nicely up to date, and most have ocean views.

Spend the late afternoon on the hotel's rattan chair-lined verandah with a drink in hand, just as Clark Gable and Carole Lombard once did. Service is friendly. The hotel's Speakeasy Restaurant plays off the Georgian's one-time reputation as a hideaway for gangsters.

✚ 205 E2 ⊠ 1415 Ocean Avenue, Santa Monica, CA 90401 ☎ (310) 395-9945 or (800) 538-8147; fax: (310) 451-3374; email: georgianhotel@georgianhotel.com

☞☞☞ Hotel Villa Portofino $-$$$

This Italian-style hotel fits in well with the Mediterranean feel of Avalon, Santa Catalina Island's main town. Located along Avalon's main street, it's convenient to the harbor, beach, restaurants and shops. Rooms have cable TV, and many have good views of the water; some come with fireplaces and refrigerators. You can also lounge on a private guest sundeck with harbor view. The hotel's restaurant,

Ristorante Villa Portofino, serves good Italian food.

✚ 205 E1 ⊠ 111 Crescent Avenue, Santa Catalina Island, CA 90704 ☎ (310) 510-0555; fax: (310) 510-0839; email: hotelvip@catalinas.net

☞☞☞ Inn at Laguna Beach $$-$$$

This three-story hotel, situated atop a cliff overlooking the Pacific Ocean, with flower-filled grounds, offers easy access to both beach and town. Many of the 70 rooms have ocean views. The wealth of room amenities is a big plus here: refrigerators, VCRs, bathrobes, hair dryers, irons and ironing boards, and complimentary newspaper and Continental breakfast are all included. There's also a heated swimming pool and a hot tub on a sunny terrace.

✚ 205 E2 ⊠ 211 N. Pacific Coast Highway, Laguna Beach, CA 92651 ☎ (949) 497-9722 or (800) 544-4479; fax: (949) 497-9972; email: info@innatlagunabeach.com

☞☞☞ Loews Santa Monica Beach Hotel $$$

You can stay in the city and still feel like you're at a beach resort at this hotel whose rear terrace opens right onto the beach, just two blocks from Santa Monica Pier. The design is eye-catching: A glass atrium towers above the lobby, while a glass-domed pool offers Pacific views and both indoor and outdoor swimming. Most of the airy rooms also have ocean vistas, some from private balconies. Color schemes mirror the hues of sand and sky.

✚ 205 E2 ⊠ 1700 Ocean Avenue, Santa Monica, CA 90401 ☎ (310) 458-6700 or (800) 235-6397; fax: (310) 458-6761

☞☞☞ Sunset Plaza Hotel $-$$

Though several of LA's priciest hotels are on the Sunset Strip, you don't have to pay top dollar to stay there. This Best Western property combines reasonable rates with a raft of amenities in the clean, attractively decorated rooms –

refrigerators, phones with voice mail, cable TV and complimentary newspapers among them. Many rooms have kitchens.

✚ 205 E2 ⊠ 8400 Sunset Boulevard, West Hollywood, CA 90069 ☎ (323) 654-0750 or (800) 421-3652; fax: (323) 650-6146

☞☞☞ Valadon Hotel $$

A pleasant refuge amid the hubbub of West Hollywood, the Valadon is run with verve by an expert staff. The look here is country French, a bit of an anomaly in groovy LA, but instead of seeming outré, the hotel is decidedly cozy and even a tad luxurious (not bad for the price). The rooms are spacious and many have the advantage of a balcony with city views; if your room doesn't, there's always the delightful rooftop garden.

✚ 205 E2 ⊠ 8822 Cynthia Street, West Hollywood, CA 90069 ☎ (310) 854-1114 or (800) 835-7997; fax (310) 657-2623; email: reservations@valadonhotel.com

Where to...
Shop

The range of merchandise in Los Angeles is staggering, whether you're looking for ultra-chic or retro fashions, fine antiques or Hollywood memorabilia, Mexican imports or surfer gear.

The best-known shopping area is swanky **Beverly Hills**, particularly high-gloss **Rodeo Drive** between Santa Monica and Wilshire boulevards, where you'll find an array of pricy jewelry and clothing stores: Cartier, Christian Dior, Harry Winston, Tiffany & Co., Van Cleef & Arpels, Battaglia, Bernini, BCBG Max Azria, Bijan (by appointment only), Prada, Chanel, Giorgio Armani, Gucci, Hermes and Versace. Brighton Way, just off Rodeo, has an Emporio Armani boutique and other noted retailers.

For all-purpose shopping, head to the huge **Beverly Center** (8500 Beverly Boulevard, West Hollywood, tel: 310/854-0070), home to some 200 stores, including Macy's, Bloomingdales and many boutiques.

Several big department stores are found along the 9500–9900 blocks of **Wilshire Boulevard**, including Barneys New York, Neiman-Marcus, Robinsons-May and Saks Fifth Avenue.

One of the funkiest, and sometimes trendiest, shopping streets is **Melrose Avenue**, between Fairfax and La Brea, where a variety of clothing stores carry both retro and new fashions. **Miu Miu** (8025 Melrose Avenue, tel: 323/651-0073) sells both women's and men's sportswear, while **Maxfield** (8825 Melrose Avenue, tel: 310/274-8800) sells cutting-edge designer gear. On the west end of Melrose, Tony Melrose Place, made famous by a TV show of the same name, is lined with high-end antiques shops.

Trendy areas come and go in LA, but three hot areas for clubwear, retro fashions and quirky boutiques are **North La Brea Avenue** and **Robertson Boulevard** in West Hollywood, and **Sunset Boulevard** in Los Feliz.

Farther west, on West Hollywood's famous Sunset Strip, Sunset Plaza offers a pleasant mix of sidewalk cafés and high-end shops. LA's best bookstore, **Book Soup** (8818 Sunset Boulevard, tel: 310/659-3110), is open till 11 pm and has a huge newsstand, carrying both domestic and foreign publications. A Virgin Megastore offers CDs and tapes.

Hollywood Boulevard, now rebounding from decades of seediness, is still a good place to comb stores for movie memorabilia and appropriately tacky souvenirs. **Frederick's of Hollywood** (6608 Hollywood Boulevard, tel: 323/466-8506) is legendary for lingerie.

The Citadel Factory Stores (5675 E. Telegraph Road, tel: 323/888-1220) are located in a landmark building off 1-5 and carry a wide selection of discount brand-name clothing.

The venerable **Farmers Market** (6333 W. 3rd Street) has dozens of stores and a top-flight food court.

Olvera Street, in the city's historic El Pueblo de Los Angeles downtown, is the place to find Mexican-style trinkets and souvenirs. The colorful **Grand Central Market** (317 S. Broadway), also downtown, is filled with exotic produce stands and food booths.

Universal CityWalk near Universal Studios has a number of offbeat stores, many geared toward kids, and a lively, offbeat ambience.

In **Santa Monica**, the pedestrian-only **3rd Street Promenade** is lined with a mix of boutiques, restaurants and movie theaters. At one end of it is **Santa Monica Place** (3rd St. and Broadway), which has three stories of shops and a huge food court.

Where to...
Be Entertained

For entertainment listings, check the free tabloid *LA Weekly*, the weekend Calendar section of the *Los Angeles Times*, or the *Los Angeles* magazine. For information on music and theater call the Music Center of Los Angeles County (tel: 213/972-7211), which gives 24-hour recorded information about the productions at the Dorothy Chandler Pavilion, the Ahmanson Theater and the Mark Taper Forum, among others. The Los Angeles Philharmonic performs at the Walt Disney Concert Hall.

NIGHTCLUBS

Hollywood and West Hollywood are the centers of nightlife. Nightclubs usually close by 2 am, when it's no longer legal to serve liquor. Remember that this week's hot, trendy club is next week's fading memory.

One of the enduring areas for action is West Hollywood's famed Sunset Strip, where you'll find **Whisky A Go Go** (8901 Sunset Boulevard, tel: 310/652-4202), the **Viper Room** (8852 Sunset Boulevard, tel: 310/358-1880), the **Key Club** (9039 Sunset Boulevard, tel: 310/786-1712) and the **House of Blues** (8430 Sunset Boulevard, tel: 323/848-5100), which all present big-name acts from rock, blues

and jazz, depending on the venue. The **Comedy Store** (8433 Sunset Boulevard, tel: 323/656-6225) has spawned a number of star stand-up comics.

Los Feliz and Silver Lake are two trendy areas for bars and clubs. Several gay and lesbian clubs are located along Santa Monica Boulevard in West Hollywood.

Classic movie theaters are attractions in and of themselves in Hollywood. Watching a flick at **Mann's Chinese Theatre** (6925 Hollywood Boulevard, tel: 323/464-8111) or **El Capitan** (6838 Hollywood Boulevard, tel: 323/467-7674) adds a touch of class and cachet to the experience.

THEATER AND CONCERT MUSIC

Tickets by telephone, with a service charge, are available through **Ticketmaster** (tel: 213/365-3500 or 714/740-2000).

Concerts and operas are held at the **Walt Disney Concert Hall** (111 S. Grand Avenue, tel: 323/850-2000) and the **Dorothy Chandler Pavilion** (135 N. Grand Avenue) in the Los Angeles Music Center. The season for the famous **Hollywood Bowl** (2301 Highland Avenue, tel: 323/850-2000), which presents open-air concerts by the LA Philharmonic Orchestra, is June to mid-September.

Major venues for stage include two theaters at the Los Angeles Music Center on Grand Avenue: the **Ahmanson Theater** and the **Mark Taper Forum**. The **Pantages** (6233 Hollywood Boulevard, Hollywood, tel: 323/468-1700) and the **Wiltern Theater** (3790 Wilshire Boulevard, Beverly Hills, tel: 213/380-5005) are both splendid art-deco theaters that present Broadway-style musicals and other productions.

The **John Anson Ford Amphitheater** (2580 Cahuenga Boulevard East, Hollywood, tel: 323/461-3673) is a pleasant place to watch a production under the stars in summer.

Southern California

In Four Days 154 – 155
Don't Miss 156 – 170
At Your Leisure 171 – 172
Where To 173 – 178

Getting Your Bearings

Southern California encompasses the state's two largest cities, Los Angeles and San Diego, but away from the coast much of the region is arid desert, where the color brown comes in more shades than you might imagine possible. The quest for water has in many ways defined Southern California, though with plentiful sources having been tapped in Northern California and points east, many people here take the continued flow of water for granted.

Such was not the case in the mid-1800s, when a band of 100 gold-seekers got lost and stumbled across a long, low valley. The giant lake it once held had long since dried up. The group suffered a torturous month of heat and dehydration. The one who didn't survive inspired the region's name: Death Valley.

Death Valley presents perhaps the desert's harshest face, but this land that at first glance appears so barren illustrates the resilience of living things: About 900 plant varieties and several rare wildlife species flourish here. In the Coachella Valley, which contains Palm Springs and other resort communities and is part of a different desert zone, the numbers are even higher.

As you head west to the coast, sagebrush and other low-lying desert shrubs give way to greenery and pinyon pines. You sense the moisture in the air and fog occasionally rolls in. Though San Diego has its hot days, ocean breezes often cool the air. Pleasant weather and dry skies have made San Diego a vacation mecca for outdoorsy types and families headed for the many theme parks. But this is a cultural oasis as well, with a slew of museums and an active performing arts scene.

The main north–south highway through Southern California is I-5, which connects Los Angeles and San Diego and ends at the U.S. border with Mexico. I-15 heads north and east from San Diego through the desert and beyond to Las Vegas, Nevada. I-10 heads east from Los Angeles into the Palm Springs area and then on to Arizona. Except in parts of San Diego and downtown Palm Springs, a car is pretty much essential.

Previous page: Death Valley

The Agua Caliente originally settled in the Coachella Valley centuries ago

⭐ **Don't Miss**
- **1** San Diego ➤ 156
- **2** Palm Springs ➤ 165
- **4** Death Valley National Park ➤ 168

At Your Leisure
- **3** Sequoia and Kings Canyon National Parks ➤ 171
- **5** Mojave Desert ➤ 171
- **6** Anza-Borrego Desert State Park ➤ 172

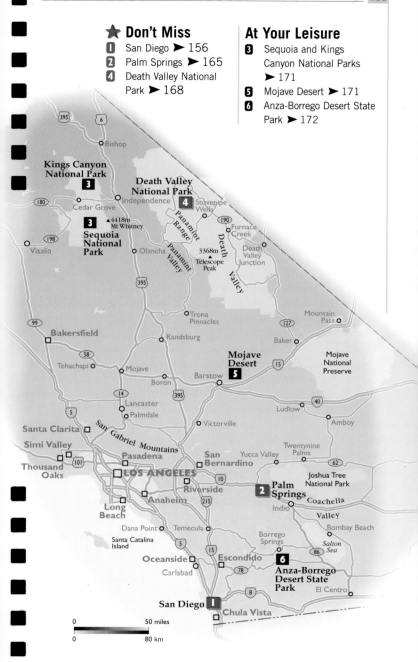

Southern California in Four Days

You could zip past Southern California's highlights in three days, but most people spend at least two days each in San Diego, Palm Springs and Death Valley. The one-day and two-day itineraries below will provide a rousing introduction to the three areas.

Two Days in ❶ San Diego (➤ 156–164)

Day 1

Morning
Begin your day by arriving early at the world-famous **San Diego Zoo**.

Afternoon
Slip up to **La Jolla** for a late lunch, then explore the area around La Jolla Cove. As the afternoon winds down, head south along Coast Boulevard, La Jolla Boulevard and then Mission Boulevard to **Pacific Beach**. Walk out on the Crystal Pier, fun anytime and a magical place at sunset.

Evening
Have dinner at Anthony's Star of the Sea Room (➤ 173), where the seafood's as peerless as the sea views. After dinner stroll the **Gaslamp Quarter,** stopping at a nightclub to hear some jazz or blues.

Day 2

Morning
Wake yourself up for a two-hour harbor cruise, then walk south along the Embarcadero for a peek at **Seaport Village**.

Afternoon
Have lunch in the Gaslamp Quarter at the Sammy's Woodfired Pizza (➤ 174), then take the San Diego Trolley to **Old Town State Historic Park**.

Evening
If the weather's fine and you're feeling romantic, take a gondola ride in Mission Bay (book in advance to ensure a slot) and have dinner at Parallel 33 (reservation recommended; ➤ 173); otherwise head directly to Montanas.

Day 3

A Day in **2** Palm Springs (➤ 165–167)

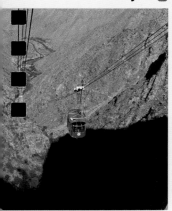

Morning
Board the **Palm Springs Aerial Tramway** (left) for breathtaking views of the Coachella Valley. Back near sea level, view the natural history and art exhibits at the **Palm Springs Desert Museum**.

Afternoon
Have lunch at Edgardo's Café Veracruz (494 N. Palm Canyon Drive, tel: 760/320-3558), known for its Mexican specialties. Afterward, stroll a bit of Palm Canyon Drive. If it's not too hot, visit the **Indian Canyons** and walk one of the shorter loop trails within Palm Canyon.

Evening
A light snack will get you through the Fabulous Palm Springs Follies (show starts at 7 pm), after which you can have a late and ritzy dinner at Le Vallauris (385 W. Tahquitz Canyon Way, tel: 760/325-5059).

Day 4

A Day in **4** Death Valley (➤ 168–170)

Morning
Few experiences inspire awe as thoroughly as a Death Valley sunrise – catch the moment at **Zabriskie Point**. The thrills continue to the south on a drive through Twenty Mule Team Canyon and farther on at Dante's View. Reverse course and head north to the Furnace Creek Ranch, where you can have breakfast or an early lunch.

Afternoon
Head south again, this time on Badwater Road. Go all the way to Badwater (right), stopping at Artists Palette and Golden Canyon on the way back. Stop for lunch or a snack at the Furnace Creek Ranch before heading up to the Harmony Borax Works and the Sand Dunes near Stovepipe Wells.

Evening
Have dinner at the Furnace Creek Inn (➤ 174) or the steakhouse at the Furnace Creek Ranch (➤ 176).

San Diego

California's sunny, second largest city has long played a role in the state's history. Spanish friars established the first of their California missions in San Diego. Most people come for the near-perfect climate and attractions – the zoo, Old Town and La Jolla are among the must-sees – but you may find yourself wanting to learn more about this city's rich heritage.

San Diego County sprawls across 4,255 square miles (11,020 sq kilometers) that include, among others, the cities of San Diego, Del Mar, Carlsbad, Coronado and Escondido. The major sights to see lie north of San Diego's downtown – especially on a first visit you'll be unlikely to head south of downtown unless you're making a shopping excursion to Tijuana, Mexico. Balboa Park is due north of downtown, Coronado is west of downtown, and Old Town, Mission Bay and La Jolla are to its northwest.

🔲 206 A1

Maritime Museum of San Diego
✉ 1492 N. Harbor Drive, at Ash Street
☎ (619) 234-9153 🕐 Daily 9–8
🚌 Bus 7/7A/7B; Trolley (Santa Fe Depot) 🚹 Moderate

San Diego Aircraft Carrier Museum
✉ 1335 N. Harbor Drive, at Navy Pier
☎ (619) 702-7700 🕐 Daily 10–5
🚌 Bus 7/7A/7B, Trolley (Santa Fe Depot) 🚹 Moderate

Harbor Cruises
Hornblower Cruises ✉ 1066 N. Harbor Drive, near Broadway (cruises only) ☎ (619) 686-8715 San Diego Harbor Excursions ✉ 1050 N. Harbor Drive, Broadway Pier (cruises, Coronado Ferry) ☎ (619) 234-4111
🚌 Bus 7/7A/7B, Trolley (Santa Fe Depot) 🚹 Moderate–expensive

Seaport Village
✉ Harbor Drive from Pacific Highway to Market Place ☎ (619) 235-4014
🚌 7/7A/7B; Trolley (Seaport Village)

Gaslamp Quarter
✉ 4th, 5th and 6th avenues between Broadway and Harbor Drive 🚌 Bus 1, 3/3A, 4, 5/5A, 16; Trolley (5th Avenue)

The Waterfront and Downtown San Diego

Several points of interest lie along the **Embarcadero**, south from Ash Street on N. Harbor Drive and then southeast on Harbor Drive to the San Diego Convention Center.

The **Maritime Museum of San Diego** maintains the *Star of India*, a restored 1863 bark, on board which you'll get a vivid sense of life at sea. Moored to the north is the *Berkeley*, an 1898 steam-powered ferry with deluxe appointments – don't miss that stained glass. Nearby is the USS *Midway*, home to the **San Diego Aircraft Carrier Museum**, which has engaging exhibits about naval aviation. You can tour the mess hall, crew berths, bomb-making area, and more. One- and two-hour **harbor cruises** sail from piers south of the museum. The longer trips, which take in more of the harbor and swing by Point Loma, are best. Ferries to Coronado also depart from here.

A touristy collection of shops, restaurants and other diversions, among them street artists, **Seaport Village** has a winning design and fine harbor views going for it.

The reclamation of San Diego's 19th-century **Gaslamp Quarter** is one of urban America's great success stories. Cast-iron and other buildings, many of which had been slated for demolition, were converted into stores, restaurants and nightclubs. The district, whose liveliest streets are 4th and 5th avenues between Market Street and Harbor Drive, is more fun by night (➤ 178), but there are a few historic sights to visit by day. You can learn about these at the **William Heath Davis House** (410 Island Avenue, at 4th Avenue, tel: 619/233-4692). Hours vary, so call ahead. The bar at the **U.S. Grant Hotel** (326 Broadway) is a swank, old-timey place for a cocktail.

Facing page: San Diego commerce shifted to the waterfront in the 1800s

Beyond Downtown
Coronado

For a low-key excursion, take a 15-minute ferry to Coronado. The sights to see include Victorian-era mansions along the waterfront, the stores and small parks along Orange Avenue, the 19th-

Multi-Horticultural

Two restful stops near El Prado are the **Alcazar Garden** and the **Japanese Friendship Garden.** Tropical and subtropical plants inhabit the **Botanical Building,** a large open-air structure made of redwood lathing.

century Hotel Del Coronado and Silver Strand State Beach. You can rent a bicycle at the ferry landing (the terrain's mostly level).

🚌 Bus 901, 902, 903, 904

Cabrillo National Monument

The explorer Juan Rodriguez Cabrillo dropped anchor in 1542 not far from the monument that bears his name. "A very good enclosed port" was his description of San Diego Bay. Exhibits at the visitor center here will clue you into the history, but on a clear day you'll need no assistance appreciating the views of the Pacific Ocean, San Diego, the Cuyamaca Mountains and even Mexico.

✉ 1800 Cabrillo Memorial Drive (southern end of Catalina Boulevard) ☎ (619) 557-5450 🕐 Daily 9–6:15, Jul to early Sep; 9–5:15, rest of year 🚌 Bus 26 💲 Inexpensive

Balboa Park

With approximately 1,200 acres (485 hectares), Balboa Park ranks as one of the nation's largest urban park (greenswards), but attractions here are intellectual as well as natural. The **San Diego Zoo** (▶ 160) takes up most of the park's northwestern quadrant, but south of it lies **El Prado,** a long, wide promenade lined on both sides with museums and other cultural institutions. Nearly all the ornate Spanish-Moorish structures along El Prado were built for

The ornate Casa del Prado, along Balboa Park's El Prado (The Promenade)

Music Fills the Air

Free outdoor concerts take place every Sunday (2 pm) at **Spreckels Organ Pavilion**, an elevated band shell flanked by a neoclassical colonnade that curves grace-fully toward the audience. With 4,500-plus pipes a-playing, music fills the air. The organist also performs on Monday at 8 pm from mid-June through August. (Pan American Road E., tel: 619/702-8138.)

international fairs in 1915 and 1935–36. Chandeliers hang in the arched walkways that connect many of the buildings. The exterior decorative touches, such as the scallop-shaped entry arch to the San Diego Museum of Art and the accompanying heraldry, medallions and scrollwork, are quite extraordinary.

Pick up maps and events calendars at the **Balboa Park Visitor Center** (House of Hospit-ality, 1549 El Prado, open: daily 9:30–4:30).

The park's standout museums include the **Mingei International Museum** (exciting folk-art displays), the **San Diego Aerospace Museum** (surveying the complete history of flight) and the **Reuben E. Fleet Space Theater and Science Center** (home to a domed Omnimax theater and clever interac-tive exhibits). The **San Diego Automotive Museum** has captivating specimens, from Model Ts and early prototypes to Corvettes and recent sport cars.

Three facilities share space in the Casa de Balboa. The **Museum of San Diego History** and the **Museum of Photographic Arts** both mount interesting shows. Less erudite, but well worth a stop, is the **San Diego Model Railroad Museum**, where members of model-railroad clubs have erected elaborate

Legoland California

Torrey Pines State Beach and Reserve

5

S21

Birch Aquarium at Scripps

Ellen Scripps Browning Park

La Jolla Caves

Museum of Contemporary Art, San Diego

LA JOLLA

JACOB

DEKEMA FREEWAY

SAN

DIEGO FREEWAY

52

805

0 3 miles
0 5 km

PACIFIC BEACH

5

274

163

San Diego Wild Animal Park

15

Mission San Diego de Alcala

MISSION BEACH

Mission Bay Park

SeaWorld

Mission Valley

MISSION VALLEY FWY

8

SAN

Old Town

San Diego International Airport

163

San Diego Zoo

Balboa Park Museums

DIEGO

POINT LOMA

209

Maritime Museum

94

MONTGOMERY FWY

15

805

75

Cabrillo National Monument

CORONADO

San Diego Bay

5

54

Area covered by Central San Diego map

Silver Strand State Beach

exhibits of real, planned and imagined routes. The **San Diego Museum of Art** often hosts important traveling exhibits; its key holdings include Renaissance and Spanish baroque paintings and California art. The nearby **Timken Museum of Art** is known for its Russian icons. **Centro Cultural de la Raza**, on Park Boulevard south of El Prado, presents works by Mexican and Chicano artists.

Reputable but missable if you're pressed for time are the **San Diego Museum of Man**, which specializes in the anthropology of the American Southwest and Latin America, and the **San Diego Museum of Natural History** (unless the special exhibits sound appealing). The **San Diego Hall of Champions – Sports Museum** honors local sporting heroes.

✉ Balboa Park, Park Boulevard (12th Avenue), off Highway 163 or I-5
☎ (619) 239-0512 (information and museum hours) 🕐 Park: 24 hours. Museums: hours vary (a few closed Mon and/or Tue) 🚌 Bus 1, 3, 3A, 7, 7A, 7B, 25 💲 Park: free. Museums: inexpensive–expensive

> ### Don't Forget Your Passport
> The **Passport to Balboa Park** gains you entry to a dozen Balboa Park museums at a huge discount. Pick up passports at the visitor center (► 159) or at the participating museums.

San Diego Zoo

Simply put, the San Diego Zoo is one of the world's best, a carefully constructed menagerie where the flora is said to be worth even more than the fauna. The array of exotic animals staggers the mind – gazelles, meerkats, bearded pigs, Himalayan snowcats, and the showstoppers, the pandas. Large-scale environments include ones for hippos, polar bears (quite the performers), primates, denizens of the Asian rain forest and some highly colorful birds. Animal shows take place throughout the day – the schedule is on the map provided when you enter the zoo.

The zoo straddles a canyon, so you may have to cover steep terrain. Moving walkways assist you on the steepest climbs – back uphill from the pandas, for instance. For an extra fee, the **Guided Bus Tour** allows you to get an overview of the park

Colorful residents of Flamingo Lagoon at San Diego Zoo

on a 40-minute tour. You can't get off the regular bus, but several pauses along the way are long enough that you may not feel the need to return to some exhibits, saving you steps and freeing time to see other areas. Your ticket is also good for a ride on the **Express Bus**, which you can get off and reboard as you please. On both buses, if you sit on the right side, you won't have to peer over other passengers as much as on the left. The **Skyfari** aerial tram (included with the package that includes the Guided Bus Tour) crosses the canyon between the zoo entrance and the Polar Bear Plunge. The best of the zoo's cafés and restaurants is **Albert's** (seafood, steaks, pastas, chicken, salads), but also good are the **Canyon Café** (Mexican) and **Sydney's Grill** (salads, pastas, sandwiches).

> ### Kids' Delight
> Try the art projects and interactive exhibits at **Children's Museum of San Diego** reopening in 2005. (200 W. Island Avenue, tel: 619/233-8792, open: Tue–Fri 10–3, Sat–Sun 10–4. Closed Jan 1, Jul 4, Thanksgiving, Dec 25. Bus: 4; Trolley: Convention Center West. Admission: inexpensive.)

✉ Off Park Boulevard, Balboa Park ☎ (619) 718-3000 🕐 Daily 7:30 am–9 pm, late Jun to early Sep (grounds close at 10); 9–4, rest of year (grounds close at 5 or 6) 🚌 Bus 7/7A/7B
💲 Expensive

SeaWorld Adventure Park
SeaWorld's highlights include the killer-whale and dolphin shows, the shark, penguin and polar-bear exhibits, and the Journey to Atlantis thrill ride. SeaWorld serves up a reasonably good mix of education and entertainment, the latter including the thrilling Shipwreck Rapids water ride. Tickets comes at a price but you're more than likely to have a good time.

✉ SeaWorld Drive, off I-5 (follow signs), Mission Bay ☎ (619) 226-3901 🕐 Hours vary, but generally 10–dusk (late hours in summer) 🚌 Bus 9, 27 💲 Expensive

Old Town
Even many San Diegans find their city's history a tad dry in the telling, but the 19th-century highlights come to life in colorful **Old Town State Historic Park.** Restored or replicated buildings line dirt streets set around the original town plaza. You get an inkling of the past, but the feel is refreshingly un-museumlike.

The *Old California Gazette* souvenir newspaper, available for free all around Old Town, contains a map. A good starting point is the **Robinson-Rose House,** where a diorama and early photos depict Old Town in the 1800s. From here head south (to your right as you exit the front door) to the re-created **San Diego House** and what was the **Commercial House** restaurant (listed on the Gazette map as the U.S. House). East of this is **Racine & Laramie,** San Diego's

Crowd-pleasing dolphins entertain at SeaWorld

first cigar store, which has been painstakingly re-created to recall the 1870s. It is still in business.

Don't miss the no-nonsense **Mason Street School,** a one-room wooden structure built in 1865 and tucked behind the **Brick Courthouse.** It's furnished for a late-1800s schoolday, complete with a punishment chart prescribing various numbers of lashes, depending on the infraction. And speaking of torture, those leery even of today's techniques may find the exhibits in the nearby **McKinstry Dentist Office** too harrowing to view.

North of the dentist's office stands the sturdy **Casa de Estudillo** – notice the broad ceiling beams tied together

Old Town celebrates San Diego's multifaceted past

with cowhide. Furnished to illustrate the lifestyle of an important ranching family around the mid-19th century, the casa is the largest original adobe in Old Town. Across Calhoun Street is **Seeley Stables,** which contains an excellent collection of stagecoaches, some of them behind the main building.

Heading down Calhoun past the **Casa de Bandini** – a city landmark that houses a festive Mexican restaurant – you'll shortly run into the even more festive **Bazaar del Mundo.** Bright yellows, reds and oranges are among the clues that this outdoor mini-mall celebrates the city's Mexican heritage.

From Old Town head north on Taylor Street and east up Presidio Drive to the **Presidio** (great views of downtown and beyond), where the **Junipero Serra Museum,** a repository of San Diego artifacts, sits on the site of the original Mission San Diego.

✉ Old Town San Diego State Historic Park, bordered by Taylor, Juan, Twiggs and Congress streets (main parking lot off Twiggs) ☎ (619) 220-5422 🚌 Bus 5/5A, 6, 9, 26, 28, 29, 34/34A, 35/35A, 44, 81, 908; Trolley (Old Town) 🎟 Free

The Beaches

On a sunny day, with leisure sailors taking to the waters and picnickers cavorting on shore, the 4,600-acre (1,860-hectare) **Mission Bay Park** (Mission Bay Drive, off I-8) becomes a jolly place indeed. Roller-coasters zoom and carousel horses twirl at nearby **Belmont Park** (3146 Mission Boulevard, at West Mission Bay Drive, tel: 619/491-2988), which abuts wide and sandy **Mission Beach.** Immediately north lies **Pacific Beach**, where the **Crystal Pier** (Garnet Avenue, west of Mission Boulevard) juts so far into the ocean that you'll get a fascinating rear perspective on surfers as they battle the waves. (Bus: 9, 27, 30, 34/34A)

La Jolla

Linguists disagree over the origins of the name of *La Jolla* (pronounced La Hoya), some saying it derives from the Spanish word for jewel, others the one for hole. But few would dispute that this coastal town, where tall palms tower over fancy Spanish-Mediterranean and modernist homes, is one of San Diego's gems. A good walking tour might begin with the **La Jolla Caves** (1325 Coast Boulevard). Here you enter a bungalow, pay the fee and head down 133 steps to the caves (the climb back up is steep). A platform at the base of the steps has water and shoreline views – the waves break near it at high tide, a thrilling sight.

From La Jolla Caves continue west and then south past rocks inhabited by pelicans and other species. The **Brockton Villa Restaurant** (1235 Coast Boulevard, tel: 858/454-7393), great for lunch or weekend brunch, perches above these rocks and sheltered **La Jolla Cove.** Wander out among the tide pools during low tide and you'll see crabs, snails and other creatures amid the rocks and multihued seaweed.

You can explore more of the coast south past **Ellen Scripps Browning Park,** the grassy area that abuts La Jolla Cove. Or head inland a block to the **Museum of Contemporary Art,**

San Diego (700 Prospect Street, tel: 858/454-3541). The postmodern building is more noteworthy than the art collection, though significant post-World War II California artists are represented.

Prospect Street, a few blocks north of the museum, is one of several tony shopping streets. **Girard Avenue** is another. Stop for a genteel cocktail in the ocean-view lobby bar of **La Valencia Hotel** (1132 Prospect Street), built in 1926. From here or the nearby **Crab Catcher** restaurant (1298 Prospect Street, tel: 858/454-9587), which serves up tasty seafood and appetizers – happy hour's a real bargain – you might see a pod of dolphins swimming just beyond the cove.

Heading north from Prospect, follow signs off Torrey Pines Road to La Jolla Shores Drive and turn west on Avenida de la Playa. This will lead you to flat, sandy, palm-lined **La Jolla Shores Beach,** yet another of those Southern California strands that look like a movie set (which occasionally it is).

Low tide in La Jolla reveals an amazing array of creatures

Mission San Diego de Alcalá

Franciscan padres founded Mission San Diego de Alcalá in 1769 near Old Town but relocated the mission to its present site in 1774. Native Americans promptly burned down the first church, an 1803 earthquake leveled its successor, and the third building deteriorated until restoration began during the 20th century. Notable features are the 46-foot (14-meter) campanario (bell tower), gardens (roses, bougainvillea and indigenous succulents) and the long, narrow main church – constructed that way because taller trees for use as beams weren't available. (10818 San Diego Mission Road, tel: 619/281-8449, open: daily 9–4:45. Closed Thanksgiving and Dec 25. Bus: 13; Trolley: Mission San Diego. Admission: inexpensive.)

Off Torrey Pines farther north lies the **Birch Aquarium at Scripps** (2300 Expedition Way, tel: 858/534-3474), which has knockout ocean views and equally breathtaking sea-life and oceanographic exhibits. If you continue north, you'll eventually run into **Torrey Pines State Beach and Reserve** (N. Torrey Pines Road, south of Carmel Valley Road, tel: 858/755-2063), where you can investigate the many migrating shorebirds or just relax on the beach.

✉ From downtown San Diego, take I-5 north, Ardrath Road west and Torrey Pines Road (south to Coast Boulevard, north to La Jolla Shores) 🚌 Bus 30, 34/34A

Legoland California

This theme park based on the colorful snap-together toys contains rides, games, interactive attractions and other diversions for the 2-to-10 set. Everything's scaled small, and judging by the squeals of delight, this suits the target audience just right.

✉ 1 Legoland Drive, east on Cannon Road from I-5, Carlsbad ☎ (760) 918-5346 🕐 Daily 10–5 (later in summer; call for times) 🚌 County Bus 344 (from Coaster train) 💲 Expensive

San Diego Wild Animal Park

Most of the nearly 1,000 developed acres (405 hectares) of this facility associated with the San Diego Zoo are given over to large-scale environments viewed on a 55-minute railway tour. You'll see rhinos, giraffes and lesser-known creatures living more or less as they would in the wild. Back near the entrance, you can step close to giraffes and other animals in the Heart of Africa, and there's a walk-through aviary. California condors, desert bighorn sheep, burrowing owls and other North American animals inhabit the Condor Ridge exhibit. Some great stunts take place at the Bird Show Amphitheater.

✉ 15500 San Pasqual Valley Road, Escondido, Highway 78 (take Via Rancho Parkway exit east from I-15) ☎ (760) 747-8702 🕐 Daily from 9; closing times vary 🚌 Bus 307 (Mon–Sat only) 💲 Expensive

Palm Springs

When it's cloudy in San Diego or Los Angeles, or anytime Southern Californians feel the need to unwind, their thoughts often turn to Palm Springs. "Perfect climate, wonderful scenery, pure mountain air," declared an 1887 newspaper advertisement for what was briefly known as Palm Valley. The mountain and desert air may not be as pristine as they were in days past, but, except during the very hot summers, the climate is agreeable and the scenery varied.

The city of Palm Springs, the hub of the **Coachella Valley**, lies at its western edge. About 250,000 people live in the valley year-round but during the winter the population expands to about 320,000. Most of the ultrarich reside (often in gated communities) in **Rancho Mirage, Palm Desert** and **La Quinta**, all on Highway 111 east of Palm Springs. Other valley towns include the resort area of **Desert Hot Springs** and relatively laid-back **Cathedral City** and **Indio**. The southern entrance to Joshua Tree National Park (► 167) is 47 miles (75 kilometers) east of Palm Springs.

The pace in Palm Springs began to pick up in the 1920s and 1930s, when it became a favorite getaway of Hollywood's elite. Actors, directors and producers

Golfing, shopping and lounging are major activities in Palm Springs

relaxed at La Quinta Hotel (now La Quinta Resort & Club) and El Mirador Hotel and frolicked and played tennis at the Racquet Club. Radio stars such as Jack Benny sometimes broadcast their shows from their vacation paradise.

According to local surveys, shopping is the number-one tourist activity in the Palm Springs area. Three key shopping districts are **Palm Canyon Drive** in Palm Springs, **El Paseo** street in Palm Desert (The Gardens complex, at 73-585 El Paseo, is a good place to start) and the **Desert Hills Premium Outlets** (Fields Road, off I-10, tel: 909/849-6641) in Cabazon.

Golfing, sitting by the pool and taking a spa treatment are other popular diversions. **Tahquitz Creek Palm Springs Golf Resort** (1885 Golf Club Drive, tel: 760/328-1005) is a major public course. Two good spas are the moderately priced **Spa Resort Casino** (100 N. Indian Canyon Drive, tel: 760/778-1772) and the more upscale **Spa La Quinta** (La Quinta Resort & Club, 49-499 Eisenhower Drive, La Quinta, tel: 760/777-4800). The two sightseeing experiences not to miss are the Palm Springs Aerial Tramway and Joshua Tree National Park.

The Agua Caliente Band of Cahuilla Indians own much of the Coachella Valley

Palm Springs
✚ 206 A2 ✉ Highway 111, off I-10 (110 miles/177 km from Los Angeles) ☎ (800) 347-7746 (tourist information)

Palm Springs Aerial Tramway
✉ Tramway Road off N. Palm Canyon Drive (at San Rafael Road) ☎ (760) 325-1391 or (888) 515-8726 🕐 Mon–Fri 10–8, Sat–Sun 8–8 (last car down: 9:45), early Sep to late May; Mon–Fri 10–9, Sat–Sun, 8 am–9 pm (last car down: 10:45), rest of year 🚌 SunBus 24 (2-mile/3-km walk uphill to Valley Station) 💷 Expensive

Joshua Tree National Park
✉ Main entrance: Utah Trail, off Highway 62, Twentynine Palms ☎ (760) 367-5500 💷 Moderate (per carload, fee valid for one week)

With its rotating tram cars, the **Palm Springs Aerial Tramway** provides a thrilling ascent up 10,804-foot (3,293-meter) Mt. San Jacinto. At certain points along the ride from the Valley Station (elevation 2,643 feet/805 meters) to the Mountain Station (8,501 feet/2,591 meters), the tram dangles in mid air between solid slabs of grayish granite several hundred feet high. The terrain changes from desert to arctic/alpine – from cacti and yuccas to pines and firs of the type found in Alaska – and the temperature drops about 40 degrees Fahrenheit (22 degrees Celsius). You can hike or picnic (bring your own food; the restaurant's fare is mediocre).

The classy **Palm Springs Desert Museum** (101 Museum Drive, tel: 760/325-0189) provides a fine introduction to the desert's cultural and natural history. On the ground level are rooms with Native American art, furniture made by the Western film actor George Montgomery and exhibits about the desert's flora and fauna. The top level contains a representative sample of post-World War II American art.

Cacti, agave and other desert plants inhabit the marvelously overgrown **Moorten Botanical Garden** (1701 S. Palm Canyon Drive, tel: 760/327-6555).

Tall palm trees line Palm Canyon, the lushest of the **Indian Canyons** (Indian Canyon Drive, 3 miles (5 kilometers) south of E. Palm Canyon Drive, tel: 760/325-5673 for guided tour times). As you hike through the canyon, you may spot rock art and Indian food preparation areas. The most easily identified of the latter are the smooth indentations in rocks where acorns were mashed to make flour.

The 1,200-acre (485-hectare) **Living Desert Zoo & Gardens** (47-900 Portola Avenue, north of Highway 111, tel: 760/346-5694) contains impressive exotic species from around the world.

Joshua Tree National Park straddles two distinct desert regions. The more interesting terrain – lunarlike boulders towering over cacti, Joshua trees and other succulents – is in the high desert to the north.

TAKING A BREAK

Have a snack at casual **Hair of the Dog English Pub** (238 N. Palm Canyon Drive, Palm Springs, tel: 760/323-9890). In Palm Desert try the **Daily Grill** (73-061 El Paseo, tel: 760/779-9911).

Mexican wolves are among the Living Desert's denizens

PALM SPRINGS: INSIDE INFO

Top tips If you're without a car, call **VIP Express Taxi** (tel: 760/322-2264) or **SunBus** (tel: 760/343-3451).

• On Thursday night, S. Palm Canyon Drive between Tahquitz Canyon Way and Baristo Road becomes a **pedestrians-only open-air market**, with street musicians and food and crafts vendors.

Death Valley National Park

The western slopes of the barren Panamint Mountains often glow a soothing red in the early morning sun. Within an hour, red gives way to warmish browns. But as the day unfolds in Death Valley, the colors quickly mutate into brighter, more severe hues, a fitting visual metaphor for the treacherous beauty of what on many days is the hottest place on earth.

Furnace Creek, the valley's hub, contains a resort and some no-nonsense lodgings, a gas station, a grocery store and a few restaurants. Exhibits at the National Park Service visitor center describe the region's geology and wildlife; and park rangers can give you details and maps about short and long hiking possibilities. Read and heed the warnings about dealing with the heat and other conditions in Death Valley.

🞣 205 F5 ✉ Highway 190 (east and north from US 395 on Highway 178 and Panamint Valley Road; east on Highway 190) ☎ (760) 786-2331 💵 Moderate (per carload, valid for one week)

A road at the southern end of Furnace Creek leads south from Highway 190 to three points of interest: **Golden Canyon,** where a short hike will introduce you to the area's terrain; the multihued rocks of **Artists Palette**; and the salt flats of **Badwater,** at 282 feet (86 meters) below sea level the lowest point in the Western Hemisphere. (Across the Badwater Road from the parking area, look up the hillside for the sign that indicates sea level.) The unpaved loop road to Artists Palette is one-way heading north, so most people visit this sight on the way back from Badwater.

A bit farther south (and east) of Furnace Creek, Highway 190 passes serenely desolate **Zabriskie Point.** Most of the land here is sandy-colored, though to the north are some reddish-brown hills – the point at which they meet looks like a swirl of coffee and chocolate ice cream. About a mile farther is **Twenty Mule Team Canyon**, seen on an exciting unpaved loop so narrow in some places that you can touch the canyon walls from your car. Past this a few miles, Highway 190 forks left and Dante's View Road forks right, rising for 13.3 miles (21 kilometers) to more than 5,000 feet at **Dante's View,** which yields a stunning panorama (especially at sunrise or sunset) of nearly the entire valley, brown mountains rising from the white salt beds.

To the north of Furnace Creek off Highway 190 are the remains of the **Harmony Borax Works**, where 19th-century

Vital Statistics

Acreage: 3.3 million

Average annual rainfall: Less than 2 inches (5 cm)

Hottest temperatures recorded, Fahrenheit: 134 (57° C; air), 200 (93° C; ground)

Annual visitation: 1.2 million

Highest point: Telescope Peak (11,049 feet/3,367 m above sea level)

Lowest point: Badwater (282 feet (86 m) below sea level)

Death Valley looks barren at first glance, but it's not

Scotty's Castle's namesake was a swindling bon vivant

miners and processors of borax spent grueling days. A little farther north, past the road to Scotty's Castle (below), even the slightest wind alters the shape of a long stretch of sand dunes. A gravel road leads from the highway to a parking lot from which you can hike into the dunes.

The gravel road continues north past the lot to the road to **Scotty's Castle** (tel: 760/786-2395); make a left if you've come this way. The castle, 60 miles (96 kilometers) north of Furnace Creek, can only be seen on one-hour tours, with space available on a first-come, first-served basis. The Spanish-style house is named for Walter E. Scott (also known as Death Valley Scotty), the genial con man and raconteur who swindled but charmed Albert Johnson, the Chicago millionaire who actually built it. The fanciful appointments include medieval-inspired wrought-iron chandeliers, carved redwood beams and glazed ceramic tiles. Before or after your trip to the castle, take the detour to nearby **Ubehebe Crater** (follow the signs), the impressive product of a volcanic eruption a thousand years ago.

DEATH VALLEY: INSIDE INFO

Top tips Drink plenty of water (up to 2 gallons/7.6 liters per day is recommended) to **avoid dehydration.**
• Fuel up before you head into the valley – **stations are few and far between.**
• Restaurant food and groceries are expensive, so if you're on a budget, **stock a cooler in Ridgecrest** (➤ opposite) or elsewhere.
• West of the dunes on Highway 190 is **Stovepipe Wells,** a small town with basic services.

Hidden gem Not much goes on in **Death Valley Junction,** southeast of Furnace Creek where highways 190 and 127 meet, but the small town's **Amargosa Opera House** (tel: 760/852-4441) draws crowds nonetheless for engaging performances of "dance mime in a program of musical theater." Check it out.

At Your Leisure

3 Sequoia and Kings Canyon National Parks

Less-trafficked than Yosemite yet equally beautiful, these two tree-studded parks are often visited together. At Grant Grove Visitor Center, you can learn about **Kings Canyon National Park** attractions. The highlight is the scenic drive (closed in winter) along Highway 180 through the Cedar Grove area. The trip (90 minutes each way) follows the twists and turns of the south fork of the Kings River through lush and then drier terrain before deadending. Three miles (5 kilometers) east of Grant Grove Village on Highway 180 is the parking area for the short hike to **Roaring River Falls**, and farther on a 1-mile (1.6-kilometer) trail winds to scenic **Zumwalt Meadow**.

The Generals Highway leads south from Kings Canyon into **Sequoia National Park**, whose Lodgepole Visitor Center contains exhibits about both parks. Rangers sell tickets to the nearby not-to-be-missed **Crystal**

Cave, a marble cavern with several huge "rooms" that are viewable only between mid-May and late September on guided tours. The rangers can also direct you to the trails, meadows and sequoia groves of the Giant Forest area and to **Moro Rock**, a granite formation that shoots 6,725 feet (2,050 meters) from the Giant Forest floor.

🔢 205 D5 ✉ Kings Canyon National Park, Highway 180; Sequoia National Park, Highway 198 and the Generals Highway ☎ (559) 565-3134 (both parks) 💵 Moderate (per car-load, fee valid for one week at both parks)

5 Mojave Desert

The Mojave Desert wraps around the southern portion of Death Valley

Kings Canyon National Park 3

(180) Cedar Grove ○ Independence

3 ▲4418m Mt Whitney

Sequoia National Park ○ Olancha

Panamint Valley

(395)

○ Trona Pinnacles

○ Randsburg

Mojave Desert

Barstow 5 (15)

National Park. The town of **Ridgecrest**, on the desert's western side at US 395 and Highway 178, serves as a park gateway. Fuel up and buy groceries, water and ice at **Albertson's** (927 S. China Lake Boulevard) or one of the other stores – provisions are more expensive and in shorter supply in Death Valley.

Much of the Ridgecrest area lay under water eons ago, a point made clear by the **Trona Pinnacles** (RM 143, off Highway 178, 22 miles (35 kilometers) east of Ridgecrest); the road off Highway 178 is dirt

Giant sequoias in winter

(some gravel), but you can nearly always make it in a car. The pinnacles appear in sci-fi films (most notably "Star Trek V") as outer-space landscapes, but there is a similarity between these peaks and lake-bottom formations, which once they were. Likewise at parched **Fossil Falls** (Highway 395, 20 miles (32 kilometers) north of the junction of Highway 14 and US 395), a former river gorge, now completely dry, that seems in eerie, perpetual longing for the waters that once roared through it.

The **Maturango Museum** (100 E. Las Flores Avenue, off N. China Lake Boulevard, tel: 760/375-6900, open: daily 10–5), doubles as a visitor center. Museum guides lead fascinating weekend tours in spring and fall to the **Little Petroglyphs Canyon.** Book way in advance for these trips, on a restricted section of a U.S. naval base, to see rock drawings, some of which are thousands of years old.

South of Ridgecrest, off US 395, lies amusing **Randsburg**, a still-active mining town with old shacks stacked up the sides of its scruffy hills. The fun and easily walkable downtown strip, a few blocks of Butte Avenue, contains saloons, restaurants and stores selling crafts and collectibles. Burma Road, which loops above

town, provides a fine perspective on it all. Head west on the Red Rock–Randsburg Road and you'll wind up at the southern tip of **Red Rock Canyon State Park** (Abbott Road, off Highway 14, tel: 661/942-0662), used as a backdrop for the movie "Jurassic Park."

Much of the eastern Mojave lies within **Mojave National Preserve.** Rangers at the Desert Information Center (72157 Baker Boulevard, Baker, tel: 760/733-4040, open: daily 9–5), dispense maps and advice about the preserve's dunes, caverns and other natural wonders.

6 Anza-Borrego Desert State Park

Off-road vehicle enthusiasts and hikers love the vast desert that lies on the backcountry route between San Diego and Palm Springs. Except during the spring wildflower season, six weeks between late February and April (blooming time varies from year to year), hardly anyone comes here. You need a four-wheel drive to visit some sights, but you can easily hike through **Borrego Palm Canyon,** a rare oasis amid this dry and dusty expanse. Stop by the visitor center for trail maps and tips. If you're not up for a hike, pick up the brochure for the informative, self-guiding **Erosion Road** auto tour.

🕂 206 A2 ✉ Visitor Center: 200 Palm Canyon Drive, off County Road S22, Borrego Springs ☎ (760) 767-5311 💲 Inexpensive

Sand verbena adds a splash of color to mostly brown Anza-Borrego

Where to...
Eat and Drink

Prices
Expect to pay per person for a meal, excluding drinks and service
$ under $15 $$ $15–25 $$$ over $25

SAN DIEGO & AREA

☜☜☜ Anthony's Star of the Sea Room $$$

The total package here is tops of any fish restaurant in the city. The dinner-only menu changes with the seasons, assuring that preparations take advantage of the freshest ingredients. The marine-themed decor has recently been updated, the bay views are sweeping and service is polished.

➕ 206 A1 ⊠ 1360 Harbor Drive, San Diego ☎ (619) 232-7408 ◉ Daily 5:30–10. Closed Jan 1, Thanksgiving and Dec 25

☜☜ Casa de Bandini $

Housed in a historic mansion in Old Town, the colorfully decorated Casa de Bandini serves up tasty fajitas and Mexican-style seafood. It also has an inviting outdoor patio, ideal for enjoying a margarita and chips or other appetizers on warm San Diego evenings. Dress is casual; this is a good place to bring the kids. There's also a lounge with full bar.

➕ 206 A1 ⊠ 2660 Calhoun Street, San Diego ☎ (619) 297-8211 ◉ Mon–Sat 11–9:30, Sun 10–9. Closed Thanksgiving and Dec 25

☜☜ Chez Loma $$$

Coronado's Chez Loma, set in a historic 1889 Victorian home, has been serving romantic meals for three decades. The Continental-cuisine menu changes seasonally, with creative preparations of seafood, lamb, duck and pastas, as well as superb desserts. The tone is quiet and intimate but not overly formal; you can dress casually if you wish, though most diners don't. There's a small bar, and the wine list is excellent.

➕ 205 F1 ⊠ 1132 Loma Avenue, Coronado ☎ (619) 435-0661 ◉ Dinner daily 5–9. Closed Thanksgiving and Dec 25

☜☜☜ George's at the Cove $$–$$$

George's is in effect two restaurants, with two different kitchens. The first floor houses a fine indoor dining room with picture-window views of La Jolla Cove; reservations are required at weekends. The rooftop terrace, which offers inspiring open-air ocean views, is less formal and doesn't take reservations; expect a wait on warm weekend evenings, because it's a spot to see and be seen. Both kitchens produce sparkling cutting-edge California cuisine, especially the seafood.

➕ 205 F1 ⊠ 1250 Prospect Street, La Jolla ☎ (858) 454-4244 ◉ Dining room: daily; lunch 11:30–2:30, dinner 5:30–10. Terrace: daily 11–10

Parallel 33 $$–$$$

It's worth a trip Uptown to sample dishes inspired by the lands along the 33rd Parallel: China, Japan, the Middle East, Morocco and the United States. If this fusion-plus strategy strikes you a recipe for anarchy, be advised that chef-owner Amiko Gubbins pulls off the culinary journey with aplomb. Her menu changes seasonally, but lamb, ahi tuna, and (in season) soft-shell crab are among the staples. Be adventurous like Gubbins and cross national borders with your selections – you'll find yourself marveling at the diversity of flavors.

Parallel 33 is small and popular, so make a reservation.

🏠 **205 F1** ⊠ **741 W. Washington Street, San Diego** ☎ **(619) 260-0033** ⏰ **Mon–Thu 5–10, Fri–Sat 5:30–11. Closed Jan 1, Jul 4, Thanksgiving and Dec 25**

Sammy's Woodfired Pizza $-$$

For a tasty designer pizza that won't break your budget, visit the Gaslamp Quarter outpost of this homegrown chain. The inventive choices range from barbecue chicken to goat's cheese (with wild mushrooms, garlic, spinach and red onion) to duck sausage (with spinach, tomatoes, garlic and smoked gouda). No need to dress up for a meal here, as the ambience is decidedly casual. Look for Sammy's in La Jolla, Mission Valley, and elsewhere around town.

🏠 **206 A1** ⊠ **770 Fourth Avenue, San Diego** ☎ **(619) 230-8888** ⏰ **Mon–Fri 11:30–9:30, Sat 11:30–10:30, Sun noon–9:30. Closed Jan 1, Thanksgiving and Dec 25**

🍴 Blue Coyote Bar & Grill $$

The colorful and casual Blue Coyote fits in neatly with the Palm Springs scene: Southwestern and Mexican food, ranging from Yucatán fish to duck enchiladas; a cantina dispensing big margaritas; and a pleasant interior decor of whitewashed walls, ceiling fans and Native American weavings. But on warm nights the real action is in the flower-filled outdoor courtyard.

🏠 **206 A2** ⊠ **445 N. Palm Canyon Drive, Palm Springs; 72-760 El Paseo, Palm Desert** ☎ **(760) 327-1196/776-8855** ⏰ **Palm Springs: Sun–Thu 11–10, Fri–Sat 11–11. Closed Thanksgiving and Dec 25**

🍴🍴🍴 Le Vallauris $$-$$$

Le Vallauris has a longstanding reputation for its French cuisine, which now ranges from the strictly traditional to more creative California-influenced preparations of lamb, veal, beef and fish. Come here to experience a romantic, fairly formal dinner, or for a relaxing drink in the piano lounge. Things are more casual at lunch and at the Sunday brunch, especially when taken on the pretty garden patio.

🏠 **206 A2** ⊠ **385 W. Tahquitz Canyon Way, Palm Springs** ☎ **(760) 325-5059** ⏰ **Daily: lunch 11:30–2:30, dinner 5–11**

Shame on the Moon $$-$$$

The unusual name comes from an old song reworked by Bob Seger. But there's also harmony in the elegantly muted decor, the attentive but unhurried service, carefully prepared food and remarkably moderate prices in this stylish Rancho Mirage dinner house. The pastas, seafood, lamb chops and duck change seasonally. Don't overlook the excellent accompaniments: appetizers, soups and heavenly homemade desserts. Ask for a table on the heated outdoor patio – it would be a shame to miss a moonlit night here.

🏠 **206 A2** ⊠ **69-950 Frank Sinatra Drive, Rancho Mirage** ☎ **(760) 324-5515** ⏰ **Daily 5 pm–closing. Closed Jan 1–2, Thanksgiving and Dec 24–25**

🍴🍴 Furnace Creek Inn Dining Room $$$

By far the most formal restaurant in Death Valley, the Furnace Creek Inn Dining Room brings a nouvelle touch to this old-time desert oasis. Miners and desert rats of yore might be appalled, not to mention puzzled, to see such items as seared ahi tuna or sesame-encrusted salmon on the menu, when a good rattlesnake stew might do. But such seasonal dishes will soon help you forget how out of place fresh seafood and vegetables seem in this remote but attractive setting.

🏠 **205 F5** ⊠ **Highway 190, Death Valley National Park** ☎ **(760) 786-2345** ⏰ **Daily 5:30–9**

Where to... Stay

Prices

Expect to pay per room

$ under $100 per night **$$** $100–175 per night **$$$** over $175 per night

SAN DIEGO

▼▼▼ Best Western Blue Sea Lodge $$–$$$

If you like to be where the action is – to walk directly onto the beach or boardwalk from your room – you can't ask for a better location than this motor lodge on Pacific Beach. Just remember that having the often crowded beach and boardwalk practically at your doorstep doesn't promote much quiet during the day. About half the rooms have kitchenettes.

➕ 206 A1 ⊠ 707 Pacific Beach Drive, San Diego, CA 92109 ☎ (858) 488-4700 or (800) 258-3732; fax: (858)

▼▼▼ Heritage Park Inn $$–$$$

The two homes that make up this attractive bed-and-breakfast inn, the main Queen Anne-style residence and a former Italianate boarding house, were moved in pieces from downtown San Diego to Heritage Park, above Old Town. There they were carefully reassembled and decorated in Victorian style, with features such as fanciful wainscoting and stenciling and period furniture. You'll notice a similar attention to detail at the full breakfast, which is served by candlelight, and during afternoon tea.

➕ 206 A1 ⊠ 2470 Heritage Park Row, San Diego, CA 92110 ☎ (619) 299-6832 or (800) 995-2470; fax: (619) 299-9465; email: innkeeper@heritageparkinn.com

▼▼▼▼ Hotel del Coronado $$$

The West Coast's largest beach resort is also one of its most historic hotels. Dating from 1888, the "Del" has hosted U.S. presidents and British royalty, and served as backdrop for Hollywood movies. Choose from rooms in the original building – a marvel of ornate gingerbread with cupolas, verandas, a turret, shingled red roofs and white wood – or in two more recent additions. Rooms in the former are often small and lack air-conditioning, but expansive public areas, both indoor and out, help compensate.

➕ 205 F1 ⊠ 1500 Orange Avenue, Coronado, CA 92118 ☎ (619) 435-6611 or (800) 468-3533; fax: (619) 522-8238; email: delreservations@hoteldel.com

▼▼▼ Ocean Park Inn $$–$$$

You can hangout at the beach but zip easily into town from this Pacific Beach hotel. The rooms are modestly decorated, but the ocean views – ask for a second- or third-floor room facing the water – more than compensate. A complimentary Continental breakfast is served daily; coffee and juice are available all day; and several good restaurants are located nearby.

➕ 206 A1 ⊠ 710 Grand Avenue, San Diego, CA 92109 ☎ (858) 483-5858 or (800) 231-7735; fax (858) 274-0823; email: info@oceanparkinn.com

▼▼▼ La Jolla Inn $$–$$$

Lodgings in La Jolla tend to be pricy, but this 23-room inn offers good value for the locale, which is close to the beach and scenic La Jolla Cove. Not all rooms have balconies, but those that do enjoy marvelous ocean views. Otherwise, you can make use of the inn's rooftop patio, a good place to munch the free Continental breakfast while admiring the Pacific from three stories up.

✚ **205 F1** ✉ 1110 Prospect Street, La Jolla, CA 92037 ☎ (858) 454-0133 or (800) 433-1609; fax: (858) 454-2056; email: prospect@san.rr.com

San Diego Paradise Point Resort $$$

Set on a 44-acre (18-hectare) island in Mission Bay Park, this resort is geared toward active travelers. Start at one of five swimming pools, soak in an outdoor hot tub, then proceed to the resort's own sandy beaches, then rent a canoe, paddleboat or sailboat to take out on the bay. On land, you'll find gardens, tennis courts and an 18-hole putting course. Accommodations are in cottage-style rooms and suites, which all have private patios and an airy tropical ambience.

✚ **206 A1** ✉ 1404 W. Vacation Road, San Diego, CA 92109 ☎ (858) 274-4630 or (800) 344-2626; fax: (858) 581-5929; email: reservations@paradisepoint.com

PALM SPRINGS

Lake La Quinta Inn $$-$$$

It might seem odd in the desert to find a chateau built in 18th-century French style – on the edge of a man-made lake, no less – but this luxurious bed-and-breakfast delivers grand style in a remarkably cozy setting. The rooms are decorated with taste and subtle flair on themes such as "Don Quixote" and an African safari. The service is impeccable, the full breakfasts divine.

✚ **206 A2** ✉ 78-120 Caleo Bay, La Quinta, CA 92253 ☎ (760) 564-7332 or (888) 226-4546; fax: (760) 564-6356; email: stay@lakelaquintainn.com

Palm Springs Riviera Resort $-$$

Good value, especially for its standard rooms, this resort keeps regulars coming back year after year with its breezy décor, large pool and attractive layout. The spacious

rooms and suites (from "Petite Suites" to large ones with hot tubs) occupy eight buildings on 24 landscaped acres (8 hectares). Activities here include golf (on an 18-hole course), tennis, volleyball and basketball, and there's an exercise room.

✚ **206 A2** ✉ 1600 North Indian Canyon Drive, Palm Springs, CA 92262 ☎ (760) 327-8311; fax (760) 325-8572; email: reservations@psriv.com

Rancho Las Palmas Marriott Resort and Spa $$-$$$

Recently upgraded, with a 27-hole golf course, 25 tennis courts, three swimming pools (one with a 100-foot/30-meter water slide), three hot tubs, a newly added luxury spa, a health club, children's programs, four restaurants, a bar with entertainment and dancing, and the requisite desert palms, this sprawling 450-unit Spanish-style resort is designed to keep you on the premises from morning till night. You'll find your room to

be luxurious, spacious and further enlarged by your own patio or balcony.

✚ **206 A2** ✉ 41000 Bob Hope Drive, Rancho Mirage, CA 92270 ☎ (760) 568-2727 or (800) 458-8786; fax: (760) 568-5845

DEATH VALLEY

Furnace Creek Inn and Ranch Resort $-$$$

A felicitous mix of history, rusticity and casual elegance lends the Furnace Creek Inn, Death Valley's luxury lodging, much of its appeal. Soft colors, swaying palms, gardens, a spring-fed pool and an attentive staff keep the mood here upbeat despite often blisteringly hot weather. All the rooms have a contemporary, stylish look. The nearby Ranch, under the same management, offers less expensive motel-style lodging.

✚ **205 F5** ✉ Highway 190, Death Valley National Park, CA 92328 ☎ (760) 786-2361/786-2345; fax: (760) 786-2423 (Inn); (760) 786-9098 (Ranch)

Where to... Shop

Southern California offers an eclectic array of potential purchases: antiques, discounted clothing, imports from Mexico, Native American jewelry and crafts, and desert-grown dates among them. San Diego and the Palm Springs region are the two top shopping areas.

SAN DIEGO

Scattered around San Diego are boutiques, shopping centers and specialty shops. Several malls are located in the general area of Mission Valley and Hotel Circle. **Fashion Valley** (452 Fashion Valley; tel: 619/297-3381) and **Westfield Shoppingtown Mission Valley** (1640 Camino del Rio North; tel: 619/296-6375) are two of the largest. The city's most interesting shopping center, convenient to downtown hotels, is **Horton Plaza** (bounded by Broadway, G Street, 1st and 4th avenues; tel: 619/238-1596), acolorful, multilevel complex of department stores, shops, restaurants, snack bars and theaters.

For the most concentrated selection of antiques and art galleries, head for downtown's renovated historic **Gaslamp Quarter** (bounded by 4th, 5th and 6th avenues and Broadway). On the waterfront, **Seaport Village** (Harbor Drive at Kettner Boulevard, tel: 619/235-4014) is a tourist-oriented open-air mall built to resemble a century-old fishing village. In Old Town, the plaza-like **Bazaar del Mundo** (Juan Street; tel: 619/296-3161) is a colorful place to hunt for mostly inexpensive Mexican folk art, crafts, pottery and textiles. The increasingly hip **Hillcrest** section north of downtown has a good selection of music and bookstores, as well as the bulk of the city's shops oriented toward gays and lesbians.

In **Coronado**, you can comb the boutiques along Orange Avenue for upscale clothing. The **Ferry Landing Marketplace** has more than two dozen stores along with terrific views of San Diego. **La Jolla** is home to numerous ritzy boutiques, especially along Prospect and nearby streets.

PALM SPRINGS AREA

In the Palm Springs area, the top shopping venue is the town of **Palm Desert**. El Paseo, an avenue enlivened by splashing fountains and Mediterranean-style courtyards, is lined with clothing boutiques, art galleries, department stores and restaurants. When it's too hot to shop outdoors, or when some stores close entirely for the summer, head for **Palm Desert Town Center**, a big enclosed mall that harbors about 150 department stores and specialty shops, along with eating places and movie theaters.

In the town of **Palm Springs** itself, the prime shopping street is **Palm Canyon Drive**, where the Palm Springs Promenade offers a collection of chic boutiques and larger stores. **North Palm Canyon Drive** is a good place to hunt for antiques and collectibles.

If you have a hankering for dates (the edible kind) head southeast to the towns of **Thermal** and **Indio**. There you can buy dates to snack on (date shakes – a whipped concoction of ice cream, milk and chopped dates – are a hit) or to ship home at **Oasis Date Gardens** (59-111 Highway 111, Thermal; tel: 760/399-5665) or **Shields Date Gardens** (80-225 Highway 111, Indio; tel: 760/347-0996).

A few miles northwest of Palm Springs, in **Cabazon**, you'll find more than 100 factory clothing discount outlet centers at **Desert Hills Premium Outlets** (48-400 Seminole Drive; tel: 909/849-6641).

Where to...
Be Entertained

Southern California offers an intriguing mix of nightlife, the arts and outdoor activities, centered primarily in the San Diego and Palm Springs areas. In San Diego, check entertainment listings in the *San Diego* magazine, or pick up a copy of *The Reader*, a free weekly. In Palm Springs, *Palm Springs Life* magazine has entertainment listings, as does the Friday edition of the *Palm Desert Sun* newspaper. Call (619) 497-5000 for recorded information sponsored by the San Diego Performing Arts League; this is also the number for Arts Tix, the discount, same-day ticket service whose main office is at Horton Plaza downtown.

THEATER

San Diego

Get half-price, same-day tickets for San Diego theater performances at Arts Tix (Broadway Circle, Horton Plaza, tel: 619/497-5000).

San Diego is rich in theater. Balboa Park's **Old Globe Theater** (tel: 619/239-2255) is one of the state's oldest professional theater groups, and stages summertime Shakespeare plays. Also during summer in Balboa Park, the **Starlight Musical Theater** (tel: 619/544-7827) produces outdoor musicals. The Gaslamp Quarter Theatre Company, La Jolla Playhouse (May to November only), Coronado Playhouse and the Theatre in Old Town are other top venues.

MUSIC AND NIGHTLIFE

San Diego

San Diego's **Gaslamp Quarter,** especially along 4th and 5th avenues, has the city's greatest concentration of bars and nightclubs. The areas around Pacific, Mission and Ocean beaches also harbor lively nightspots. Options range from dance clubs to those offering rock, jazz and blues. The **Hillcrest** section, especially University Avenue, Park Boulevard and 5th Avenue, is the focus of gay and lesbian nightlife.

The town of **La Jolla** is known for its singles bars. Some of the San Diego area's top hotels have piano bars. The **San Diego Opera** (tel: 619/570-1100) season runs from January to April in the downtown Civic Theatre.

Palm Springs

The hot-ticket theater event in Palm Springs, from November to May, is the **Fabulous Palm Springs Follies** (Plaza Theater, 128 S. Palm Canyon Drive, tel: 760/327-0225), a vaudeville-style revue starring singers and dancers over age 50. More traditional performances take place at the **McCallum Theatre** (73-000 Fred Waring Drive, Palm Desert, tel: 760/340-2787) and the **Annenberg Theater** (101 Museum Drive, Palm Springs, tel: 760/325-4490).

SPORT

The Palm Springs region is best known for its dozens of golf courses, many open to the public. Other activities include hiking, horseback riding and bicycling; you can also fish in nearby lakes.

San Diego is blessed with a wealth of good swimming beaches; the largest and most popular include Coronado, Mission, Ocean, Pacific and Silver Strand beaches. Smaller, more secluded beaches include La Jolla Cove, La Jolla Shores and Torrey Pines State beaches.

Tours

1 Coast Highway 1 & Point Reyes
   National Seashore 180 – 182
2 Santa Barbara & the San Marcos
   Pass 183 – 185
3 Mulholland Drive 186 – 188

1 COAST HIGHWAY 1 AND THE POINT REYES NATIONAL SEASHORE

DISTANCE 57 miles/91 km (one way) **TIME** 6–8 hours
START POINT Golden Gate Bridge (US 101 off Doyle Drive)
🕂 202 B1
END POINT Point Reyes Lighthouse 🕂 202 B1

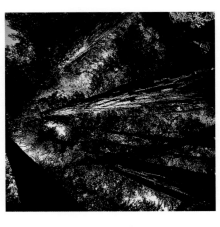

The theme for this tour is stunning vistas – San Francisco, the Golden Gate, towering redwoods, rolling ranchland and a wind-sculpted stretch of the Pacific Coast. On a map it may not look as if you are covering much terrain, but it will take you the better part of an exhilarating day to make this drive. Get an early start, and bring your camera.

Planning note: The roads to Muir Woods and Stinson Beach can be crowded on sunny weekends, and the last stop, Point Reyes Lighthouse, is closed on Tuesday and Wednesday.

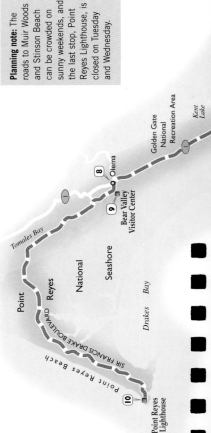

Above: Centuries-old redwoods soar skyward from the Muir Woods valley floor
Previous page: Point Reyes Lighthouse

5 miles

8 km

Tiburon

101

Angel
Island

Sausalito

Vista Point

2

SAN
FRANCISCO

Golden Gate
Bridge

1

Golden Gate
National
Recreation Area

PANORAMIC
HIGHWAY

Muir
Woods
Nat Mon

3

Muir Beach

Alpine
Lake

Stinson
Beach

5

4

Bolinas
Lagoon

Bolinas

6

HORSESHOE
HILL ROAD

7

Duxbury
Reef

1–2
Head north on US 101 across the **Golden Gate Bridge** (► 55). Stop at the **vista point** at the northern end for a look at San Francisco's skyline.

2–3
Follow US 101 north to the Mill Valley/Stinson Beach exit. You will exit to the right, pass under

Looking out across Golden Gate National Recreation Area

US 101, veer around to the right past some small shopping areas, then make a left on Highway 1. Continue west on Highway 1, make a right on Panoramic Highway and after a mile (1.6 kilometers) turn left on Muir Woods Road, following the signs to **Muir Woods National Monument** (► 61). Take one of the shorter hikes through its old-growth redwoods.

3–4
Continue west on Muir Woods Road until it runs into Highway 1, make a right and drive north about 7 miles (11 kilometers) to **Stinson Beach**. Park the car in the beach's lot (just west of the small downtown) and take a short stroll.

4–5
As you continue north out of Stinson, you'll pass the **Bolinas Lagoon**, where even on a slow

day you're likely to see white cranes, ducks and sea lions without leaving your car.

5–6
It's a time-honored tradition of some Bolinas residents to destroy signs to their town to keep out tourists, though most folks are actually friendly. Make the first left after the lagoon and another quick left after a short distance onto Olema–Bolinas Road. Make another left at the stop sign at Horseshoe Hill Road (though you'll still be on Olema–Bolinas Road). This leads into

Bolinas' small commercial strip, where you'll find the Bolinas Bakery and Café, Smiley's Schooner Saloon and a few galleries.

6–7

Reverse course north out of town on Olema–Bolinas Road. At Mesa Road make a left, then another left on Overlook Drive and a right on Elm Road (all this covers less than 2 miles/3 kilometers). Here you'll see the parking area for **Duxbury Reef**, where sea creatures galore live among the tide pools.

7–8

Head back out of Mesa to Olema–Bolinas Road and make a left. Continue north on Horseshoe Hill Road, which shortly thereafter runs into Highway 1. Make a left, and continue north to **Olema**. If you didn't have lunch in Bolinas, stop for a bite at the **Olema Farm House** (10005 Highway 1, tel: 415/663-1264). The barbecued oysters and oyster stew here are sublime.

8–9

A few blocks to the north, make a left on Bear Valley Road, which leads to the Bear Valley

Visitor Center of the **Point Reyes National Seashore** (▶ 61).

9–10

Keep track of the time. It takes nearly an hour to drive north and west along Sir Francis Drake Boulevard to **Point Reyes Lighthouse**. You need to arrive at least a half-hour – preferably an hour –

before closing (5 pm). The setting's worth the trip, though, even if you don't make it down to the lighthouse.

Alternatively take the easier but still scenic route of Sir Francis Drake Boulevard heading east out of the seashore. It eventually runs into US 101, which you can take south back to San Francisco.

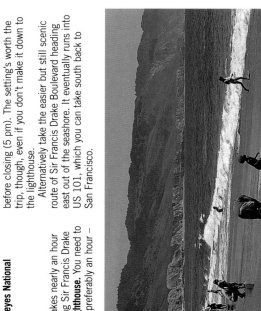

Limantour Beach is one of several long strands at Point Reyes

SANTA BARBARA AND THE SAN MARCOS PASS

2

DISTANCE 51 miles/82 km (one way) **TIME** 3–5 hours
START POINT Mission Santa Barbara ⊞ 204 C3
END POINT Solvang ⊞ 204 C3
Please note that the scale of the Santa Barbara map on page 185 is different to the scale of the map on page 184

You'll come to appreciate Santa Barbara County's varied splendors on this excursion, which begins in the city of Santa Barbara's colorful foothills and winds past its waterfront. The terrain alters abruptly along an old stagecoach pass – green giving way to nearly barren brown – then mellows as you head into the Santa Ynez Valley vineyard region. The last transformation may confound you the most: the Danish-style village called Solvang.

You could easily drive the route in two hours, leaving plenty of time for gazing at the view, stopping for lunch and tasting a little wine. For the first nine stages of the tour – those in Santa Barbara – the city's "Scenic Drive" signs, which have white letters on a dark-blue background, will provide additional guidance.

View from a ridge in Montecito

1–2
Follow the Scenic Drive signs east from **Mission Santa Barbara** (▶ 112) on Alameda Padre Serra. Bougainvillea and other colorful plants brighten the street as it edges along the foothills. Catch the view of downtown and the waterfront at a small **vista point** just past the Brooks Institute's Jefferson campus (near Dover Road).

2–3
At Salinas Street, Alameda Padre Serra runs into a roundabout. Follow the circle three-quarters of the way around to the continuation of Alameda Padre Serra. Shortly after this, the street name becomes Alston Road; continue east on it.

3–4
Follow Alston to Olive Mill Road and make a right. Several blocks south make another right on Coast Village Road. Galleries, chic shops and outdoor cafés line tony **Montecito's** petite commercial zone.

4–5

Stroll Coast Village Road or continue west to Hot Springs Road, where you'll make a left and follow the road as it passes under US 101 and loops around the southern edge of the **Andree Clark Bird Refuge** (▶ 111).

5–6

You are now on Cabrillo Boulevard as it passes west along the palm-lined waterfront past **Stearns Wharf** (▶ 110) and the **Santa Barbara Yacht Harbor** (▶ 111).

6–7

By the time you see thin, green **Shoreline Park**, you're atop a cliff and now on Shoreline Drive. Slip into the parking area to take in the sweeping ocean view.

7–8

Shoreline Drive runs into Meigs Road (make a right), shortly after which you'll make a left on Cliff Drive. This leads into the exclusive **Hope Ranch** housing development.

8–9

Along the way, Cliff Drive becomes Marina Drive, which becomes Roble Drive before running into Las Palmas Drive (now heading north). Just keep following the Scenic Drive signs to State Street (right after

you pass over US 101), by which time you're on La Cumbre Road. Here's where you depart from the Scenic Drive.

9–10

Make a left on State and shortly thereafter a right on Highway 154 – the sign reads "San Marcos Pass/Lake Cachuma." Vibrant greenery quickly gives way to stark browns and the muted tones of coyote bush, sage and coastal live oaks as you head through the **San Marcos Pass.**

10–11

Highway 154 winds resolutely up the Santa Ynez Mountains before plunging nearly straight down toward **Lake Cachuma**, which shortly comes into view after you reach the mountain peak. You can interrupt the steep decline by stopping at the vista point a bit past Stagecoach Pass Road.

11–12

Stay on Highway 154 for a few miles past the intersection with Highway 246. Head south (left) on Grand Avenue, the main street of **Los Olivos,** where you can have smoothies or sandwiches at **Panino** (2900 Grand Avenue, tel: 805/688-9304) or a gourmet meal at **Los Olivos Café** (2879 Grand Avenue, tel: 805/688-7265).

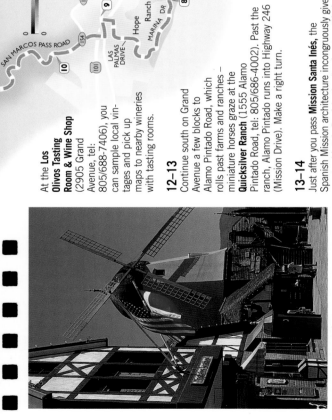

At the **Los Olivos Tasting Room & Wine Shop** (2905 Grand Avenue, tel: 805/688-7406), you can sample local vintages and pick up maps to nearby wineries with tasting rooms.

12–13

Continue south on Grand Avenue a few blocks to Alamo Pintado Road, which rolls past farms and ranches – miniature horses graze at the **Quicksilver Ranch** (1555 Alamo Pintado Road, tel: 805/686-4002). Past the ranch, Alamo Pintado runs into Highway 246 (Mission Drive). Make a right turn.

13–14

Just after you pass **Mission Santa Inés**, the Spanish Mission architecture incongruously gives way to old-style Danish, the dominant motif of cheery **Solvang**. Park at meters or in the plentiful public lots. Two key streets for browsing and

munching (Solvang is well known for its delicious Danish pastries and buttermilk pancakes) are Copenhagen Drive and Alisal Road.

14–15

To return to Santa Barbara, follow Mission Drive (Highway 246) west. At US 101 head south. (**Mission La Purísima Concepción,** ▶ 24, is 20 miles (32 kilometers) west of Highway 246 and US 101.)

Solvang is an architectural non-sequitur in a region where Spanish Colonial design dominates

3 MULHOLLAND DRIVE

Mulholland Drive, named for William Mulholland, who stole – er, developed – Los Angeles' water supply, snakes 55 miles (88 kilometers) along the ridge of the Santa Monica Mountains from Hollywood to the Pacific Ocean. The spectacular route yields 360-degree views of the best (rugged canyons, movie-star mansions, cacti and sometimes even coyotes) and worst (traffic-clogged freeways) Los Angeles has to offer. But mostly the best, and for long stretches you'll have the road pretty much to yourself.

A few of the directions may seem peculiar, but this drive really is worth tackling. Here's the quick version: Mulholland Drive west until it becomes dirt. Detour north on the paved roads – Encino Hills and Hayvenhurst to the Ventura Freeway heading west. At Topanga Canyon

DISTANCE 77 miles/124 km (one way) **TIME** 3–5 hours
START POINT North Highland Avenue and Hollywood Boulevard ✚ 205 E2
END POINT Santa Monica ✚ 205 E2

Boulevard head south back to Mulholland Drive. Turn west (right) on Mulholland Drive. When you see signs for Mulholland Highway, continue southwest on that to Malibu.

1–2

Finding the very beginning of Mulholland Drive is your first challenge. Head north past Hollywood Boulevard on **Highland Avenue.** Near the Hollywood Freeway (US 101) there's a merge onto **Cahuenga Boulevard West** (the sign reads Cahuenga Blvd. West/Barham Blvd.), which slithers along the west side of the freeway to Mulholland Drive, where you make a left.

(If you end up on Cahuenga Boulevard East, which is east of the freeway, don't fret. Make a right at Lakeridge Road, in the 2700 block of Cahuenga, just before it looks as if you're

Take to the open road and enjoy the ride

getting onto the freeway. Then take an immediate left on Lakeridge Place, which winds around left to a bridge that crosses over US 101. A sign points the short way to Mulholland Drive.)

2–3

Mulholland begins its twisting ways immediately, but your first respite – and photo opportunity – comes in less than a mile at the **Hollywood Bowl Overlook.** Signs tell a bit of William Mulholland's story, but here and at future stops the view's the thing.

3–4

This is the busiest stretch of Mulholland, with stars and regular folk rushing to and fro. (Past and present residents include the actors Errol Flynn and Warren Beatty, and Walt Disney Company chief Michael Eisner.) Pull over when possible and let traffic pass, and don't

drive too fast or you may miss the small overlooks, some of them official and others just dirt pullouts. Just past 7701 Mulholland is the **Universal City Overlook** and farther on, and certainly worth a stop, the **Fryman Canyon Overlook.** Still farther on there's a pullout just past Bowmont Drive and yet another across from 13810 Mulholland. All have sterling views.

4–5

About 2 miles (3 kilometers) west of the 405 (the San Diego Freeway), Mulholland Drive becomes a dirt road for 7 miles (11 kilometers). (You can drive a short way to a Cold War relic, the former **San Vicente Nike Missile Site**, but eventually a gate will stop you.) After taking in the incredible vista of the San Fernando Valley from where the dirt road begins, continue down the paved road you were on.

5–6

You may think you're still on Mulholland, but you're actually on Encino Hills Drive, part of a detour into the suburban **San Fernando Valley** that will bring you back to Mulholland. When you get to Haywenhurst Avenue, make a left.

6–7

Follow Haywenhurst north to Ventura Boulevard. Turn west onto Ventura Boulevard and shortly after north onto Balboa Boulevard. Join US 101, now called the **Ventura Freeway**, and get on the freeway for 5 miles (8 kilometers). At Topanga Canyon Boulevard (Highway 27), turn south.

7–8

Less than a mile south on Topanga, you'll come to **Mulholland Drive**. Make a right.

8–9

In less than a mile you come to the intersection of several roads. Topanga continues south, Mulholland Drive heads northwest, and Mulholland Highway (hey, where'd that come from?) heads southwest. Take **Mulholland Highway**.

9–10

Mulholland Highway winds west through increasingly desolate terrain, looking so 19th-century American West that Paramount Pictures shot many a Western out here. The studio even built a fake town that you can explore. To do so, make a right turn on Cornell Road and follow the signs a short distance to the **Paramount Ranch**, now run by the National Park Service. When the wind blows a few leaves and makes an unpainted, rusty-hinged door creak, you'll half expect Henry Fonda or John Wayne to whirl on you, gun cocked, and challenge you to a draw.

10–11

Backtrack on Cornell Road to Mulholland Highway and make a right. You'll eventually pass the **Peter Strauss Ranch** and **Rocky Oaks**, both of which have hiking trails and picnic areas. Browns and muted greens become more the norm in this area formed by a volcanic eruption approximately 13 to 16 million years ago.

11–12

Just past Mile Marker 13.58 is a super overlook with a view back toward the Strauss Ranch and man-made Malibu Lake. As you continue toward the coast you'll notice the air becoming cooler and moister, a sign that you're entering **Malibu** (▶ 140). (Another indication will be the sign that reads Malibu.)

12–13

Mulholland Highway intersects the Pacific Coast Highway (PCH) at **Leo Carrillo State Beach** (▶ 140), where you can rest for a moment and watch the surfers take their waves.

13–14

Head south on PCH through Malibu's main commercial district. If you're hungry, make a left at Cross Creek Road and, as celebrities often do, stop by the **Marmalade Café** (tel: 310/317-4242) or one of the other eateries in the Malibu Country Mart. Continue south through Pacific Palisades to **Santa Monica** (▶ 141), where you can catch I-10 heading back toward LA.

Practicalities

GETTING ADVANCE INFORMATION

Websites

- The Official California Web Site (with links to San Francisco, LA, San Diego and other sites): www.gocalif.com
- California State Parks: www.parks.ca.gov
- National Park Service: www.nps.gov
- Travel California: www.travelcalifornia.com

BEFORE YOU GO

WHAT YOU NEED

- ● Required
- ○ Suggested
- ▲ Not required
- △ Not applicable

	U.K.	Germany	U.S.A.	Canada	Australia	Ireland	Netherlands	Spain
Passport/National Identity Card	●	●	▲	○	●	●	●	●
Visa (waiver form to be completed)	▲	▲	▲	▲	▲	▲	▲	▲
Return Ticket	●	●	▲	▲	●	●	●	●
Health Inoculations (tetanus and polio)	▲	▲	▲	▲	▲	▲	▲	▲
Health Documentation (➤ 194, Health)	▲	▲	▲	▲	▲	▲	▲	▲
Travel Insurance	●	●	●	○	●	●	●	●
Driving License (national)	●	●	●	●	●	●	●	●
Car Insurance Certificate	△	△	●	●	△	△	△	△
Car Registration Document	△	△	●	●	△	△	△	△

WHEN TO GO

San Francisco

⬜ High season   ⬜ Low season

JAN	FEB	MAR	APR	MAY	JUN	JUL	AUG	SEP	OCT	NOV	DEC
13°C	14°C	17°C	18°C	20°C	21°C	23°C	23°C	24°C	21°C	18°C	14°C
55°F	58°F	62°F	64°F	67°F	70°F	72°F	72°F	74°F	71°F	64°F	57°F

☀ Sun   ☁ Cloud   🌧 Wet   ⛅ Sun/Showers

Temperatures are the **average daily maximum** for each month. **Average daily minimum** temperatures are approximately 14 to 18 degrees Fahrenheit (8 to 10 degrees Celsius) lower. The weather varies from region to region in California. Late spring and early fall are **generally pleasant** throughout the state, and even in winter it's nice in Palm Springs, Santa Barbara and other Southern California locales. During summer, temperatures can range from 60 to 90 degrees Fahrenheit (16 to 32 degrees Celsius) in the coastal regions to well over 100 (37 degrees Celsius) inland in the deserts, Central Valley and the Gold Country. In San Francisco, Monterey and other coastal cities **fog** often rolls in during the summer, making them quite cool. The **rainy season** in California is usually from November through April.

In the U.S.A.
- California Division of Tourism
  P.O. Box 1499
  Sacramento, CA 95812
  ☎ (800) 462-2543

In the U.K.
- California Tourism Information Office
  High Holborn House
  52–54 High Holborn
  London WC1V 6RB
  ☎ (44) 20 7242 3131

In Germany
California Tourism Information Office,
c/o Touristikdienst Truber,
Schwarzwaldstrasse 13
D-63811 Stockstadt
☎ (49) 6027 401108

GETTING THERE AND AROUND

By Air California has two main **airports**, San Francisco International (SFO) and Los Angeles (LAX), both served by most major international carriers that fly to the United States and by the major and some smaller U.S. domestic carriers.

There are **direct flights** to Los Angeles and San Francisco from London's Gatwick and Heathrow airports and from Dublin, Montreal, Toronto and Vancouver. **Nonstop flights** to California originate from Auckland, Sydney and Melbourne, usually to Los Angeles, with connections from there to San Francisco. Flights from Germany often route through Frankfurt, but might instead stop at some other European airport (e.g. Heathrow from Berlin). All **airport taxes** (which are nominal) are included in the price of your ticket.

By Car Interstates 10, 15, 40 and 80 are the main routes into the state from the east; I-5 and US 101 are the principal routes from the north. Except when signs instruct otherwise, you can turn right on a red light after stopping. At intersections with three- or four-way stop signs, the first to arrive is the first to go. Children under age 6 who weigh less than 60 pounds (27 kilograms) must sit in an approved child-restraint seat. All passengers must wear seatbelts.

By Rail and Bus Alternative options for travelers from Canada or elsewhere in the United States are **Amtrak trains** (tel: 800/872-7245; www.amtrak.com), which stop in San Diego, Los Angeles, Santa Barbara, Emeryville (shuttle bus to San Francisco provided), Sacramento and many other towns, and long-distance buses of **Greyhound Lines** (tel: 800/231-2222; www.greyhound.com).

TIME

California is on Pacific Standard Time (PST), eight hours behind Greenwich Mean Time (GMT -8). Daylight Savings Time (GMT -7) operates from early April (when clocks are advanced one hour) through late October.

CURRENCY AND FOREIGN EXCHANGE

Currency The basic unit of currency in the United States is the dollar ($1). One dollar is 100 cents. **Notes** (bills) come in denominations of $1, $5, $10, $20, $50 and $100. All bills are green and the same size, so look carefully at the dollar amount on them. **Coins** are 1 cent (penny), 5 cents (nickel), 10 cents (dime), 25 cents (quarter), 50 cents (half-dollar) and one-dollar, though the latter two are not as common. An unlimited amount of U.S. currency can be imported or exported, though amounts over $10,000 have to be declared.

U.S. dollar **travelers' checks** are the best way to carry money and they are accepted as cash by most businesses, as are credit cards (Amex, Visa, MasterCard, Diners Club).

Exchange The best place to exchange non-U.S. currency is at a bank. Automated teller cards can be used to withdraw money from your account in U.S. currency. Your bank will provide you with details of where your cards will be accepted in California.

TIME DIFFERENCES

GMT	California	New York	Germany	Spain	Australia
12 noon	← 4 am	← 7 am	→ 1 pm	→ 1 pm	→ 10 pm

WHEN YOU ARE THERE

CLOTHING SIZES

U.K.	Rest of Europe	U.S.A.	
36	46	36	
38	48	38	
40	50	40	
42	52	42	Suits
44	54	44	
46	56	46	
7	41	8	
7.5	42	8.5	
8.5	43	9.5	
9.5	44	10.5	Shoes
10.5	45	11.5	
11	46	12	
14.5	37	14.5	
15	38	15	
15.5	39/40	15.5	
16	41	16	Shirts
16.5	42	16.5	
17	43	17	
8	34	6	
10	36	8	
12	38	10	
14	40	12	Dresses
16	42	14	
18	44	16	
4.5	38	6	
5	38	6.5	
5.5	39	7	
6	39	7.5	Shoes
6.5	40	8	
7	41	8.5	

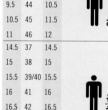

NATIONAL HOLIDAYS

Jan 1	New Year's Day
Third Mon Jan	Martin Luther King Day
Third Mon Feb	Presidents' Day
Mar/Apr	Easter
Last Mon May	Memorial Day
Jul 4	Independence Day
First Mon Sep	Labor Day
Second Mon Oct	Columbus Day
Nov 11	Veterans' Day
Fourth Thu Nov	Thanksgiving
Dec 25	Christmas Day

Boxing Day (Dec 26) is not a public holiday in the U.S. Some stores open on National Holidays.

OPENING HOURS

○ Stores   ● Post Offices
● Offices   ● Museums/Monuments
● Banks   ● Pharmacies

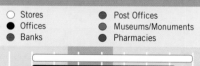
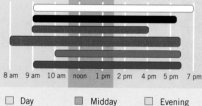

8 am   9 am   10 am   noon   1 pm   2 pm   4 pm   5 pm   7 pm

☐ Day   ■ Midday   ☐ Evening

Stores Hours vary greatly, but most open between 9 and 6 or 7, and many have evening hours until 9 pm. Some stores close on Sunday.
Banks Most are open between 9 or 10 and 3 or 4; some open until 6 pm. Most are closed on Saturday. All are closed on Sunday.
Post Offices Open from 8 or 8:30 until 5 or 6 on weekdays; many open until 1 pm on Saturday.
Museums Hours vary. Most open by 10 and close at 5 or 6. Late opening often Thursday or Friday.

POLICE 911

FIRE 911

AMBULANCE 911

PERSONAL SAFETY

Crime is not a problem in most tourist-frequented areas of California, but it is still wise to take precautions especially in urban areas:

- Carry only the cash you need; leave other cash and valuables in the hotel safe.
- If you have a waist pack, keep the part with your valuables in front of your body.
- When driving keep all car doors locked.
- Keep an eye on your belongings at all times in public places.
- Report theft or mugging to the police to provide a reference for insurance claims.

Police assistance:
 911 from any phone

TELEPHONES

There are pay-phones on many street corners and most are coin oper-ated. From public phones dial 0 for the operator and give the name of the country, city

and number you are calling. You will need at least $5.50 in quarters for an overseas call. Some phones take prepaid phone cards, available at drug-stores and newsstands, and some take credit cards. Dial 1 plus the area code for numbers within the U.S. and Canada. Dial 411 to find U.S. and Canadian numbers.

**International Dialling Codes
Dial 011 followed by**

U.K.:	**44**
Ireland:	**353**
Australia:	**61**
Germany:	**49**
Netherlands:	**31**
Spain:	**34**

POST

You can find listings of U.S. Postal Service facilities in the U.S. Government section of the White Pages of the local tele-phone directory.
Mail boxes can be found on street corners, often near trash cans.

ELECTRICITY

The power supply is 110/120 volts AC (60 cycles).
Sockets take two-prong, flat-pin plugs. An adaptor is needed for appliances with two-round-pin and three-pin plugs.
European appliances also need a voltage transformer.

TIPS/GRATUITIES

Tipping is expected for all services. As a general guide:
Yes ✓   No ✗

Restaurants (service not included)	✓	15–20%
Bar service	✓	15%
Tour guides	✓	discretion
Hairdressers	✓	15%
Taxis	✓	15%
Chambermaids	✓	$1 per day
Porters	✓	$1 per bag

CONSULATES

U.K.
(310) 481-0031
(415) 617-1300

Ireland
(415) 392-4214

Canada
(213) 346-2700

Australia
(310) 229-4800
(415) 536-1970

New Zealand
(310) 207-1605

HEALTH

 Insurance Medical insurance cover of at least $1 million is strongly recommended; medical fees in the United States are unregulated. If you are involved in an accident in California, you will be cared for by medical services and charged later.

 Dental Services Your medical insurance cover should include dental treatment, which is readily available but expensive. Many dentists will accept credit cards, but most prefer cash or travelers' checks. To find a dentist, look under "Dentists" in the Yellow Pages telephone directory.

 Weather The sun shines brightly for long periods during the summer. Throughout the state, but especially in the desert and Southern California, use a good sunscreen, cover up and drink plenty of fluids.

 Drugs Pharmacies dispensing prescription and over-the-counter treatments are plentiful throughout the state. If you need regular medication, take your own drugs and prescription (for U.S. Customs). The Rite Aid chain (tel: 800/748-3243 for nearest location) has branches throughout the state; some are open 24 hours.

Safe Water Drinking unboiled tap water is safe. Mineral water is cheap and readily available.

CONCESSIONS

Students/children Holders of an International Student Identity Card (ISIC) are entitled to discounts on many attractions. Children under 3 are generally allowed into attractions free; children's tickets are usually available up to age 12. Teenagers often have to pay the full adult rate.

Senior Citizens Discounts on many services and attractions, and reductions on hotel room rates during the low season, are available to seniors. Qualifying age varies from 55 to 65. You need to request a discount up front and may be asked to show proof of age and identity.

TRAVELING WITH A DISABILITY

Public facilities must, by California and U.S. federal law, be accessible to people with disabilities. The only exceptions tend to be small, older buildings such as Victorian B&Bs, where the cost to comply would be very high. Most public buses have elevators and wheelchair spaces, and subway and other rail stations provide wheelchair access.

CHILDREN

Baby-changing facilities are provided in many restrooms in hotels, restaurants and attractions. Children's events are listed in the Friday and/or Sunday sections of metropolitan daily newspapers.

LAVATORIES

The cleanest and safest lavatories are in large hotels, chain bookstores and department stores.

LOST PROPERTY

If something is stolen from your hotel or car, contact the police (tel: 911) and get a copy of the paperwork for your insurance company.
Airports
SFO ☎ (650) 821-7014
LAX ☎ (310) 417-0440
Trains
Amtrak ☎ (800) 872-7245

accommodations 36
see also individual
regions
Adams, Ansel 26
Adamson House 141
admission charges 35
Ahwahnee 24
airports and air
services 32, 191
Alcatraz Island 46
Allensworth 25
Andree Clark Bird
Refuge 111, 184
Angel Island 47
Anza-Borrego Desert
State Park 172
Aquarium of the
Pacific 141
Arcata 90
Artists Palette 169
Asian Art Museum of
San Francisco 59
Asilomar State Beach
105
Auburn 85
Autry Museum of
Western Heritage
129
Avenue of the Giants
90
Avila Beach 115

baby-changing
facilities 194
Badwater 169
Balboa Island 143
Balboa Park 158–160
Balboa Peninsula 142
banks 192
Battery Point
Lighthouse 90
bed-and-breakfast
inns 36
Bel-Air 131
Benziger Family
Winery 79
Beringer Vineyards
81–82
Beverly Hills 130–131
Museum of
Television and
Radio 131
Rodeo Drive 130–131
Big Sur 107
Birch Aquarium at
Scripps 164
Bird Rock 106
Bixby Bridge 107
Black Bart 15
Bodega 76
Bodie Ghost Town
State Historic Park
25
Bolinas 181–182
Borrego Palm
Canyon 172
Brannan, Sam 14
Buena Vista Carneros
Winery 78
buses, long-distance
33, 191

Cable Car Museum
58
Cabrillo National
Monument 158
Calaveras Big Tree
State Park 85
California Academy
of Sciences 50, 51
California Carnivores
81
California Gold Rush
12–15, 19, 24, 25,
85
California Palace of
the Legion of Honor
55
California Sea Otter
Game Refuge 114
California State
Indian Museum 84
California State
Railroad Museum
84
Calistoga 81
Cambria 114
Cannery Row
104–105
Carmel 106
Carmel Mission 106
Carmel River State
Beach 106
Carrillo State Beach
140
Cartoon Art Museum
50, 51
Catalina Island 142
Avalon Theatre 142
Casino 142
Cathedral City 165
Central Coast 99–120
accommodations
118–119
Big Sur 107
Cambria 114
eating out 116–117
entertainment 120
Harmony 114
Hearst Castle
108–109
map 100–101
Monterey Peninsula
100, 104–106
Morro Bay 114–
115
Ojai 115
Santa Barbara
110–113,
183–184
Santa Cruz 114
shopping 120
three-day itinerary
102–103
Chandler, Raymond
26
Chateau Montelena
81
children's entertain-
ment 194
Children's Museum
of San Diego 161
Children's
Playground 54

Chinatown
Los Angeles 139
San Francisco
48–49
Cliff House 55–56
climate and seasons
190
Clos Pegase 81
clothing sizes 192
Coachella Valley 152,
165, 166
Collins, Jackie 26–27
Columbia State
Historic Park 85
concessions 194
Conservatory of
Flowers 53–54
consulates 194
Coronado 158
credit cards 38, 191
Crescent Bay 143
"Crookedest Street in
the World" 56
Crumb, R. 27
Crystal Cave 171
Crystal Cove State
Park 143
Culinary Institute of
America 82
culture and the arts
26–29
currency 191

Dana, Richard Henry
27
Dante's View 169
Death Valley 152,
155, 168–170
DeMille, Cecil B. 9,
10, 128, 129
dental services 194
Desert Hot Springs
165
Didion, Joan 27
Diebenkorn, Richard
27
disabilities, travelers
with 194
Disneyland Park
134–135
drinking water 194
driving 34–35, 83,
190
drugs and medicines
194
Duncan, Isadora 27
Duxbury Reef 182

earthquakes 16–18
eating out 37–38
see also individual
regions
El Capitan 88
El Matador State
Beach 140
electricity 193
Elk 77
Ellen Scripps
Browning Park 163
Emerald Bay 92

emergency telephone
numbers 193
Empire Mine State
Historic Park 84
entertainment 40
see also individual
regions
Eureka 90

Ferndale 90
film industry 8–11
Filoli 62–63
food and drink 37–38
see also eating out
foreign exchange
191
Fort Ross 24, 25
Fossil Falls 172
Furnace Creek 168

Gamble House 136
Gary Farrell
Vineyards &
Winery 80–81
George C. Page
Museum of La Brea
Discoveries 138
Getty Center
132–133
Goat Rock Beach 76
Gold Bug Mine 85
Gold Country 84–85
Golden Canyon 169
Golden Gate Bridge
55, 181
Golden Gate Park
52–54
Grace Cathedral 58
Grateful Dead 27–28
Griffith Park 127,
129
Gualala 77

Haas-Lilienthal
House 57
Harley-Davidson
Museum 114
Harmony 114
Harmony Borax
Works 169–170
Harte, Bret 15
Healdsburg 80
health 190, 194
Hearst, William
Randolph 108–109
Hearst Castle
108–109
Heavenly Ski Resort
92
Hess Collection 83
history of California
30
Hollywood
126–129
Autry Museum of
Western Heritage
129
Egyptian Theatre
127

El Capitan Theatre 127
Griffith Park 127, 129
Hollywood Entertainment Museum 129
Hollywood Forever 129
Hollywood Roosevelt Hotel 127
HOLLYWOOD sign 129
Hollywood Walk of Fame 28, 126, 127
Mann's Chinese Theatre 126, 127
Sunset Strip 137
hostels 36
hot-air ballooning 82
hotels and motels 36
Humboldt Redwoods State Park 90
Huntington Library, Collections and Botanical Gardens 136–137

Indian Canyons 167
Indio 165
insurance 190, 194

Jack London State Historic Park 79
Jackson, Helen Hunt 28
Japanese American National Museum 140
Japanese Tea Garden 53, 54
Joshua Tree National Park 166, 167
Joss House 91
Julia Pfeiffer Burns State Park 107
Junipero Serra Museum 162

Kennedy, Robert F. 21–22
Kerouac, Jack 28
Kings Canyon National Park 171
Kruse Rhododendron State Park 76
Kule Loklo 61
Kunde 79

La Brea Tar Pits 138
La Jolla 162–164
Birch Aquarium at Scripps 164
Ellen Scripps Browning Park 163
La Jolla Caves 163

La Jolla Cove 163
La Jolla Shores Beach 163
Museum of Contemporary Art 163
La Quinta 165, 166
Laguna Beach 143
Lake Cachuma 184
Lake Shasta Caverns 90
Lake Tahoe 91–92
Lassen Volcanic National Park 91
lavatories 194
Legoland California 164
Leo Carrillo State Beach 188
Little Petroglyphs Canyon 172
Living Desert Zoo & Gardens 167
London, Jack 76, 79
Lone Cypress 106
Los Angeles
Bradbury Building 140
Cathedral of Our Lady of the Angels 138
Chinatown 139
downtown Los Angeles 138–140
Getty Center 132–133
Japanese American National Museum 140
Los Angeles County Museum of Art 138
Million Dollar Theatre 140
MOCA at The Geffen Contemporary 139–140
Museum of Contemporary Art 139
Museum of Tolerance 138
Olvera Street 139
orientation 34
Petersen Automotive Museum 138
Union Station 139
Walt Disney Concert Hall 138
Los Angeles area 121–150
accommodations 147–148
Beverly Hills 130–131
Catalina Island 142
Disneyland Park 134–135
eating out 144–146
entertainment 150

Hollywood 126–129
La Brea Tar Pits 138
Laguna Beach 143
Malibu 140–141
map 122–123
Newport Beach 142–143
Pasadena 136–137
public transportation 32–33, 35
Queen Mary 141
Santa Monica 141
shopping 149
Sunset Strip 137
three-day itinerary 124–125
Universal Studios 137
Venice Beach 141
Los Olivos 184–185
Los Padres National Forest 115
lost property 194
Lotusland 113

MacKerricher State Park 77
Malakoff Diggins 24–25
Malibu 140–141, 188
Malibu Lagoon State Beach 141
Mann's Chinese Theatre 126, 127
Manson, Charles 22
Marshall, James 14
Marshall Gold Discovery State Historic Park 85
Maturango Museum 172
Mendocino 77
Mendocino Coast Botanical Gardens 77
M.H. de Young Memorial Museum 53, 54
Miller, Henry 28
Mingei International Museum 159
Mission Bay Park 162
Mission Dolores 60
Mission La Purísima Concepcion 24
Mission Santa Inés 185
Miwok Indian village 24
MOCA at The Geffen Contemporary 139–140
Mojave Desert 171–172
Mojave National Preserve 172
Monarch Grove Sanctuary 105
money 191
Mono Lake 92

Montecito 113, 183
Monterey 104–106
Monterey Bay Aquarium 101, 105
Monterey Bay Recreational Trail 104–105
Monterey Peninsula 100, 104–106
Carmel 106
Monterey 104–105, 106
Pacific Grove 105
17-Mile Drive 105–106
Monterey State Historic Park Visitor Center 104
Montez, Lola 14
Moorten Botanical Garden 167
Morro Bay 114–115
Mosley, Walter 28
Mount Shasta 90
Muir Woods National Monument 61, 180, 181
Mulholland Drive 186–188
Mumm Napa Valley 82
Murieta, Joaquin 13, 14–15
Muscle Beach 141
museum opening hours 192
Museum of Photographic Arts 159
Museum of Television and Radio 131
Museum of Tolerance 138

National AIDS Memorial Grove 54
national holidays 192
Native Americans 19, 24
Nevada City 84
Newport Beach 142–143
Niebaum-Coppola Estate 82
North Beach 49, 69
Northern California 71–98
accommodations 95–97
eating out 93–95
entertainment 98
five-day itinerary 74–75
Gold Country 84–85
Lake Tahoe 91–92
map 72–73
Mono Lake 92
Mount Shasta 90

Redwood Country 90
Sacramento 84
shopping 98
Sonoma–Mendocino Coast 76–77
Wine Country 78–83
Yosemite National Park 86–89
Norton Simon Museum 136

Ojai 115
Olema 182
opening hours 192

Pacific Beach 162
Pacific Coast Highway 140
Pacific Grove 105
Palace of Fine Arts 56
Palm Desert 165, 166
Palm Springs 155, 165–167
Palm Springs Aerial Tramway 166, 167
Palm Springs Desert Museum 167
Paramount Ranch 188
Paramount's Great America 63
Pasadena 136
    Gamble House 136
    Huntington Library, Art Collections and Botanical Gardens 136–137
    Norton Simon Museum 136
passports and visas 190
Patrick's Point State Park 90
personal safety 35, 193
Peter Strauss Ranch 188
Petersen Automotive Museum 138
Pfeiffer-Big Sur State Park 107
pharmacies 194
Pismo Beach 115
Placerville 85
Point Arena Lighthouse 77
Point Lobos State Reserve 106
Point Reyes Lighthouse 61, 182
Point Reyes National Seashore 61, 182
Point Sur Lighthouse 107
police 193
Pope-Baldwin Recreation Area 92

postal services 192, 193
Precita Eyes Mural Arts & Visitors Center 60
public transportation 32–33, 34–35

Queen Mary 141
Quicksilver Ranch 185

Rabbit Ridge Vineyards 80
Rancho Mirage 165
Randsburg 172
Red Rock Canyon State Park 172
Redwood National and State Parks 90
Restless Sea 106
Reuben E. Fleet Space Theater and Science Center 159
Ridgecrest 171
Roaring River Falls 171
Robert Mondavi 82
Rocky Oaks 188
Rodriguez, Richard 28
Rosicrucian Egyptian Museum and Planetarium 63

Sacramento 84
    California State History Museum 84
    California State Railroad Museum 84
    State Capitol 84
    State Indian Museum 84
    Sutter's Fort State Historical Park 84
San Diego 152, 154, 156–164
    Balboa Park 158–160
    Bazaar del Mundo 162
    Cabrillo National Monument 158
    Casa de Estudillo 162
    Centro Cultural de la Raza 159
    Children's Museum of San Diego 161
    Coronado 158
    Gaslamp Quarter 156, 157–158
    harbor cruises 156, 157
    Junipero Serra Museum 162

La Jolla 162–164
    Legoland California 164
    McKinstry Dentist Office 162
    Maritime Museum of San Diego 156, 157
    Mason Street School 162
    Mingei International Museum 159
    Museum of Photographic Arts 159
    Museum of San Diego History 159
    Old Town 161–162
    Old Town State Historic Park 161
    orientation 34
    Presidio 162
    public transportation 33, 35
    Reuben E. Fleet Space Theater and Science Center 159
    Robinson-Rose House 161
    San Diego Aerospace Museum 159, 160
    San Diego Aircraft Carrier Museum 156, 157
    San Diego Automative Museum 159
    San Diego Hall of Champions – Sports Museum 160
    San Diego Model Railroad Museum 159
    San Diego Museum of Art 159
    San Diego Museum of Man 160
    San Diego Museum of Natural History 160
    San Diego Wild Animal Park 164
    San Diego Zoo 158, 160–161
    Seaport Village 156, 157
    SeaWorld Adventure Park 161
    Seeley Stables 162
    Timken Museum of Art 159
    William Heath Davis House 158
San Fernando Valley 188

San Francisco
    Alcatraz Island 46
    cable cars 58
    California Palace of the Legion of Honor 55
    Castro District 59–60
    Chinatown 48–49
    Civic Center 58–59
    Cliff House 55–56
    CoitTower/Telegraph Hill 56–57
    "Crookedest Street in the World" 56
    Ferry Building 57
    Fisherman's Wharf 46–47, 69
    Golden Gate Bridge 55, 181
    Golden Gate Park 52–54
    Haas-Lilienthal House 57
    Haight Street 59
    Hayes Valley 59
    Mission District 60
    Mission Dolores 60
    Nob Hill 58
    North Beach 49, 69
    orientation 33
    Palace of Fine Arts 56
    public transportation 32, 34–35
    San Francisco Museum of Modern Art 50, 51
    SkyDeck 57
    SoMa 50–51
    Twin Peaks 59
    Union Square 58, 68
San Francisco and Bay Area 41–70
    accommodations 67–68
    eating out 64–66
    entertainment 69–70
    Filoli 62–63
    map 42–43
    Muir Woods National Monument 61, 180, 181
    Point Reyes National Seashore 61, 182
    San Jose 63
    Sausalito 62
    shopping 68–69
    three-day itinerary 44–45
    Tiburon 62
San Jose 63
    Cathedral Basilica of St. Joseph 63
    Rosicrucian Egyptian Museum and Planetarium 63

San Jose Museum of Art 63
Tech Museum of Invention 63
Winchester Mystery House 63
San Simeon State Park 114
San Vicente Nike Missile Site 188
Santa Barbara 110–113, 183–185
Andree Clark Bird Refuge 111, 184
East Beach 111
Lotusland 113
Mission Santa Barbara 111, 112
Montecito 113, 183
Santa Barbara Botanic Garden 111, 112–113
Santa Barbara County Courthouse 111, 112
Santa Barbara Yacht Harbor 111
Sea Lab 111
Santa Cruz 114
Santa Monica 141
Santa Rosa 80
Sausalito 62
Scotty's Castle 170
Seal Rock 56
SeaWorld Adventure Park 161
senior citizens 194

Sequoia National Park 171
Seventeen-Mile Drive 105–106
Shasta Dam 90
shopping 39, 192
see also individual regions
Simi Winery 80
Simpson, O.J. 22
Sinclair, Upton 28–29
Six Flags Marine World 63
smoking etiquette 38
Solvang 185
Sonoma–Mendocino Coast 76–77
Southern California 151–178
accommodations 175–176
Anza-Borrego Desert State Park 172
Death Valley 152, 155, 168–170
eating out 173–174
entertainment 178
four-day itinerary 154–155
Kings Canyon National Park 171
map 153
Mojave Desert 171–172
Palm Springs 155, 165–167
San Diego 152, 154, 156–164

Sequoia National Park 171
shopping 177
spas 81
sports and activities 40, 82
State Capitol 84
Steinbeck, John 29, 104–105
Sterling Vineyards 81
Strybing Arboretum and Botanical Gardens 53, 54
students and young travelers 194
sun protection 194
Sutro Baths 56
Sutter, John 14
Sutter's Fort State Historic Park 84

Tahquitz Creek Palm Springs Golf Resort 166
Tan, Amy 29
taxis 35
Tech Museum of Invention 63
telephones 193
Tiburon 62
time differences 191, 192
Timken Museum of Art 159
Tin How Temple 49
tipping 38, 193

Torrey Pines State Beach and Reserve 164
tourist information 190–191
trains 33, 191
travelers' cheques 38, 191
Trona Pinnacles 171–172
Twenty Mule Team Canyon 169

Ubehebe Crater 170
Universal Studios 137

Venice Beach 141
Vikingsholm 92

Walker, Alice 29
Warner Bros. 137
Weaverville 91
websites 190
Winchester Mystery House 63
wineries 77, 78–83, 106

Yerba Buena Gardens 50
Yosemite National Park 24, 86–89

Zabriskie Point 169

Picture credits

Abbreviations for terms appearing below: (t) top; (b) bottom; (l) left; (r) right; (c) center.

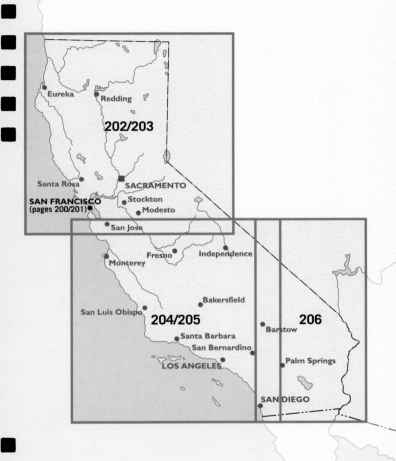

Eureka

Redding

202/203

Santa Rosa

SAN FRANCISCO
(pages 200/201)

SACRAMENTO

Stockton

Modesto

San Jose

Fresno

Independence

Monterey

Bakersfield

San Luis Obispo

204/205

206

Santa Barbara

Barstow

San Bernardino

Palm Springs

LOS ANGELES

SAN DIEGO

Regional Maps

—··—··—	International boundary	☐	City
—·—·—	State boundary	▫	Major town
⑤	Interstate highway	∘∘	Other town
㊿	Federal highway	**City Plan**	
①	Other highway	——	Cable Car line
	National Park	●	BART station
▪	Place of interest	▨	Featured place of interest

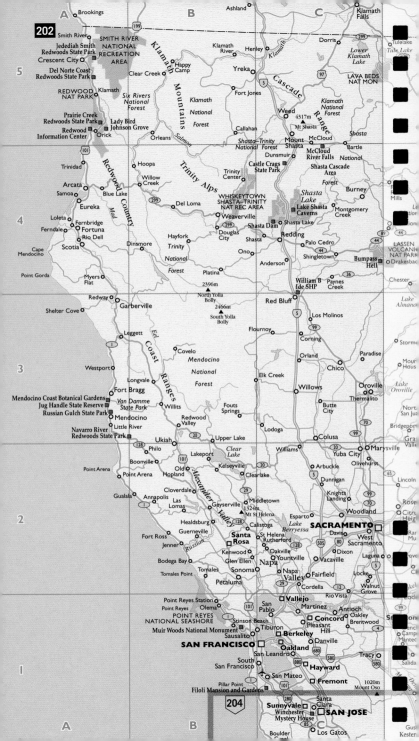

A | **B** | **C**

Brookings

Ashland

Klamath Falls

Smith River

Dorris

Tulelake
Tide Lake

Jedediah Smith
Redwoods State Park
Crescent City

SMITH RIVER
NATIONAL
RECREATION
AREA

Klamath
River

Henley

Lower
Klamath
Lake

LAVA BEDS
NAT MON

Del Norte Coast
Redwoods State Park

Clear Creek

Happy
Camp

Yreka

REDWOOD
NAT PARK

Klamath

Six Rivers
National
Forest

Fort Jones

Prairie Creek
Redwoods State Park

Lady Bird
Johnson Grove

Klamath
Mountains

Callahan

Weed
4317m
Mt Shasta

Klamath
National
Forest

Redwood
Information Center

Orick

Klamath
National
Forest

Orleans

Salmon

Mount
Shasta

McCloud

Shasta

Trinidad

Hoopa

Shasta–Trinity
National Forest

Dunsmuir

McCloud
River Falls

Bartle

Arcata

Willow
Creek

Del Loma

Trinity
Center

Castle Crags
State Park

Shasta Cascade
National

Shasta Cascade
Forest

Burney

Samoa

Blue Lake

Trinity Alps

WHISKEYTOWN
SHASTA–TRINITY
NAT REC AREA

Shasta
Lake

Montgomery
Creek

Eureka

Loleta

Fernbridge
Fortuna

Weaverville

Lake Shasta
Caverns

Ferndale

Rio Dell

Hayfork

Douglas
City

Shasta Dam

Shasta Lake

Palo Cedro

LASSEN
VOLCANIC
NAT PARK

Scotia

Dinsmore

Trinity

Redding

Drakesbac

Cape
Mendocino

National

Shasta

Anderson

Shingletown

Bumpass
Hell

Point Gorda

Forest

Ono

Chester

Myers
Flat

Platina

William B
Ide SHP

Paynes
Creek

Lake
Almano

Redway

2396m
North Yolla
Bolly

Red Bluff

Los Molinos

Shelter Cove

Garberville

2466m
South Yolla
Bolly

Flournoy

Storm

Leggett

Covelo

Corning

Paradise

Mour

Westport

Mendocino
National

Elk Creek

Orland

Chico

Lake
Oroville

Longvale

Forest

Fort Bragg

Willits

Fouts
Springs

Willows

Butte
City

Oroville

Thermalito

Nort
San Ju

Mendocino Coast Botanical Gardens
Jug Handle State Reserve
Russian Gulch State Park

Van Damme
State Park

Redwood
Valley

Lodoga

Colusa

Bridgepor

Mendocino

Little River

Ukiah

Upper Lake

Williams

Yuba City

Marysville

Gra
Valle

Navarro River
Redwoods State Park

Philo

Coast Ranges

Lakeport

Clear
Lake

Arbuckle

Olivehurst

Rose

Boonville

Kelseyville

Dunnigan

Knights
Landing

Lincoln

Point Arena

Point Arena

Alexander Valley

Clearlake

Woodland

Citr
Heig

Gualala

Annapolis

Cloverdale

Middletown

Esparto

Davis

West
Sacramento

Rar
Mu

Las
Lomas

Geyserville

1324m
Mt St Helena

Lake
Berryessa

SACRAMENTO

rov

Healdsburg

Calistoga

St Helena

505

80

Locke

Fort Ross

Guerneville

Russian

Santa
Rosa

Rutherford

Dixon

Vacaville

Laguna

S

Jenner

Kenwood

Oakville
Yountville

Napa

128

Fairfield

Bodega Bay

Glen Ellen

Sonoma

Napa
Valley

Cordella

Walnut
Grove

Cl

Tomales Point

Tomales

Petaluma

29

Vallejo

Rio Vista

12

Point Reyes Station

San
Pablo

Martinez

Antioch

99

Point Reyes

Olema

Concord

Oakley

Campi

POINT REYES
NATIONAL
SEASHORE

Stinson Beach

Tiburon

Berkeley

Pleasant
Hill

Brentwood

Mantec

Muir Woods National Monument

Sausalito

Oakland

Danville

680

580

Tracy

SAN FRANCISCO

San Leandro

880

Salida

South
San Francisco

Hayward

580

1020m
Mount Oso

San Mateo

Fremont

S

Pillar Point

101

Filoli Mansion and Gardens

Santa
Clara

Gus
Kester

Sunnyvale

Winchester
Mystery House

SAN JOSE

85

Boulder

Los Gatos

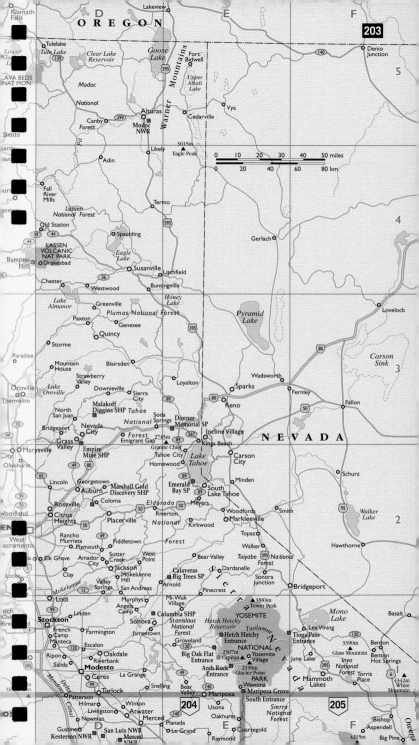

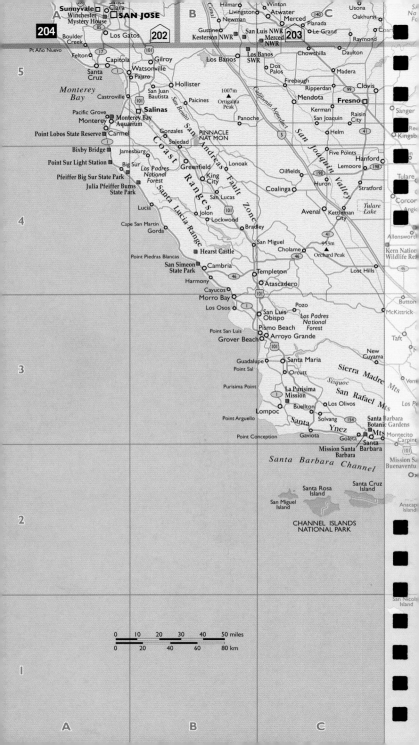

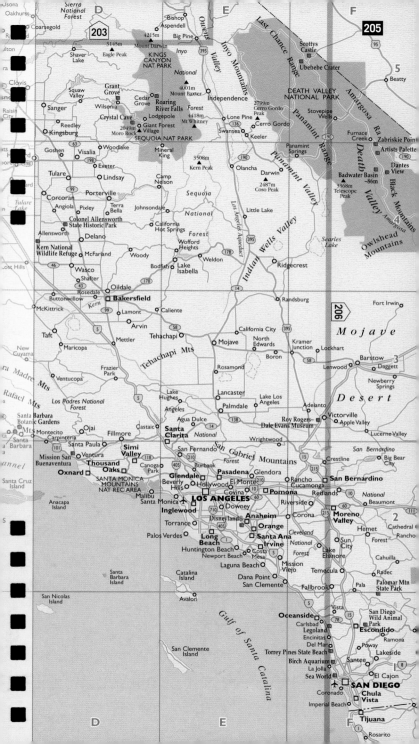

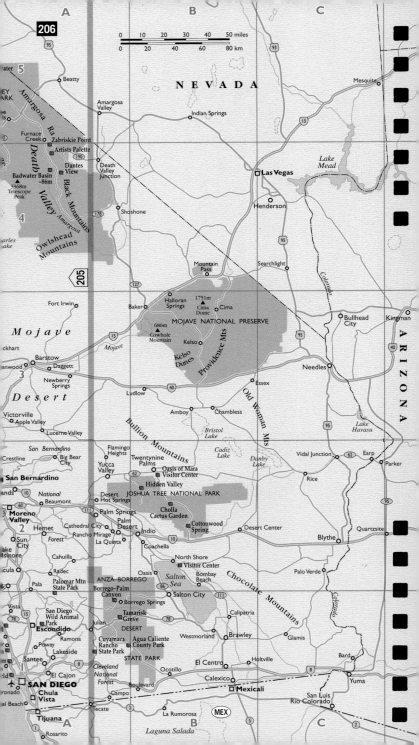

SPIRAL GUIDES

Questionnaire

Dear Traveler

Your comments, opinions and recommendations are very important to us. So please help us to improve our travel guides by taking a few minutes to complete this simple questionnaire.

Send to: Spiral Guides, MailStop 66, 1000 AAA Drive, Heathrow, FL 32746–5063

Your recommendations…

We always encourage readers' recommendations for restaurants, nightlife or shopping – if your recommendation is added to the next edition of the guide, we will send you a FREE AAA Spiral Guide of your choice. Please state below the establishment name, location and your reasons for recommending it.

_____

_____

_____

_____

_____

Please send me AAA Spiral _____

(see list of titles inside the back cover)

About this guide…

Which title did you buy?

_____ AAA Spiral

Where did you buy it? _____

When? mm/ y y

Why did you choose a AAA Spiral Guide? _____

_____

_____

_____

Did this guide meet your expectations?

Exceeded ☐   Met all ☐   Met most ☐   Fell below ☐

Please give your reasons _____

_____

_____

_____

continued on next page…

Were there any aspects of this guide that you particularly liked?

_____

_____

_____

_____

Is there anything we could have done better?

_____

_____

_____

_____

About you...

Name (Mr/Mrs/Ms)_____

Address_____

_____

_____ **Zip**_____

Daytime tel nos._____

Which age group are you in?

Under 25 ☐   25–34 ☐   35–44 ☐   45–54 ☐   55–64 ☐   65+ ☐

How many trips do you make a year?

Less than one ☐   One ☐   Two ☐   Three or more ☐

Are you a AAA member? Yes ☐   **No** ☐

Name of AAA club_____

About your trip...

When did you book? m m/ y y   **When did you travel?** m m/ y y

How long did you stay?_____

Was it for business or leisure?_____

Did you buy any other travel guides for your trip? ☐ **Yes** ☐ **No**

If yes, which ones?_____

Thank you for taking the time to complete this questionnaire.